AFTA SpringerBriefs in

A publication of the American Family Therapy Academy

Founded in 1977, the **American Family Therapy Academy** is a non-profit organization of leading family therapy teachers, clinicians, program directors, policymakers, researchers, and social scientists dedicated to advancing systemic thinking and practices for families in their social context.

Vision

AFTA envisions a just world by transforming social contexts that promote health, safety, and well-being of all families and communities.

Mission

AFTA's mission is developing, researching, teaching, and disseminating progressive, just family therapy and family-centered practices and policies.

More information about this series at http://www.springer.com/series/11846

Carmen Knudson-Martin · Melissa A. Wells
Sarah K. Samman
Editors

Socio-Emotional Relationship Therapy

Bridging Emotion, Societal Context,
and Couple Interaction

Editors
Carmen Knudson-Martin
Graduate School of Education
    and Counseling
Lewis & Clark College
Portland, OR
USA

Sarah K. Samman
Department of Counseling and Family
    Sciences
Loma Linda University
Loma Linda, CA
USA

Melissa A. Wells
Department of Counseling and Family
    Sciences
Loma Linda University
Loma Linda, CA
USA

ISSN 2196-5528   ISSN 2196-5536 (electronic)
AFTA SpringerBriefs in Family Therapy
ISBN 978-3-319-13397-3   ISBN 978-3-319-13398-0 (eBook)
DOI 10.1007/978-3-319-13398-0

Library of Congress Control Number: 2014960138

Springer Cham Heidelberg New York Dordrecht London

Printed on acid-free paper

Springer International Publishing AG Switzerland is part of Springer Science+Business Media
(www.springer.com)

Series Foreword

The *AFTA SpringerBriefs in Family Therapy* series is an official publication of the American Family Therapy Academy. Each volume focuses on the practice and policy implications of innovative systemic research and theory in family therapy and allied fields. Our goal is to make information about families and systemic practices in societal contexts widely accessible in a reader friendly, conversational, and practical style. We have asked the authors to make their personal context, location, and experience visible in their writing. AFTA's core commitment to equality, social responsibility, and justice are represented in each volume.

Socio-Emotional Relationship Therapy: Bridging Emotion, Societal Context, and Couple Interaction is an important step in translating theory about equity and social justice into actual clinical practice. The authors in this volume have taken the rare step of systematically studying their own work with couples to identify the clinical processes involved in identifying how the larger societal context is present in the moment by moment of clinical practice and how to address these issues. Rather than simply adding a cultural component to their work, they *begin* with attunement to each partner's socio-contextual experience and the societal and relational power processes involved.

The approach, referred to as SERT by the authors, innovatively integrates recent advances in neurobiology with social constructionist sensibilities regarding how personal identities, gender and couple relationships, and cultural norms and expectations are constructed through interaction and are fluid and open to change, while also maintaining a clear critical contextual lens that keeps attention to societal-based power dynamics at the forefront. The authors report and apply their groundbreaking clinical process research, taking care to also share their personal insights and struggles as practitioners. Each chapter offers rich case examples and step-by-step guidelines that detail how practitioners can resist sociocultural stereotypes and inequities and empower couples to transform destructive societal discourses and power differentials to create new relational possibilities.

The critical socio-contextual approach to couple therapy described in this volume exemplifies the progressive, just family therapy and family-centered practices and policies central to AFTA's mission. Readers across disciplines and clinical models will find the findings and strategies applicable and valuable to efforts that advance health, safety, and well-being for couples and their families across diverse contexts and circumstances.

Portland, OR   Carmen Knudson-Martin
                                                                              Series Editor

Acknowledgments

The approach to therapy presented in this book began when Carmen Knudson-Martin and Douglas Huenergardt and a group of marital and family therapy doctoral students at Loma Linda University decided to meet regularly to study and reflect on our own clinical work with couples. At the beginning it was not a formal research project. The weekly meetings were outside our regular student and faculty course loads. We came together around a shared interest in better articulating how to work with gender, culture, power, and other larger context issues in the moment by moment of couple therapy. Though we evolved our work into an action research study approved by the Loma Linda University Institutional Review Board (IRB), the group meetings were a labor of love and commitment to the ideals of relational justice, the relatively simple conviction that intimate relationships should equally serve the well-being of each partner, and a passion for improving clinical practice. Every chapter here is the product of each author's engagement with the larger clinical study group and reflects the ongoing experience and contributions of all who participated.

Douglas Huenergardt has been a major contributor and pillar of the group. He is convinced of the value of watching live sessions as a foundational legacy of family therapy and is adamant that the group maintain this essential characteristic. He loves watching therapy and observing clinical process. The women in the group often joke that Doug is the most feminist of all of us. He recognizes the subtle ways gender inequality infuses relationships and he never lets go of the potential for couples to experience something new.

Since the group started meeting in October 2008, some students have left the regular group meetings and others have joined. As our project evolved, new participants became part of what we now call the *Socio-Emotional Relationship Therapy* clinical research group. We developed a set of clinical competencies that we continue to evolve. Other participants to date have included Adrian Avila, Les Bishop, Carizma Chapman, Jessica ChenFeng, Elisabeth Esmiol Wilson, Julie Estrella, Aimee Galick, Horatius Gittens, Young Joo Kang, Christian Kim, Grace Kim, Lana Kim, Veronica Kuhn, Ketsia Lafontant, Elsie Lobo, A'verria Martin, Jessica Moreno, Caroline Nyairo, Mia Pandit, Jason Richards, Hans Schaepper, and Kirstee Williams. Together with Doug and Hans, Melissa and Carmen have been part of the group since the beginning. Sarah joined in 2012. We are grateful for the willingness of each participant to be vulnerable in exposing their clinical work to scrutiny and being personally open to a shared developmental process.

We are also deeply indebted to the couple clients who consented to work with our team of in-session therapists and observers. Often they came to know many of us as therapists rotated in-session or observers shared their reflections. Couples willingly opened the most sensitive parts of themselves to participate in the clinical endeavor and engaged in the often difficult process of confronting the influence of destructive societal discourse and structures in their lives.

The work of our group evolved out of so many other dedicated couple and family therapists. We were especially influenced by the Women's Project in Family Therapy (Walters et al. 1988) and the many groundbreaking authors in McGoldrick et al. (1989). Virginia Goldner and Rachel Hare-Mustin guided our work conceptually; Marianne Walters felt almost physically present to us through her previous mentorship of Doug Huenergardt. He shared Marianne's wisdom with us often. We are also indebted to Judith Jordan and the work of the Stone Center at Wellesley College. Their emphasis on relational connection and mutuality is at the heart of our socio-emotional approach.

We are grateful to the American Family Therapy Academy for highlighting the importance of the larger social context in family and intimate life and for sponsoring the AFTA Springer Briefs in Family Therapy that makes it possible for us to share our work with a network of colleagues who "envision a just world by transforming social contexts that promote health, safety, and well-being of all families and communities" (AFTA Vision Statement). Thank you to Jennifer Hadley and the team at Springer Science for shepherding our book every step of the way. Jennifer has been wonderfully responsive in guiding us through the publishing process.

Thank you to Loma Linda University for providing the facilities, intellectual space, and the commitment to service and professional excellence that made our weekly meetings possible. Randall Walker, Heidi Robbins, and Carizma Chapman at the LLU Behavioral Health Institute were especially helpful and supportive in managing the logistics of the clinical space and client contacts. They accommodated our special clinical needs and interests with graciousness and attention to detail.

We are family members as well as researcher–clinicians. Our own families of origin are always close to our hearts in so many ways as we and the other authors in this book join with our couple clients to build on strengths and catalyze new possibilities. Melissa and Carmen are parents and grandparents. Sarah became a mother just as this book is published. We are motivated by our love and hope for our children and grandchildren. Drawing on the legacy of family therapists such as Ivan Boszormenyi-Nagy, we feel accountable to the next generation. We are also each blessed by loving partners committed to the task of transforming societal gender inequalities as we try to work these through in our own relationships. Shagy, Gary, and John have been tremendously supportive as we put this book together. We thank you for sharing our vision and encouraging our work.

A final thanks to each chapter author. We asked you to write in an accessible and personal style, to make your ideas as applicable as possible. You rose to the challenge and willingly made numerous revisions. We think your work is outstanding! We are inspired by you and your clinical wisdom and invite readers to share in your journey and experience translating concepts of diversity, equality, and relational justice into clear guidelines for practice, even as each of you continues to discover more. Thank you for engaging in this important work.

Carmen Knudson-Martin
Melissa A. Wells
Sarah K. Samman

References

McGoldrick, M., Anderson, C., & Walsh, F. (Eds.). (1989). *Women in families: A framework for family therapy*. New York: Norton.
Walters, M., Carter, B., Papp, P. & Silverstein, O. (1988). *The invisible web: Gender patterns in family relationships*. New York: Guilford Press.

Contents

Editors and Contributors

Editors

Carmen Knudson-Martin Ph.D., LMFT, is internationally recognized for her work regarding gender, marital equality, and relational health. She has published over 60 articles articulating the importance of the larger social context on issues such as marital equality, relational development, postpartum depression, women's health, and couple therapy. Together with Douglas Huenergardt, she founded the Socio-Emotional Clinical Research group at Loma Linda University. Carmen is currently Professor and Director of the Marital, Couple, and Family Therapy program at Lewis & Clark College in Portland, OR. She serves on the Board of directors of theFamily Process Instituteand theAmerican Family Therapy Academyand is series editor of the AFTA Springer Briefs in Family Therapy.

Melissa A. Wells M.S., Ph.D.(c), is a Marital and Family Therapy doctoral student at Loma Linda University in Loma Linda, CA. She works with individuals, couples, and families at Mt. Vision Family Therapy in Redlands, CA. Her research interests and clinical specialties include medical family therapy, especially perinatal bereavement and postpartum depression, as well as sensitively addressing with couples the particular relational stressors resulting from a traumatic history of childhood abuse. She previously worked for more than two decades as a journalist, and in her free time enjoys writing screenplays.

Sarah K. Samman M.S., M.A., CCRP, is a third-year Ph.D. student in the Marital and Family Therapy Program at Loma Linda University. She has presented at national and international conferences on issues related to the impacts of gender, power, and chronic illnesses on couple and family relationships. She came to doctoral study with a strong interdisciplinary background in health psychology, experience as a research coordinator at the Neurosciences Center, King Fahad Medical City, Riyadh, Saudi Arabia, as well as a deep commitment to social justice nurtured by her second master's degree from Lewis & Clark College. Sarah is currently the Clinicians Coordinator of the Socio-Emotional Relationship Therapy (SERT) Clinical Research group at the Behavioral Health Institute as well as a Medical Family Therapist (MedFT) Intern at the Transplantation Institute at the Loma Linda University Medical Center in Loma Linda, CA.

Contributors

Jessica L. ChenFeng Department of Educational Psychology and Counseling, California State University, Northridge, CA, USA

Julie Estrella Department of Counseling and Family Sciences, Loma Linda University, Loma Linda, CA, USA

Mona DeKoven Fishbane Couple Therapy Training, Chicago Center for Family Health, Chicago, IL, USA

Cassidy J. Freitas Department of Counseling and Family Sciences, Loma Linda University, Loma Linda, CA, USA

Aimee Galick School of Health Professions, University of Louisiana-Monroe, Monroe, LA, USA

Douglas Huenergardt Department of Counseling and Family Sciences, Loma Linda University, Loma Linda, CA, USA

Naveen Jonathan Frances Smith Center for Individual and Family Therapy, Crean College of Health and Behavioral Sciences Chapman University, Orange, CA, USA

Young Joo Kang Department of Counseling and Family Sciences, Loma Linda University, Loma Linda, CA, USA

Lana Kim Marriage and Family Therapy Department, Valdosta State University, Valdosta, GA, USA

Carmen Knudson-Martin Counseling Psychology Department, Lewis and Clark College, Portland, OR, USA

Veronica P. Kuhn Department of Counseling and Family Sciences, Loma Linda University, Loma Linda, CA, USA

Mayuri (Mia) Pandit Loma Linda University Behavioral Medicine Center, Outpatient Services, Redlands, CA, USA

Jason C. Richards Department of Counseling and Family Sciences, Loma Linda University, Loma Linda, CA, USA

Sarah K. Samman Department of Counseling and Family Sciences, Loma Linda University, Loma Linda, CA, USA

Melissa A. Wells Department of Counseling and Family Sciences, Loma Linda University, Loma Linda, CA, USA; Marital and Family Therapy Intern, Mt. Vision Family Therapy, Redlands, CA, USA

Kirstee Williams Behavioral and Social Sciences Department, Lee University, Cleveland, TN, USA

Elisabeth Esmiol Wilson Department of Marriage and Family Therapy, Pacific Lutheran University, Tacoma, WA, USA

Bridging Emotion, Societal Discourse, and Couple Interaction in Clinical Practice

Carmen Knudson-Martin and Douglas Huenergardt

So much is on the line when intimate partners respond to each other. A simple ignored request to "please turn off the light" may involve so much—each person's identity, their value and worth, what is right or wrong, and their capacity to influence the other and be cared about. Over time, the consequences of these relational patterns have profound implications for the health and well-being of each partner, as well as for the success of the relationship over all. When we (Carmen and Doug) began to work together at Loma Linda University, we discovered a shared interest in how gender, culture, and societal power contexts affect these relationship processes.

Doug had been part of a supervision group with Marianne Walters, a key voice in the Women's Project that took on the impact of patriarchy on the practice of family therapy (e.g., Walters et al. 1988). He had worked with many couples and had considerable experience helping men overcome gender stereotypes to relationally engage. Carmen had been writing on the politics of gender in couple therapy (Knudson-Martin 1997) and challenging the applicability of some of the field's dominant theories for women and people from less individualistic cultures (Knudson-Martin 1994, 1996). Together with an international team of students and sociologist Anne Rankin Mahoney, she had been studying the processes by which couples across diverse cultural and life contexts reproduce gendered power inequities or transform them (Knudson-Martin and Mahoney 2009).

For over six years, we have been meeting weekly with a clinical study team to conduct therapy and systematically review our own practice in order to improve our

C. Knudson-Martin (✉)
Graduate School of Education and Counseling, Lewis & Clark College,
Portland, OR, USA
e-mail: carmen@lclark.edu

D. Huenergardt
Department of Counseling and Family Sciences, Loma Linda University,
Loma Linda, CA, USA
e-mail: dhuenergardt@LLU.edu

© American Family Therapy Academy 2015   1
C. Knudson-Martin et al. (eds.), *Socio-Emotional Relationship Therapy*,
AFTA SpringerBriefs in Family Therapy, DOI 10.1007/978-3-319-13398-0_1

ability to work with the societal context in couple therapy. Our diverse group includes 28 marital and family therapy faculty and doctoral students, with some participants leaving as others join the team. We are 8 men and 20 women. Sixteen are persons of color. Eleven immigrated to the USA or are international students. Fourteen are licensed MFTs; 14 are doctoral MFT interns. Our goal has been to document and reflect upon the skills needed to practice socio-contextually aware couple therapy and teach it to others. We call our approach Socio-Emotional Relationship Therapy (SERT) (e.g., Knudson-Martin and Huenergardt 2010; Knudson-Martin et al. 2014).

In this chapter, we illustrate five principles that guide SERT, present our model of the conditions that promote mutual support, and preview the clinical competencies involved. We use the example of Shana and Sean, a working-class unmarried heterosexual European American couple in their late 20s expecting their second child. Shana initiated therapy because she was unhappy. Sean came "at her pleasure." The case has been modified to protect confidentiality.

Five Foundational Principles

Context Structures Personal Identities and Relational Processes

SERT begins with therapist attunement to how each partner's identity is connected to sociocultural ideas about who they are in relation to others and how this invites them to think, feel, and behave. As will be detailed in the chapter "SERT Therapists' Experience of Practicing Sociocultural Attunement" (Pandit et al. 2015), we want to "get" their experience as sociocultural persons, to resonate with them as they are situated in a particular social location. The concept of societal discourse helps us identify cultural messages and shared ways of thinking that inform personal experience. Like the air we breathe, societal discourses are often so taken for granted that people are not really aware of them. Moreover, these cultural identity messages are intricately connected to a wider set of intersecting power differentials depending on one's gender, socioeconomic status, sexual orientation, age, ability/disability, religion, ethnicity, indigenous heritage, and national origin, among other social locations (McDowell and Fang 2007).

As therapy begins, SERT therapists listen for the sociocultural discourses implicit in clients' stories. For example, when Sean says, "She doesn't tell me what she's thinking! How am I supposed to know why she's upset?" we want to take in his experience as a man, to understand the societal messages that invite his frustration. We are especially interested in discourses about relational responsibilities such as what he has a right to expect in a relationship and who is responsible for noticing and attending to the other. The salience of gender discourses such as "women are responsible for relationship maintenance" or "men are supposed to have the answers" is especially relevant to heterosexual couple therapy and is expanded upon in "How Gender Discourses Hijack Couple Therapy—And How to Avoid It" (ChenFeng and Galick 2015).

People are informed by many societal discourses, and identities may change depending on the context (Knudson-Martin and Huenergardt 2010; Winslade 2009). Binary societal scripts (such as men are from one planet and women from another) seldom capture the full range of experience. Moreover, internalized discourses oftentimes contradict each other. Sean's emotional response to Shana is catalyzed by European American societal messages that encourage male autonomy and do not invite him to focus on her. But he also endorses societal ideals of equal partnership and does not want to view himself as dominating her. Thus, he expects her to tell him what she thinks or needs, but does not actively seek to notice or resonate with her experience or consider how his actions may limit her voice. Like other social constructionist approaches (e.g., Dickerson 2013), SERT locates problems in the larger context rather than the individual, or even the relationship. We seek to map out and address how these societal processes are embodied in emotion and the couple's interaction patterns.

Emotion Is Contextual

Something that is complex or detailed,

A common view is that emotions are inside us, and then, we express them or let them out. This view does not capture the intricacies of emotion. Emotion involves a neurobiological state in response to a social situation and thus represents the interface between the individual and the outside world (Siegel 2001). It is how larger societal processes are personally and relationally experienced. Attuning to emotion is thus an important source of contextual information and meaning and a way by which new experience is constructed, not only in language, but also in the body.

As described by Fishbane and Wells ("Toward Relational Empowerment: Interpersonal Neurobiology, Couples, and the Societal Context," 2015), the brain is intuitively social and dependent on emotional information. When people affectively respond to each other and their situations, meaning is created and neural connections are reinforced or modified. Shana experiences significant emotional pain because Sean does not seem to care about her. Her intensely "personal" feelings of disappointment are invited by relational societal discourses that say intimate partners should reciprocally focus on and attune to each other. Sean, on the other hand, responds to societal messages that say he is supposed to have the answers and not be questioned. His quick counter-arguments when Shana tries to raise relationship issues are connected to this sense of authority, but tell Shana that her voice is not valued. This reinforces the societal gender hierarchy and leaves Shana increasingly depressed and withdrawn. The confluence of societal, relational, and emotional processes is the site of our clinical work.

Social engagement at the neurological level requires each partner to be open to influence—neurologically changed by—the other (Porges 2009). It cannot be based on unequal power positions (Hughes 2009). When they began therapy, Shana was highly attuned to Sean. She actively noticed and tried to respond to his emotions and needs. Sean said he cared about Shana but did not take in her experience. A lot of what she was feeling went unnoticed. When she expressed her distress, Sean tried to unilaterally take charge of the situation. These stereotypic

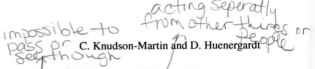

[handwritten annotations: "acting seperatly from other things or people", "impossible to pass or seep through"]

gender enactments made him seem impenetrable and autonomous, left her vulnerable with little way to influence him, and limited reciprocal emotional engagement.

Power Is Relational

In SERT, we define power as the ability to influence the other. It is a dynamic, fluid process between people. We explore the balance of power by considering the following: "Who notices? Who feels entitled to express their needs or have them fulfilled? Who accommodates or organizes around the other? Who responds to provide care? The less powerful tend to automatically… accommodate the other" (Knudson-Martin 2013, p. 6). People in powerful positions may not be aware of how others accommodate and do not necessarily *feel* powerful (Kimmel 2011). The intricacies and consequences of these power processes are detailed in the chapter "When Therapy Challenges Patriarchy: Undoing Gendered Power in Heterosexual Couple Relationships" (Knudson-Martin 2015).

Sean was not aware of his power position until we tracked the couple's power dynamics in session. For example, when asked about her distress, Shana said she felt anxious about how they would manage when the new baby was born. Sean immediately dismissed her concerns and began to explain that it would be fine and that in fact he thought it would be fun. When the therapist (Carmen) asked Sean what he thought her concerns were, he again very quickly said there was no basis for concern. At this point, Shana began to visibly retreat. When Carmen walked the couple through what had just happened, how Sean's quick take-charge response left Shana feeling unable to influence him, Sean was concerned. He did not want to dominate Shana in that way.

Most people have more access to power in some settings than others. The intersections of power sources in intimate relationships are complex; however, power differences associated with binary societal gender processes are particularly salient and surprisingly difficult to recognize and change (see ChenFeng and Galick, "How Gender Discourses Hijack Couple Therapy—And How to Avoid It," 2015). Though access to money and other societal resources such as prestige certainly impacts intimate power dynamics, a number of studies have documented that in heterosexual relationships these often do not trump gender. Tichenor (2005) found that when women earned more than their partners, both persons did things to maintain key aspects of male power. Similarly, Stuchell (2013) found no examples in which female physicians exerted the kind of power over their partners that many of the male physicians did.

Study of committed same-sex couples helps to clarify the distinctions between power and gender (Jonathan 2009; Richards et al., "Building a Circle of Care in Same-Sex Couple Relationships: A Socio-Emotional Relational Approach," 2015). Jonathan found that same-sex partners tend to actively engage in discussions to ensure that partners carry equal weight. In contrast, like Sean and Shana above, heterosexual couples often fall into stereotypic gender patterns that perpetuate gendered power without discussion or awareness (Knudson-Martin and

Different from each other

Mahoney 2005). Some same-sex partners in Jonathan's study experienced power disparities based on work and family roles and income, but they seemed to be more aware of these differences and the benefitting partner was likely to acknowledge them and take at least a few steps to address them. There were also a few same-sex couples in which one partner appeared less attuned to the other and not willing to accommodate to meet the other person's interests. For example, one woman expected her partner to follow her job moves and did not seem aware of what this sacrifice meant to her partner. When influence is relatively equal, each partner feels free to express their needs, goals, and interests, and each attends to and accommodates the other (Knudson-Martin and Mahoney 2009).

Relationships Should Mutually Support Each Partner

We tell client couples that we work from the premise that relationships should equally support each partner and ask whether they agree. In our experience, they always do. Though how it is expressed may vary, ideals of reciprocity and mutual respect extend across cultures and religions. Considerable research suggests that relationships do better when partners are able to notice and respond to each other, attune to emotion, and accept influence (e.g., Gottman 2011; Greenberg and Goldman 2008; Mirgain and Cordova 2007). When the power to influence each other is not reciprocal, these foundational relationship capacities are thwarted (Jonathan and Knudson-Martin 2012).

to prevent from doing something

Therapists Must Actively Intervene in Social Processes

When working with Sean and Shana, Carmen needed a guiding lens (Esmiol et al. 2012) that enabled sociocultural attunement to each partner and also actively resisted the limiting effects of dominant gender and cultural discourses on the couple's ability to create a mutually supportive relationship. She wanted to understand Sean's experience as a working man who had learned that it was his role to provide financially for his family and solve problems for them but had little control over his hours, pay, and environment outside the home. In his world, a person was either "one-up" or "one-down." Challenging patriarchy in this family was a societal as well as relationship intervention.

Conditions that Foster Mutual Support: The Circle of Care

In order to resist taken-for-granted gender norms that are difficult to see or to avoid inadvertently following a more powerful partner's definition of the problem or societal discourses that may obscure inequities between partners, SERT therapists use a model of mutual support based on equality to guide case

Fig. 1 Elements of mutual support

conceptualization and planning. We call it the "Circle of Care" (see Fig. 1). It emphasizes four interrelated processes: shared relational responsibility, mutual vulnerability, mutual attunement, and mutual influence (Knudson-Martin and Huenergardt 2010). Though what these look like in practice will vary considerably depending on the couple's context and preferences, focusing on reciprocity in each of these areas creates the conditions that enable couples to envision and experience new, mutually supportive ways of relating.

Shared Relational Responsibility

When responsibility for the relationship is shared, each partner is sensitive to and accountable for the effect of their actions on the other and takes an active interest in doing what is necessary to maintain their relationship. When Shana and Sean began couple therapy, Shana carried most of this responsibility. Even though Sean held a strong sense of economic responsibility for the family, he often behaved as though his needs and perspectives were more important than Shana's or their son's.

Mutual Vulnerability

Mutual vulnerability means that each person brings a spirit of openness, curiosity, and self-honesty to the relationship. Each can experience the other in ways that make space for mistakes, weakness, or uncertainty without fearing the other's condemnation. When therapy began, Shana was in a much more vulnerable position than Sean. Though she had begun distancing from him to protect herself, she readily expressed her relational needs and desire for connection and had not given up making these moves toward relationship. Sean's experience growing up in a family and community organized around male dominance did not permit him to question himself or express his innermost thoughts, feelings, and concerns with Shana.

Mutual Attunement

Mutual attunement means that each partner is sensitive and responsive to the needs of the other. Carmen listened for and observed how interested each partner was in knowing and understanding the other's experience and perspectives and to what extent each listened to, noticed, and responded to the other's feelings and needs. At the start of therapy, attunement was out of balance. As a result, Shana did not feel important or supported. Though both partners needed to eventually better understand the other's perspective, attending to the societal and power processes that limited Sean's attunement was a key to clinical progress.

Mutual Influence

Mutual influence involves making an impression and impact on each other's thoughts, feelings, and actions. Each is willing to accommodate for the sake of the relationship and open to being changed by the other. Decision-making is shared. When therapy started, Shana was not able to engage Sean in addressing issues that concerned her. Sean felt freer to directly express his opinions or make requests. The family tended to organize around his interests and schedule. Without conscious intention on either part, Shana was more likely to accommodate than Sean.

SERT Clinical Competencies

Through ongoing reflection, evaluation, and action, our team identified a set of clinical competencies for addressing gender, culture, and societal power in couple therapy (Knudson-Martin et al. 2014). These are depicted in Fig. 2. Though each is relevant throughout therapy, they emerge in three phases as therapy progresses: (1) establishing an equitable foundation for therapy, (2) deconstructing and interrupting the flow of power, and (3) facilitating alternative experience. The overall goal is to empower couples to cocreate new relational experiences based on mutual support.

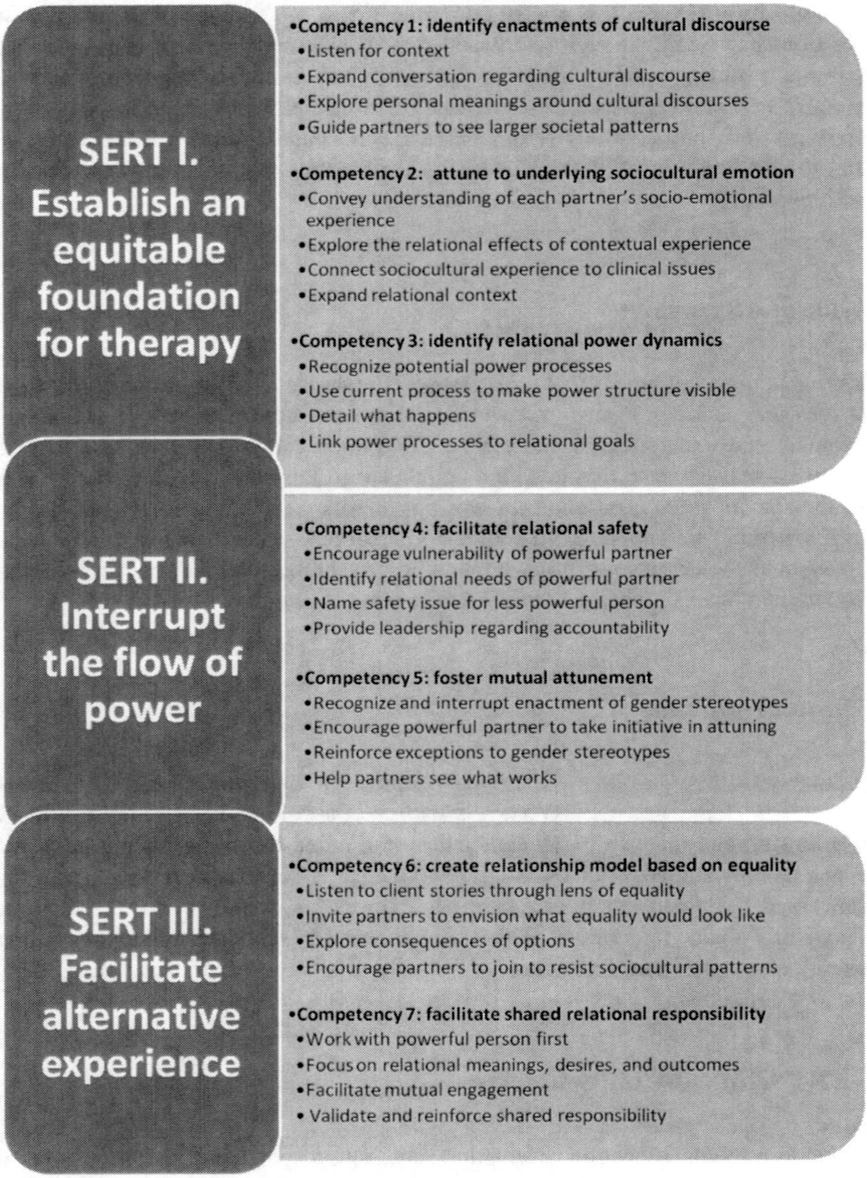

SERT I. Establish an equitable foundation for therapy

- **Competency 1: identify enactments of cultural discourse**
  - Listen for context
  - Expand conversation regarding cultural discourse
  - Explore personal meanings around cultural discourses
  - Guide partners to see larger societal patterns

- **Competency 2: attune to underlying sociocultural emotion**
  - Convey understanding of each partner's socio-emotional experience
  - Explore the relational effects of contextual experience
  - Connect sociocultural experience to clinical issues
  - Expand relational context

- **Competency 3: identify relational power dynamics**
  - Recognize potential power processes
  - Use current process to make power structure visible
  - Detail what happens
  - Link power processes to relational goals

SERT II. Interrupt the flow of power

- **Competency 4: facilitate relational safety**
  - Encourage vulnerability of powerful partner
  - Identify relational needs of powerful partner
  - Name safety issue for less powerful person
  - Provide leadership regarding accountability

- **Competency 5: foster mutual attunement**
  - Recognize and interrupt enactment of gender stereotypes
  - Encourage powerful partner to take initiative in attuning
  - Reinforce exceptions to gender stereotypes
  - Help partners see what works

SERT III. Facilitate alternative experience

- **Competency 6: create relationship model based on equality**
  - Listen to client stories through lens of equality
  - Invite partners to envision what equality would look like
  - Explore consequences of options
  - Encourage partners to join to resist sociocultural patterns

- **Competency 7: facilitate shared relational responsibility**
  - Work with powerful person first
  - Focus on relational meanings, desires, and outcomes
  - Facilitate mutual engagement
  - Validate and reinforce shared responsibility

Fig. 2 Socio-Emotional Relationship Therapy competencies

Phase I: Establishing an Equitable Foundation for Therapy

Therapists begin by intentionally positioning themselves in relation to the larger societal context. The challenge is to validate and support each partner without inadvertently organizing therapy around the dominant partner's view and to explore client goals in the context of mutual support. Three competencies are particularly important.

Identify enactments of cultural discourse. Clients usually tell their stories from their own individual perspective. Therapists must listen for how the larger context is present in the issues they raise. For example, Shana said she felt constrained and wanted more independence. She also hesitated to leave Sean in charge of their son. Carmen recognized cultural discourses about both individuality and motherhood in her experience and was curious about what these meant to her. While some therapists might have focused on her personal inconsistency or ambivalence, Carmen expanded the conversation about these multiple discourses in ways that affirmed her social identities and helped the couple begin to see their connection to larger societal patterns.

Attune to underlying sociocultural emotion. We have learned that it is not enough to understand clients' social contexts; therapists must also convey that they "get" each partner's socio-emotional experience. This provides a foundation from which therapists can explore the relational effects of sociocultural experience and connect them to clinical issues. Shana seemed particularly distressed when Sean did not take her worries about the need to plan seriously. Carmen gently sought to take in the socio-contextual experience of each of them around this issue. She wanted to understand what it felt like to be a mother who had learned she needed to sacrifice all for her children, including her own personal goals and financial stability. She wanted to experience the pressure Sean felt that he was supposed to have answers and how he had learned to rely on himself growing up in poverty. As each partner felt understood, they became interested in the consequences of these sociocultural experiences in their marriage.

Identify relational power dynamics. Identifying relational power dynamics works best when using current process. As therapy began, Carmen was attentive to how the partners attuned to and influenced each other. She watched for the extent to which both partners were vulnerable and taking responsibility for relational change. As she tracked their relational process in the room, she was able to help the couple detail how Sean ended up determining which issues were important and how that left Shana unable to get her concerns addressed. The couple was able to join together around a shared goal of how to create a more balanced relationship that supported each of them.

Phase II: Interrupting the Flow of Power

We found that identifying power issues does not in and of itself create change. Before other significant progress can be made, therapists need to provide leadership that interrupts the flow of power so that partners can begin to experience relating from more equitable positions. Though this is an ongoing process, two competencies are especially relevant:

Facilitate relational safety. This competency expands the idea of safety beyond issues of physical safety and the potential for violence and encourages partners to be accountable for the relational effects of their actions. When power is skewed, it is not safe for the more vulnerable person. Thus, we first explore the vulnerabilities of the more powerful partners, identifying their relational needs. This helps equalize the playing field. We also name the vulnerability of less powerful partners. Carmen reflected, "I know that both of you want this relationship to work, but somehow Shana's pain is really taking a toll on her. Your need for her is less visible. She's a lot more vulnerable in that way." To help counter this imbalance, Carmen engaged with Sean about his need for relationship, which was hard for him to express. As Carmen also helped him consider what it must be like for Shana, he expressed new awareness of her experience and accountability to make it safer for her.

Foster mutual attunement. When the ability to influence each other is not equal, the flow of attention is toward the powerful person. Since gender-stereo-typic behavior tends to reinforce this disparity, SERT therapists interrupt these patterns and encourage the more powerful partner to take initiative in attuning. Thus, when Sean quickly stepped in with answers, Carmen asked him what he thought Shana might feel. It is especially helpful to reinforce exceptions to gender stereo-types and make visible the positive effects of the powerful person's attempts to attune. When Sean told Shana he thought it must be hard for her to be so finan-cially dependent on him, that it might make her afraid for her future, Carmen emphasized his positive impact on her: that Shana visibly brightened and turned toward him. She helped him process what enabled him to take in her perspective and encouraged Shana to share what it felt like to be heard.

Phase III: Facilitating Alternative Experience

It is also not enough to identify and interrupt the flow of power. Therapists need to provide leadership in facilitating alternative experience (Williams et al. 2013). Shana and Sean needed to expand and solidify their new experiences of mutual support. Two clinical competencies facilitate this work.

Create relationship model based on equality. Despite egalitarian ideals, cou-ples often do not have a model for an equal relationship (Gerson 2010). As Shana and Sean spoke about their day-to-day life, Carmen listened through a lens of equality. She encouraged them to envision what equality would look like for them and helped them explore the consequences of options. For example, what did it mean to them that Sean had more personal time than Shana or that Shana was financially depend-ent on him? Carmen helped them detail what happened when they made decisions and invited them to think about how they could approach decisions and structure their time as partners. This intentional conversation was important in enabling the couple more flexibility in response to taken-for-granted gender patterns.

Facilitate shared relational responsibility. Shana and Sean began to address how she could fulfill her dream of nursing school and he could be more engaged with her and the family. Their discussions were difficult and reengaged socio-emotional issues for each partner regarding sacrifice, independence, selfishness, and commitment. Attention to shared relational responsibility throughout the process required ongoing attention to the gendered power dynamics that threatened to limit mutual engagement. It was especially important to validate and reinforce the couple's new experiences of shared relational responsibility as they attempted to address sociocultural, family of origin, and economic issues from more equal power positions.

Therapy as a Social Intervention

Though most therapists know that sociocultural contexts such as gender, sexual orientation, culture, race, and class affect couple dynamics, most practice models do not explicate how to actually address these issues. Attention to the larger societal context must somehow be added. Socio-Emotional Relationship Therapy is different because it *begins* with attunement to sociocultural experience and societal power disparities. SERT expands the lens outward to examine how sociocultural processes are present, reinforced, or modified in the moment by moment of couple therapy (see Estrella et al., "Expanding the Lens: How SERT Therapists Develop Interventions That Address the Larger Context," 2015). It integrates recent advances in neurobiology with social constructionist understandings of gender, culture, personal identities, and relationship processes.

In contrast to most models of therapy that proceed as though partners are equal (Leslie and Southard 2009; Williams and Knudson-Martin 2013), SERT involves ongoing attention to power imbalances between partners. Positive relational change happens when persons in powerful positions share responsibility for maintaining the relationship and initiating relational connection (Knudson-Martin and Huenergardt 2010). When Sean intentionally focused on engaging with Shana and listening to her, Shana described feeling more loved and less fearful about the future. Doing so meant that he had to recognize and challenge societal gender discourses that pressured him to have quick answers and privileged his experience and knowledge over hers. Shana reported feeling less depressed and less likely to give up when Sean did not seem to value her perspective. This shift in the power dynamic was an important foundation for addressing other issues such as different perspectives on parenting, unresolved issues with their families of origin, and how to manage work and family roles.

The authors in this volume explore the processes involved as therapists seek to bridge societal discourse, emotion, and couple interaction across many different kinds of cases and contexts. With the exception of Mona Fishbane's contribution on neurobiology in collaboration with Melissa Wells ("Toward Relational Empowerment: Interpersonal Neurobiology, Couples, and the Societal Context"), the chapters that follow are written by members of the SERT study team. We describe what we have learned and experienced, offering specific practice guidelines and many case examples on topics such as how gender hijacks couple therapy, how to practice sociocultural attunement, how to work with power and engage powerful partners, and how to apply SERT to issues such as same-sex relationships, the influence of childhood trauma, infidelity, and relational spirituality.

References

ChenFeng, J. L., & Galick, A. (2015). How gender discourses hijack couple therapy and how to avoid it. In C. Knudson-Martin, M. A. Wells, & S. K. Samman (Eds.), *Socio-emotional relationship therapy: Bridging emotion, societal context, and couple interaction* (pp. 41–52). New York, NY: Springer.

Dickerson, V. (2013). Patriarchy, power, and privilege: A narrative/poststructural view of work with couples. *Family Process, 52*, 102–114.

Esmiol, E., Knudson-Martin, C., & Delgado, S. (2012). How MFT students develop a critical contextual consciousness: A participatory action research project. *Journal of Marital and Family Therapy, 38*, 573–588.

Estrella, J., Kuhn, V. P., Freitas, C. J., & Wells, M. A. (2015). Expanding the lens: How SERT therapists develop interventions that address larger context. In C. Knudson-Martin, M. A. Wells & S. K. Samman (Eds.), *Socio-emotional relationship therapy: Bridging emotion, societal context, and couple interaction* (pp. 53–65). New York, NY: Springer.

Fishbane, M. D., & Wells, M. A. (2015). Toward relational empowerment: Interpersonal neurobiology, couples, and the societal context. In C. Knudson-Martin, M. A. Wells & S. K. Samman (Eds.), *Socio-emotional relationship therapy: Bridging emotion, societal context, and couple interaction* (pp. 27–40). New York, NY: Springer.

Gerson, K. (2010). *The unfinished revolution: How a new generation is reshaping family, work, and gender in America.* New York: Oxford University Press.

Gottman, J. M. (2011). *The science of trust: Emotional attunement for couples.* New York. NY: Norton.

Greenberg, L. S., & Goldman, R. N. (2008). *Emotion-focused couples therapy: The dynamics of emotion, love, and power.* Washington DC: American Psychological Association.

Hughes, D. (2009). The communication of emotions and the growth of autonomy and intimacy in family therapy. In D. Fosha, D. J. Siegel, & M. F. Solomon (Eds.), *The healing power of emotion: Affective neuroscience, development and clinical practice* (pp. 280–304). New York, NY: Norton.

Jonathan, N. (2009). Carrying equal weight: Relational responsibility and attunement among same-sex couples. In C. Knudson-Martin & A. R. Mahoney (Eds.), *Couples, gender and power: Creating change in intimate relationships* (pp. 79–104). New York, NY: Springer Publishing Company.

Jonathan, N., & Knudson-Martin, C. (2012). Building connection: Attunement and gender equality in heterosexual relationships. *Journal of Couple and Relationship Therapy, 11*, 95–111.

Kimmel, M. (2011). *The gendered society* (4th ed.). New York, NY: Oxford University Press.

Knudson-Martin, C. (1994). The female voice: Applications to Bowen's family systems theory. *Journal of Marital and Family Therapy, 20*, 35–46.

Knudson-Martin, C. (1996). Differentiation and self-development in the relationship context. *The Family Journal, 4*, 188–198.

Knudson-Martin, C. (1997). The politics of gender in family therapy. *Journal of Marital and Family Therapy, 23*, 431–447.

Knudson-Martin, C. (2013). Why power matters: Creating a foundation of mutual support in couple relationships. *Family Process, 52*, 5–18.

Knudson-Martin, C. (2015). When therapy challenges patriarchy: Undoing gendered power in heterosexual couple relationships. In C. Knudson-Martin, M. A. Wells & S. K. Samman (Eds.), *Socio-emotional relationship therapy: Bridging emotion, societal context, and couple interaction* (pp. 15–26). New York, NY: Springer.

Knudson-Martin, C., & Huenergardt, D. (2010). A socio-emotional approach to couple therapy: Linking social context and couple interaction. *Family Process, 49,* 369–386.

Knudson-Martin, C., Huenergardt, D., Lafontant, K., Bishop, L., Schaepper, J., & Wells, M. (2014). Competencies for addressing gender and power in couple therapy. *Journal of Marital and Family Therapy (Advance online publication),*. doi:10.1111/jmft.12068.

Knudson-Martin, C., & Mahoney, A. (2005). Moving beyond gender: Processes that create relationship equality. *Journal of Marital and Family Therapy, 31,* 235–246.

Knudson-Martin, C., & Mahoney, A. (2009). *Couples, gender, and power: Creating change in intimate relationships.* New York, NY: Springer Publishing Company.

Leslie, L. A., & Southard, A. L. (2009). Thirty years of feminist family therapy: Moving into the mainstream. In S. A. Lloyd, A. L. Few, & K. R. Allen (Eds.), *Handbook of feminist family studies* (pp. 328–339). Los Angeles, CA: Sage Publications.

McDowell, T. M., & Fang, S. S. (2007). Feminist-informed critical multiculturalism. *Journal of Family Issues, 28,* 549–566.

Mirgain, S. A., & Cordova, J. V. (2007). Emotion skills and marital health: The association between observed and self-reported emotion skills, intimacy, and marital satisfaction. *Journal of Counseling and Clinical Psychology, 26,* 983–1009.

Pandit, M., ChenFeng, J. L., & Kang, Y. J. (2015). Becoming socioculturally attuned: A study of therapist experience. In C. Knudson-Martin, M. A. Wells & S. K. Samman (Eds.), *Socio-emotional relationship therapy: Bridging emotion, societal context, and couple interaction* (pp. 67–78). New York, NY: Springer.

Porges, S. W. (2009). Reciprocal influences between body and brain in the perception and expression of affect. In D. Fosha, D. J. Siegel, & M. F. Solomon (Eds.), *The healing power of emotion: Affective neuroscience, development and clinical practice* (pp. 27–54). New York, NY: Norton.

Richards, J. C., Jonathan, N., & Kim, L. (2015). Building a circle of care in same-sex couple relationships: A socio-emotional relational approach. In C. Knudson-Martin, M. A. Wells & S. K. Samman (Eds.), *Socio-emotional relationship therapy: Bridging emotion, societal context, and couple interaction* (pp. 93–105). New York, NY: Springer.

Siegel, D. J. (2001). *The developing mind: How relationships and the brain interact to shape who we are.* New York, NY: Guilford Press.

Stuchell, S. (2013). *Physician couples: A qualitative inquiry focused on gendered power and marital equality (Unpublished doctoral dissertation).* Loma Linda, CA: Loma Linda University.

Tichenor, V. J. (2005). *Earning more and getting less: Why successful wives can't buy equality.* New Brunswick, NJ: Rutgers University Press.

Walters, M., Carter, B., Papp, P., & Silverstein, O. (1988). *The invisible web: Gender patterns in family relationships.* New York, NY: Guilford Press.

Williams, K., Galick, A., Knudson-Martin, C., & Huenergardt, D. (2013). Toward mutual support: A task analysis of the relational justice approach to infidelity. *Journal of Marital and Family Therapy, 39,* 285–298. doi:10.1111/j.1752-0606.2012.00324.x.

Williams, K., & Knudson-Martin, C. (2013). Do therapists address gender and power in infidelity? A feminist analysis of the treatment literature. *Journal of Marital and Family Therapy, 39*(3), 271–284. doi:10.1111/j.1752-0606.2012.00303.x.

Winslade, J. (2009). Tracing lines of flight: Implications of the work of Gilles Deleuze. *Family Process, 48,* 332–346.

When Therapy Challenges Patriarchy: Undoing Gendered Power in Heterosexual Couple Relationships

Carmen Knudson-Martin

Transforming power imbalances is at the heart of Socio-Emotional Relationship Therapy (SERT), an approach that addresses sociocultural processes that perpetuate inequality and interfere with mutual care and support (see Knudson-Martin and Huenergardt, "Bridging Emotion, Societal Discourse, and Couple Interaction in Clinical Practice," 2015). Working with power in couple therapy raises many challenging questions. What is power? How can we recognize it? Isn't this a personal values issue? What if people don't want equal power? Why would someone give up power? Addressing gendered power associated with patriarchy can be particularly challenging.

Although I have studied gendered power and practiced couple therapy for a long time, I still struggle with all these concerns and experience them daily from my vantage point as a married heterosexual woman. As part of the SERT clinical research team, I have observed countless therapy sessions, tracked and coded the clinical processes involved, explored my own personal responses, and engaged in an ongoing effort to recognize and address power disparities (see Estrella et al. "Expanding the Lens: How SERT Therapists Develop Interventions that Address the Larger Context," 2015; Knudson-Martin et al. 2014). In this chapter, I address some of the most common questions. The case examples, which have been modified to protect confidentiality, illustrate the hidden and complex nature of gendered power.

Why Is Power a Relationship Issue?

Because people influence each other, power is an inherent part of all relationships. Among intimate partners, power "refers to the ability of one person to influence a relationship toward his own goals, interests, and well-being" (Mahoney

C. Knudson-Martin (✉)
Counseling Psychology Department, Lewis & Clark College, Portland, OR, USA

© American Family Therapy Academy 2015
C. Knudson-Martin et al. (eds.), *Socio-Emotional Relationship Therapy*,
AFTA SpringerBriefs in Family Therapy, DOI 10.1007/978-3-319-13398-0_2

15

and Knudson-Martin 2009, p. 10). When power is relatively well balanced, each partner is able to engage the other around issues that are important to them and they feel equally entitled to express their ideas, needs, and feelings. Both partners notice and attend to the needs of the other and each is likely to accommodate.

When power is not equal, the more powerful partner will be less aware of the other's experience. What makes it more complicated is that people in higher power positions generally are not aware of their power; they may not even realize that others are attentive to their needs or that their interests are dominating the agenda. On the other hand, people in less powerful positions are likely to automatically take into account the desires or expectations of the more powerful. People in powerful roles (i.e., teacher, employer, physician, and husband) may take for granted that others accommodate them—or become distressed when they do not. Conflict may be reduced, but at the expense of a limited voice for the less powerful.

Contemporary intimate relationships generally presume mutuality; partners expect that the relationship will equally support each of them (Knudson-Martin 2013). Enacting the qualities that comprise the Circle of Care described in "Bridging Emotion, Societal Discourse, and Couple Interaction in Clinical Practice," (Knudson-Martin and Huenergardt, 2015) requires a relatively equal balance of power and reciprocity. Unless power imbalances are identified and transformed, other desired clinical change is likely to be difficult. Figure 1 includes a list of assessment questions developed by Mahoney and Knudson-Martin (2009, p. 11–12).

The power processes in a relationship can be surprisingly difficult to assess, especially among heterosexual partners. This is because a power hierarchy is implicit in how binary gender is socially constructed and maintained. Even in Western contexts where ideas of gender have changed considerably in recent decades, people get mixed social messages. On the one hand, both men and women increasingly seek equal relationships (Sullivan 2006); at the same time, transforming hierarchical gender patterns turns out to be much more difficult than people realize (Coontz 2005; Gerson 2010; Knudson-Martin and Mahoney 2009). People, including therapists, often believe that women and men are equal now and may not recognize how communication patterns tend to remain gendered such that men are less likely to tune into, notice, and accommodate to female partners. Or if they do, masculine gender norms tell them they have given up too much.

Why Is Power So Difficult to Recognize?

Gendered Individualism

At first, Lila (58) and Lance (61) appeared to epitomize equality. Both previously divorced with grown children, they met when each returned to graduate school. Now married for five years, this European American couple held identical jobs, strongly professed values of gender equality, and appeared to make decisions

WHAT IS THE BALANCE OF POWER?

RELATIVE STATUS
- Whose interests shape what happens in the family?
- To what extent do partners feel equally entitled to express and attain personal goals, needs, and wishes?
- How are low-status tasks like housework handled?

ATTENTION TO OTHER
- To what extent do both partners notice and attend to the other's needs and emotions?
- Does attention go back and forth between partners? Does each give and receive?
- When attention is imbalanced do partners express awareness of this and the need to rebalance?

ACCOMMODATION PATTERNS
- Is one partner more likely to organize his or her daily activities around the other?
- Does accommodation often occur automatically without anything being said?
- Do partners attempt to justify accommodations they make as being "natural" or the result of personality differences?

WELL-BEING
- Does one partner seem to be better off psychologically, emotionally, or physically than the other?
- Does one person's sense of competence, optimism, or well-being seem to come at the expense of the other's physical or emotional health?
- Does the relationship support the economic viability of each partner?

Fig. 1 Assessment of relationship power positions

and manage household responsibilities together. Lila spoke assertively while Lance spoke more softly. In fact, he proclaimed that he did not want to be one of those men who took over conversations. For a while, we wondered whether Lila may be in the more powerful position. But when we used the assessment guide offered in this chapter and focused on who had the ability to impact the other, it became clear that a major part of Lila's distress was that though the couple would "talk," she was unable to get him to respond to things that mattered to her. When we tracked this power dynamic in session and repeatedly observed Lance pulling away from Lila's concerns, he reported that he did not see what he could do or resisted the idea that he had any responsibility for her problems.

Though at first difficult to see, Lance and Lila demonstrated "gendered individualism" (Loscocco and Walzer 2013, p. 7), a common pattern that inadvertently perpetuates male power. We see it often in the USA. Men internalize the culture of individualism, while women are still socialized to accommodate and are held responsible for relationship maintenance. This individualistic focus discourages men from taking relationship-directed actions. According to Loscocco and Walzer, this is one of the major reasons women are less satisfied with their marriages than men. They further argue that self-help books and other relationship experts often encourage women to be the ones to change. If we had done that, we would have encouraged Lila to take more responsibility and expected less of Lance. That would have even further perpetuated the power imbalance.

Instead, we worked first with Lance to help him become more aware of internalized messages that told him to resist relational responsibility. We also helped him get more in touch with his genuine concern and care for Lila and to express it. It was slow work and sometimes frustrating for Lila, with whom we maintained a supportive balance that validated her right to expect responsiveness from Lance while helping both partners understand the societal context of his disengagement and their shared desire to transform it. At one point, Lance actually identified that his struggle was more with the voices of other men than with her. Throughout his life, he had "failed" to live up to masculinity. Yet masculine ideals of individuality were threatening their marriage.

Latent Power

Another reason power is so hard to assess is that it is built into societal gender norms that guide how partners respond to each other. As a result, shared decisions may reflect male interests and women may unwittingly subordinate their needs. This works well to reduce conflict, but limits intimacy, mutual support, and well-being. Carole and Carl, an African American couple in their late twenties sought counseling in their first year of marriage. Both medical students, this couple generally demonstrated one of the most equal communication patterns we have seen. Each seemed attentive and responsive to the well-being of the other. Yet, Carole was in tears and Carl did not know what to do. During the process of matching for residencies, the couple had tried to list only preferences that would work for both of them. However, Carl included one choice on his list that both partners knew was not really a good option for her. It turned out that this was the only offer Carl received and Carole automatically told him it would be okay. He accepted the offer, and now the couple had to live with the unequitable decision. How did this happen? How could they move forward and prevent future inequities like this?

Carl had latent power (Komter 1989) so that shared decisions ended up favoring him. Though Carole had quietly hoped that Carl would resist taking an option that was such a poor choice for her, it seemed natural to both of them to support his career. Though they did not discuss it, they took for granted that ultimately she would likely take time away from work when they had children and therefore made an almost automatic decision that limited her career options and maximized his.

Of course, in all relationships, sometimes one person has to sacrifice for the good of the other. Gender theory suggests that most often these sacrifices will support the male partner's goals (Komter 1989; Zvonkovic et al. 1996). What was unusual was that the couple recognized the potential long-term inequity and sought help to deal with the issue. When they discussed it, they learned that Carole had approached the residency matching from a relationship-directed position that prioritized what was best for the relationship as a whole (see Silverstein et al. 2006), and Carl had automatically accepted her sacrifice as natural without noticing or attending to what she was giving up—a reflection of latent power.

Invisible Power

Overt power—such as access to resources or physical strength—is more easily recognized. But many aspects of power in a relationship are less visible. According to Komter (1989), invisible power is connected to how societal patterns affect each partner's internal sense of self, their hopes and dreams, and the skills and competencies they develop. The couple is most likely not aware of how these create power differences in what each partner feels entitled to and how much each partner acknowledges needing the other. In heterosexual relationships, these tend to be gendered. Even when the female partner makes more money or has rigid time demands from her work, other relational processes may still privilege the male partner (Tichenor 2005).

For example, women are more likely to internalize blame (Gross and Hansen 2000), putting them in a (invisible) one-down power position. When Jose and Karina, a Mexican American couple in their thirties with two young children, began therapy Karina immediately took responsibility for their relationship problems by saying that she was probably codependent. Karina was the sole breadwinner of the family and Jose was a stay-at-home dad. The couple said they made this decision for practical reasons because Karina was able to earn more money than Jose and they were able to save on childcare expenses. Both agreed he was a good father. Yet, when it came to the couple relationship, Jose seemed almost entirely self-focused. When Karina raised concerns that mattered to her, Jose consistently invalidated her perspective or took the discussion in a different direction. Even though Karina made the family income, the relationship dynamics organized around what mattered to Jose. Jose held both latent and invisible power.

What About Role Reversals?

As suggested above, even when women at first appear to have the dominant voice or most income in a heterosexual relationship, the relational processes are never as simple as a role reversal. To understand each partner's experience and the power dynamics associated with it, it is necessary to expand the lens to the larger societal gender context. Everyone lives in a world in which gender still structures economic, social, and political institutions. This larger social context shapes the meaning of behavior and influences all relationships, at least to some extent. For example, Belle, a 36-year-old African American woman married to John, a 38-year-old European American man, complained that John was not interested enough in sex. This sounds like Belle is the more sexually demanding partner and a role reversal from what couple therapists more typically see. But when the meaning of her sexual demands was explored in relation to the wider social context, it turned out that what Belle really wanted was more engagement from John, for him to show more interest in her. Since she had internalized societal gender prescriptions, she viewed sexual interest from men as the way they showed interest in women. When John did not seem to fit this expectation, she felt devalued. When the therapist helped the couple explore how they related to societal gender expectations, the nuances of their responses to each other and how these connected to power processes became clearer. Belle's plea was not really coming from a power position.

Similarly, Frank, a 42-year-old European American elementary teacher, sought therapy because he wanted more closeness with his wife, Joan, a company administrator. At first, Joan refused to attend the sessions, usually a sign of a power position. So the therapist used the Circle of Care (see Knudson-Martin and Huenergardt, "Bridging Emotion, Societal Discourse, and Couple Interaction in Clinical Practice," 2015) to help Frank assess their relationship and how he attended to and engaged his wife. Frank discovered that even though he did much of the childcare for their eight-year-old son, he really had always expected that Joan would take the relational lead. When asked about how he tuned into her or what she would find engaging, Frank was dumbfounded. He had enjoyed their relationship, which he thought had been good for most of their 20 years of marriage. It was only recently that Joan seemed to "not care" about him or not have as much time for him.

As Frank began to attend more to Joan and increase his responsibility for the relationship, Joan agreed to participate in couple therapy. Viewing her apparent power position in relation to the larger societal gender context and the history of their relationship, her current responses were better understood as a way to take a more equal position in the marriage. She tearfully described how when they were dating she had had sex with Frank when she really did not want to, but felt that she had no choice "if she wanted to please a man." She spoke of years of accommodating him and working hard to make the relationship flourish. She was tired and not interested in that anymore. However, as Frank began to carry more of the relationship burden, each of them expressed new life in their relationship and renewed desire for each other.

As the example of Frank and Joan suggests, by the time a couple seeks therapy, the power dynamic may have taken a turn, especially if a hurt or angry woman is no longer willing to play the role of keeping the relationship alive. She has temporarily increased her power position because she is no longer relationship oriented. This dynamic may be exacerbated when one or both partners has experienced a history of abuse (see Wells and Kuhn, "Couple Therapy with Adult Survivors of Child Abuse: Gender, Power, and Trust," 2015) or if a woman has an affair (see Williams and Kim, "Relational Justice: Addressing Gender and Power in Clinical Practices for Infidelity," 2015). However, we have found that for the relationship to resurrect, the previous underlying power dynamic between the partners must be addressed and this usually means helping men engage from a more relationship-oriented position (see Samman and Knudson-Martin, "Relational Engagement in Heterosexual Couple Therapy: Helping Men Move from "I" to "We"," 2015).

What if Men Don't Feel Powerful?

When couples come to therapy, both partners may feel helpless. Sometimes heterosexual men are frustrated or puzzled because they do not understand why their partner is so distressed. Either way, men are more likely to feel incompetent than powerful (Shepard and Harway 2012). Being in a societal power position discourages men from attuning to others, but puts them at a disadvantage if they want to build relationship. Feeling incompetent is a primary hurdle because people on the top are supposed to know what they are doing. Thus, societal gender processes set couples up for failure by limiting the options for women and men. Each does better when relationships are more equal (Knudson-Martin 2013; Steil 1997). Therapy that helps each partner take a more relationally oriented position can be empowering to both (Fishbane 2011; Fishbane and Wells, "Toward Relational Empowerment: Interpersonal Neurobiology, Couples, and the Societal Context," 2015).

SERT begins by attuning to the sociocultural experience of each partner. Attention to the societal power context is an important aspect of this process. Power associated with various societal positions (i.e., age, ethnicity, social class, ability/disability, sexual orientation, religion, national origin, indigenous heritage, and other social locations) intersects with gender in many different ways and influence how intimate partners respond and react to each other. The goal is to first understand each partner's contextual experience and then to use the position of the therapist to counteract societal power processes in ways that empower couples to create more equitable, mutually supportive relationship patterns.

In the case of Belle and John, the mixed-race couple introduced earlier, John maintained a power position that kept him disengaged from his wife and children. Yet with limited formal education and an injury that placed him on disability, he experienced himself as powerless within the family and even less powerful in the larger society. However, as a European American male, he was socialized to believe that he *should* occupy a position of respect from others. He attempted to maintain a position of personal respect by disparaging other authorities (doctors, school officials, and government policies) and, according to Belle and the children, focused mostly on his own interests at home. If he accommodated Belle's ideas or requests, he felt diminished. He was in pain, depressed, and avoided social situations.

Belle was also in physical pain but continued her job as a teacher. Belle's experience as an African American woman was that you had to push through whatever hardships came your way. She expected disrespect, and said she had learned not to let that hold her back from doing things she wanted to do. She was therefore impatient with John's approach to life and vacillated between trying to understand his situation and anger that he did not carry more of the load in the family. One of the most important challenges in the therapy was to believe that John was capable of engaging with his wife and family and empowering him to do this, while also recognizing his disempowered societal experience.

Do Men Always Have Power?

Gender is a societal process that organizes human relationships; thus latent and invisible power accompanies membership in the male social category. This is a collective process, not an individual one. However, as in the cases described above, individual women and men respond in many different ways to male power and partners frequently have more power in some aspects of their lives than in others. In healthy relationships, power is relatively equal and ideally flows back and forth reciprocally. Though few couples fully attain this ideal, many couples are making progress toward it (Knudson-Martin and Mahoney 2009).

We seldom see cases in which women dominate male partners in ways comparable to men; i.e., they do not enter the relationship with societal norms supporting latent and invisible power. But we see a lot of power struggles. In terms of undoing gender, this often is a good sign. It means there are still two active voices and one partner has not simply given up and accommodated to keep things smooth. On the other hand, power struggles can be very painful, especially when neither feels validated by the other. SERT therapists are careful to explore the socio-contextual meaning of each side of the power struggle. Power struggles and conflict may be a sign of equal power or a battle for power. It is likely to be a contest between processes undoing gendered power and those that maintain it (Deutsch 2007).

Equal Power Struggle

Yuka, a 32-year-old Christian Japanese woman who immigrated to the USA as a child, and Rahman, a 29-year-old Muslim man who emigrated from Indonesia as a teenager, were caught in a power struggle more or less as equals. Yuka was accomplished in international law, travelled and spoke frequently at conferences, and had a wide circle of friends. When she met Rahman through a friend, he was completing medical school. She took the lead in establishing their relationship. Though the couple enjoyed spirited conversations with each other, Rahman depended primarily on Yuka for his social life. Despite her clear leadership in forming the relationship, Yuka had hesitated to move in with Rahman, but did so anyway because he promised they would get married. She was also frustrated that after completing advanced fellowship training, Rahman worked in a temporary emergency room job and was not actively seeking a position more consistent with his training. The more Yuka pushed, the more Rahman seemed to resist.

Yuka had much more power in the relationship than most women do. Rahman seemed to need her more than she needed him. Still, it was Rahman who resisted deeper commitment and Yuka who ended up accommodating. Though Rahman worried often about pleasing Yuka and said he could not imagine a better partner, he feared marriage would be disappointing. Many factors were at play for this couple, including family-of-origin, cultural, and religious issues. Intersecting with all of these were the internal contradictory gender constructions with which each partner struggled. Yuka liked her independence and easily took charge, both at home and in the workplace. Yet part of her automatically accommodated her partner and also wanted him to fit masculine norms by being more proactive and assertive. Rahman valued the sense of mutuality he experienced with Yuka. It was very different from the domineering ways of his father. But internally, he also felt that that he should be "more of a man" and feared being controlled by her.

Instead of experiencing a comfortable give and take, Rahman and Yuka's internal confusion was reflected in a power struggle that was deeply hurtful to Yuka and almost immobilizing for Rahman. An important step toward mutual support was for Rahman to become comfortable expressing his real feelings to Yuka and being able to take in her perspective without feeling controlled by her. In turn, Yuka needed to recognize how her sense of needing to keep the relationship going was a part of her identity that was not consistent with her otherwise egalitarian ideals. Though Rahman and Yuka's situation was particularly interesting because of the many contextual factors involved, most contemporary couples struggle to some extent with contradictory internalized gender ideals because current societal discourses support equality even as old gender structures continue to organize relationships around male power (Knudson-Martin and Mahoney 2009).

Battle for Power

Power struggles also occur when women begin to resist male power. For example, Veronica, a 47-year-old European American woman, had been married for 17 years to Hal, a 55-year-old European American. The marriage began as a gender-traditional relationship with Hal earning a good income for the family and Veronica serving as a stay-at-home mother for their two sons and her daughter from an earlier marriage. Hal adhered to many stereotypical gender patterns that reinforce male dominance. He wanted to be recognized for his knowledge and was invested in "being right." He liked Veronica's attractive figure and monitored her appearance closely. He liked to spend time with her and expected her to be available when his schedule permitted. He felt free to criticize her values and style when they did not agree with his.

In the first years of their marriage, Veronica had also displayed many stereotypical "submissive" gender patterns. She was adept at determining what Hal and the children wanted and needed and readily responded to them. Though sometimes she found Hal's "arrogance" irritating, she appreciated his work ethic and family focus. Since she wanted to be a stay-at-home mother and had not been able to do that in her first marriage, she welcomed the opportunity Hal's income provided. However, his criticism of her hurt and she took to "walking on eggshells" to keep the peace.

Over time, Veronica became less and less willing to put her ideas on the back burner. As she expressed herself more, Hal became more critical and demanding. Veronica frequently did not feel valued or loved by him. When she tried to raise issues that concerned her, Hal dismissed them. Veronica's "solution" was an affair. Though the affair was over when Hal discovered it, he felt deeply rejected, hurt, and angry. He thought he had been a good husband. They report that for about six months, Veronica was very contrite and apologized often; she was paying a form of penance that put her back in a lower power position. But all the issues that concerned her before the affair were even greater now. She stopped being willing to accept a one-down role.

When the couple came to therapy, the couple was in a battle for power. Veronica went back and forth between guilt for what she had done and a sense that she was entitled to more voice in the marriage and respect from her husband. Sometimes she would get very angry and demanding. Over the course of therapy, both partners decided to recommit to their marriage and a new way of relating. Hal began to let go of the idea that he needed to always be right or that a question regarding his way of doing things was a sign of disrespect. He was increasingly able to validate Veronica as an equally competent partner. Veronica was more able to speak up in ways that positively influenced decisions and made it easier for her to look at Hal "with stars in her eyes" again. At this writing, the couple still gets caught in difficult power struggles from time to time, particularly when crises occur, but they have a vision of what a more mutual relationship looks like and are beginning to experience the positive benefits of shared power.

What if People Don't Want Equal Roles?

This is an important question. The kind of power emphasized here is the power that enables one person to overlook and minimize another. It is not so much about who does the dishes or is responsible to manage the children's schedule (though these are usually also important); it is about partners having equal status and worth in the relationship. The Circle of Care provides a framework for how to relate from mutual positions that is supported by research (see Gottman 2011; Knudson-Martin 2013; Knudson-Martin et al. 2014; Williams et al. 2013).

We are not neutral about facilitating a process that promotes a more equitable flow of power in couple communication processes. We see our goal as helping couples create a relationship context that enables them to make decisions about how they divide labor or resolve conflicts in ways that support each partner. We help people bring taken-for-granted gender processes into the open and discuss them so they can decide for themselves what kind of relationship they want instead of enacting cultural norms without being aware that they are doing so.

In a recent qualitative study of how long-term couples with children made their relationship work, we found that flexibility on the part of *both* partners was directly related to stability (Nicoleau et al. 2014). These couples regularly crossed gender boundaries to "do what it takes" to support the relationship and each other. Some did this within a more stereotypic general division of labor and others described an "ungendered" approach in which responsibilities were viewed as shared and interchangeable. What stood out in the stories of these women and men was that flexibility was the result of a relational focus in which both partners described a sense that the other was tuned into their needs and invested in their well-being and that of the family. In this way, couples were undoing at least some of the constraints of gendered power. It is this kind of flexibility based on mutual support that SERT promotes.

Clinician's Role

Gendered power is persistent and built into societal norms and institutions. It shapes the meaning and emotions that women and men experience as they attempt to live, love, and form families together. Undoing gendered power is a societal work in progress (Deutsch 2007). As therapists become aware that power disparities harm both women and men, inviting couples into a process that reconstructs historical gender processes becomes a fundamental part of our role. Without conscious action, therapists will inadvertently reinforce societal power inequities. The chapters that follow offer practical guidelines that help transform gendered power while being responsive to clients' personal and cultural contexts. Each illustrates ways to empower couples to create new, more equitable relationship possibilities.

References

Coontz, S. (2005). *Marriage, a history: From obedience to intimacy or how love conquered marriage.* New York, NY: Viking Press.

Deutsch, F. M. (2007). Undoing gender. *Gender and Society, 21,* 106–127. doi:10.1177/0891243206293577.

Estrella, J., Kuhn, V. P., Freitas, C. J., & Wells, M. A. (2015). Expanding the lens: How SERT therapists develop interventions that address larger context. In C. Knudson-Martin, M. A. Wells, & S. K. Samman (Eds.), *Socio-emotional relationship therapy: Bridging emotion, societal context, and couple interaction* (pp. 53–65). New York, NY: Springer.

Fishbane, M. D. (2011). Facilitating relational empowerment in couple therapy. *Family Process, 50,* 337–352.

Fishbane, M. D., & Wells, M. (2015). Toward relational empowerment: Interpersonal neurobiology, couples, and the societal context. In C. Knudson-Martin, M. A. Wells, & S. K. Samman (Eds.), *Socio-emotional relationship therapy: Bridging emotion, societal context, and couple interaction* (pp. 27–40). New York, NY: Springer.

Gerson, K. (2010). *The unfinished revolution: How a new generation is reshaping family, work, and gender in America.* New York, NY: Oxford University Press.

Gottman, J. M. (2011). *The science of trust: Emotional attunement for couples.* New York, NY: Guilford Press.

Gross, C. A., & Hansen, N. E. (2000). Clarifying the experience of shame: The role of attachment style, gender, and investment in relatedness. *Personality and Individual Differences, 28,* 897–907.

Knudson-Martin, C. (2013). Why power matters: Creating a foundation of mutual support in couple relationships. *Family Process, 52,* 5–18.

Knudson-Martin, C., & Huenergardt, D. (2010). A socio-emotional approach to couple therapy: Linking social context and couple interaction. *Family Process, 49,* 369–386.

Knudson-Martin, C., & Huenergardt, D. (2015). Bridging emotion, societal discourse, and couple interaction in clinical practice. In C. Knudson-Martin, M. A. Wells, & S. K. Samman (Eds.), *Socio-emotional relationship therapy: Bridging emotion, societal context, and couple interaction* (pp. 1–13). New York, NY: Springer.

Knudson-Martin, C., & Mahoney, A. R. (2009). *Couples, gender, and power: Creating change in intimate relationships.* New York, NY: Springer Publishing Company.

Knudson-Martin, C., Huenergardt, D., Lafontant, K., Bishop, L., Schaepper, J., & Wells, M. (2014). Competencies for addressing gender and power in couple therapy: A socio-emotional approach. *Journal of Marital and Family Therapy,* Advance online publication. doi:10.1111/jmft.12068.

Komter, A. (1989). Hidden power in marriage. *Gender and Society, 3,* 187–216.

Loscocco, K., & Walzer, S. (2013). Gender and the culture of heterosexual marriage in the United States. *Journal of Family Theory & Review, 5,* 1–14.

Mahoney, A. R., & Knudson-Martin, C. (2009). Gender equality in intimate relationships. In C. Knudson-Martin & A. Mahoney (Eds.), *Couples, gender, and power: Creating change in intimate relationships* (pp. 3–16). New York, NY: Springer Publishing Company.

Nicoleau, A., Kang, Y. J., Choau, S. T., & Knudson-Martin, C. (2014). Doing what it takes to make it work: Flexibility, relational focus, and stability among long-term couples with children. *Family Issues.* Advanced online publication, doi:10.1177/0192513X4543852.

Samman, S. K., & Knudson-Martin, C. (2015). Relational engagement in heterosexual couple therapy: Helping men move from "I" to "We." In C. Knudson-Martin, M. A. Wells, & S. K. Samman (Eds.), *Socio-emotional relationship therapy: Bridging emotion, societal context, and couple interaction* (pp. 79–91). New York, NY: Springer.

Shepard, D. S., & Harway, M. (2012). The challenges of conducting male sensitive couples therapy: Common pitfalls and recommendations. In D. S. Shepard & M. Harway (Eds.), *Engaging men in couples therapy* (pp. 13–35). New York, NY: Routledge.

Silverstein, R., Bass, L. B., Tuttle, A., Knudson-Martin, C., & Huenergardt, D. (2006). What does it mean to be relational? A framework for assessment and practice. *Family Process, 45,* 391–405.

Steil, J. (1997). *Marital equality: Its relationship to the well-being of husbands and wives.* Newbury Park, CA: Sage Publications.

Sullivan, O. (2006). *Changing gender relations, changing families: Tracing the pace of change over time.* Lanham, MD: Rowman & Littlefield Publications.

Tichenor, V. J. (2005). *Earning more and getting less: Why successful wives can't buy equality.* New Brunswick, NJ: Rutgers University Press.

Wells, M. A., & Kuhn, V. P. (2015). Couple therapy with adult survivors of child abuse: Gender, power, and trust. In C. Knudson-Martin, M. A. Wells, & S. K. Samman (Eds.), *Socio-emotional relationship therapy: Bridging emotion, societal context, and couple interaction* (pp. 107–119). New York, NY: Springer.

Williams, K., Galick, A., Knudson-Martin, C., & Huenergardt, D. (2013). Toward mutual support: A task analysis of the relational justice approach to infidelity. *Journal of Marital and Family Therapy, 39*(3), 285–298. doi:10.1111/j.1752-0606.2012.00324.x.

Williams, K., & Kim, L. (2015). Relational justice: Addressing gender and power in clinical practices for infidelity. In C. Knudson-Martin, M. A. Wells, & S. K. Samman (Eds.), *Socio-emotional relationship therapy: Bridging emotion, societal context, and couple interaction* (pp. 121–132). New York, NY: Springer.

Zvonkovic, A., Greaves, K., Schmeige, C., & Hall, L. (1996). The marital construction of gender through work and family decisions. *Journal of Marriage and the Family, 58,* 91–100.

Toward Relational Empowerment: Interpersonal Neurobiology, Couples, and the Societal Context

Mona DeKoven Fishbane and Melissa A. Wells

Our society prizes accomplishments of the strong, autonomous individual. But, this cultural emphasis on independence and self-sufficiency unwittingly marginalizes the emotional skills of interdependence involved in creating responsive, loving, and enduring couple relationships. When performing societal expectations of ultra-individualism, many couples can easily find themselves stuck in conflict that leads to negativity and reactivity. Helping couples understand the link between their gendered power interactions, emotions, and sociocultural context is vital so that they can become less reactive toward each other and more proactive in sharing relational processes of attunement and vulnerability that promote relationship satisfaction and personal well-being (Fishbane 2011; Knudson-Martin and Huenergardt 2010). Attending to the neurobiological influences on emotions involved in couple interactions is an important part of this process and can facilitate interpersonal transformation (Fishbane 2013).

Connect or Self-protect?

Neuroscience research points to the deeply social nature of the human brain; we are "wired to connect" (Fishbane 2007). Scientists have identified our prosocial "tend and befriend" instincts (Taylor 2003). While our need for intimate connection runs

M.D. Fishbane (✉)
Couple Therapy Training, Chicago Center for Family Health, Chicago, IL, USA

M.A. Wells
Department of Counseling and Family Sciences, Loma Linda University, Loma Linda, CA, USA

M.A. Wells
Marital and Family Therapy Intern, Mt. Vision Family Therapy, Redlands, CA, USA

© American Family Therapy Academy 2015
C. Knudson-Martin et al. (eds.), *Socio-Emotional Relationship Therapy*,
AFTA SpringerBriefs in Family Therapy, DOI 10.1007/978-3-319-13398-0_3

deep, the brain has also carried forward from prehistoric ages a protective fight-or-flight emotional system that is always alert for danger. This system can derail intimate partner interaction. A disagreement—even a raised eyebrow or a misconstrued word—can trigger the brain's emotional alarm. Reflexive actions of self-protection instantly override the capacity for thoughtful reflection. Furthermore, these powerful emotions are contagious. Both partners may react to one another and escalate, triggering a process we call the "amygdalae avalanche." Fortunately, principles based on neuroscience research can guide clinical interventions designed to manage the unruly emotional reactions that occur in flare-ups of the amygdalae avalanche.

In this chapter, we explore how "news from neuroscience" (Fishbane 2008) can enhance clinical work with couples. A socio-neurobiological perspective informs our theories of how relationships work and our techniques for helping couples understand and interrupt processes of emotion dysregulation. Couples can transform their reactive cycles, thanks to the power of neuroplasticity, the ability of the adult brain to change. New relational experiences can change both partners, not only socially, but also neurobiologically, as the couple's enactments of mutuality foster and sustain neural networks for connection. We will follow the relational dynamics of Drew and Nina, a mid-thirties European American heterosexual couple in therapy to address challenges in their marriage. We will examine the powerful social effects of gender socialization in this couple, exploring both neurobiological and social influences on their dance of reactivity. The case example will track socio-neurobiological change processes as the couple and therapist work to foster new interactions and new neuronal networks to support intimate connection.

Intertwining Research Interests

Throughout my career, I (Mona) have explored ways to help couples move from disempowerment and disconnection to mutual empowerment and connection. The writings of the Stone Center (e.g., Jordan 2010; Jordan et al. 1991) have been a valuable resource in my work to enhance the relational skills of couples in therapy. More recently, I have focused on integrating interpersonal neurobiology into my clinical approach. While attending to the influence of the larger societal context on couples, I find it helpful to also include neurobiological perspectives to support relational change. Addressing both the macro (cultural) and micro (neurobiological) levels is important in helping clients develop skills of "relational empowerment" (Fishbane 2011, 2013), including the shared vulnerability and empathy that supports couple intimacy.

My (Melissa) research on the effects of a history of childhood maltreatment on couple interactions has necessarily included an understanding of the socio-neurobiological influences at work between partners. Untangling the impact of the larger social context and the brain's role in emotions between partners is especially important for adult-survivor couples, who typically have an extraordinary need for relational safety. A focus on neurobiology is critical for addressing fight-or-flight responses that derail the reflective processes that otherwise help these couples experience mutual support. A member of the Socio-Emotional

Relationship Therapy research team since the group started, I have been influenced by Mona's integration of neurobiology in couple therapy. Her work has significantly informed my own research ideas and clinical approaches as I address the link between societal context, emotion, and intimate partner interactions.

Interplay of the Brain and Social Mechanisms

Neuroscience shows that we are creatures of biology and culture. Cultural messages affect each person's brain and developmental processes throughout life. It is the intermingling of these various influences—the functioning of the brain, cultural and societal contexts, and personal history—that shapes each person's identity and approach to intimate relationships.

Our Brain's Emerging Picture

An exceedingly complicated brain supports the intricacy of human experience. Harvard astrophysicist Eric Chaisson referred to the brain as "the most exquisitely complex clump of matter in the known universe" (1989, pp. 253–254). While our brain has mystified researchers for centuries, and promises to do so for some time to come, neuroscientists' ongoing discoveries can be useful to our work as couple and family therapists. In this chapter, we discuss those aspects of the brain that are most pertinent to understanding how emotions and cultural influences impact intimate relationships. (For a more detailed exploration of interpersonal neurobiology and couple therapy, see Fishbane 2013.) This narrative begins with a basic schematic of the brain's anatomy (see Fig. 1).

The brain is composed of gray and white matter. Billions of neurons (gray matter) communicate messages across trillions of interconnecting synapses. Glial

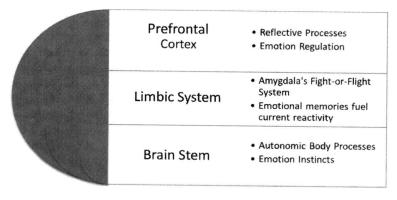

Fig. 1 The tripartite human brain

cells (white matter) enhance these synaptic communications. The brain has a three-tiered interconnected hierarchical structure composed of the brain stem at the base, the limbic system, and the neocortex at the highest level. The brain stem controls autonomic bodily functions, such as heart rate, respiration, and sleep and wake cycles. It also is implicated in emotion instincts (Panksepp and Biven 2012). We will focus on the limbic brain and the higher functioning of the neocortex, especially the prefrontal cortex (PFC), as they affect interpersonal processes. The limbic system includes the amygdala and hippocampus. The hippocampus facilitates memory and learning processes. Working beneath conscious awareness, the almond-shaped amygdala continually scans for trouble, serving as the brain's alarm system for danger. The amygdala sets off the fight-or-flight (or freeze in extreme situations) responses that fuel emotional reactivity between intimate partners. While we share much of our lower brain with other animals, the refined cognitive and reflective capabilities of the PFC distinguish us from other creatures. Crucially, emotion regulation and behavior choices depend on areas of the middle PFC. These higher brain functions of the PFC permit humans to engage in moral behavior, to flexibly respond in social situations, and to feel empathy (Siegel 2007). In times of social danger, however, the amygdala's emotional alarm can quickly overwhelm the reasoning processes of the PFC. The self-protective emotions tied to the amygdala's reactions are more brisk and automatic than the higher cognitive and affective prefrontal regions of the brain. Nonetheless, "we are not just reactive creatures wired to survive … we are thinking, meaning-make creatures" (Fishbane 2013, p. 27). There is a constant interplay in our brain between instinctual automaticity and prefrontal choice.

Biochemical players. The brain is embodied. There is a constant bidirectional influence between brain and body; the vehicles of this communication include hormones (in the blood) and neurotransmitters (in the brain). When the amygdala becomes activated, it stimulates the hypothalamic-pituitary-adrenal (HPA) axis and sympathetic nervous system to release epinephrine (or adrenalin), norepinephrine, and cortisol. The body and brain are on high alert when the amygdala senses danger. Chronic stress results in prolonged elevation of the hormone cortisol, which can kill cells in the hippocampus, negatively impacting learning and memory. Chronic elevated cortisol is also associated with reduced immune functioning, cardiovascular disease, obesity, and osteoporosis.

By contrast, oxytocin, a hormone and neurotransmitter, soothes us and contributes to human bonding processes. This hormone, part of the calm-and-connection system (Uvnas-Moberg 2003), is an antidote to stress hormones, reducing cortisol levels and lowering blood pressure and heart rate. While both sexes have oxytocin, its effect is enhanced by estrogen in women. Oxytocin, which bonds mothers and babies—and bonds lovers as well—is released with orgasm, childbirth, nursing, gentle touch, and empathy. Administering oxytocin intranasally (bypassing the blood–brain barrier) can increase trust, generosity, and empathy (Zak 2012). Hormones and neurotransmitters of passion (e.g., testosterone, dopamine), along with oxytocin, fuel sexual desire and intimate connection.

Our relational brain's culture clash. The brain does not function in isolation (Fishbane 2013). Neuroscience demonstrates that humans are relational creatures with social brains. The cultural discourse of the rugged individual self runs counter to the findings of neuroscientists that humans need others throughout life. Yet, US society privileges autonomy and competition, and these values impact us at all levels, especially our brains. This culture clash can be seen in the case of Drew and Nina, who have come to therapy for help with conflict. Nina, age 33, wants to have a baby. Drew, 34, has had challenges settling into a career. Although Nina has a graduate degree and teaches special-needs students in high school, Drew has only recently found employment as an electrician after a yearlong layoff from work. He wants to wait until he is financially stable before starting a family. He makes it clear he is not open to negotiating about this. Nina becomes upset and agitated when she cannot engage her husband in a discussion about having a baby. Drew bristles when he feels a woman (Nina) is telling him what to do; his sense of autonomy is threatened. He states emphatically, "the man needs to be the provider" and "I'm not ready yet." He shuts down, leaving Nina alone with her upset feelings. She is accustomed to processing her feelings with friends and is hurt and puzzled by Drew's shutting her out. She becomes angry and critical, which intensifies his sense of inadequacy and reinforces his defensive withdrawal from Nina. They come to therapy in an impasse, each feeling hurt and blaming the other.

Gender: A Socio-neurobiological View

Scholars have debated the relative role of nature-versus-nurture in the shaping of gender differences. Some highlight innate sex differences (Baron-Cohen 2013), while others focus on the social construction of gender (Eliot 2009; Jordan-Young 2010). In brains and abilities, women and men are more similar than different. Indeed, the genders share 99.8 % of their genes (Eliot 2009). The differences that do exist reflect complex interactions of hormones, genes, and socialization (Hines 2011). Neuroscientists have laid to rest the nature-versus-nurture controversy: Nature and nurture recursively affect each other. Experience changes the connections between neurons and even affects gene expression. Gender differences arise from a complex interplay between innate tendencies and socialization. The social construction of gender affects the brain and body, with "literal incorporation of social gender into the physical self" (Jordan-Young 2010, p. 201). Furthermore, many presumed gender differences may reflect power differences in relationships (Lips 1991).

The 0.2 % gender difference. Small innate sex differences are exacerbated by socialization (Eliot 2009). Most sex-based variations in cognitive and interpersonal skills ensue from experience and learning. The brain is shaped in childhood by play, which tends to vary according to gender as boys and girls divide into sex-segregated groups (Maccoby 1999). Drew engaged in rough-and-tumble, competitive play as a boy, while Nina played at family relationships with dolls and shared empathy talk with other girls. These varied gender activities developed brains in these partners that are focused on contrasting interests and abilities. Peer socialization in our gendered culture exaggerates small innate differences, resulting in gender stereotypes that can negatively impact adult intimate partnerships. Intimacy is challenged in heterosexual relationships when rigid gender socialization promotes polarization and unequal power between partners that frequently limit male attention to female needs while placing responsibility for relationship maintenance on women (Knudson-Martin 2012).

In our couple, Nina sharing her feelings about having a baby is experienced by Drew as pressure; he feels criticized and inadequate as a provider, and shuts down to protect himself. This increases Nina's agitation, leading to Drew storming off. Nina's gender socialization has built in the expectation that she be able to express her needs and receive empathy from her husband. Drew's gender socialization has led him to be under-skilled in empathy and prompts his reactivity at being told what to do by a woman. In response he shuts down. Both partners become frustrated as they feel misunderstood and devalued by the other. Drew's dismissal of Nina's concerns erodes their chances for intimacy and reflects societal patterns that minimize female concerns. And Nina sees Drew as selfish for focusing only on his job security, thus fueling her contempt. The emotions building between them are setting up a cycle of reactivity.

The Amygdalae Avalanche: Anatomy of Emotional Reactivity

Thinking and feeling are both necessary for healthy functioning; balance and integration between emotion and cognition are key. But when conflict occurs between partners, a cascade of negative emotions can disrupt the balance, shutting down higher processes of the brain, resulting in an "amygdalae avalanche." The trigger of an emotional response is often culturally embedded (Knudson-Martin and Huenergardt 2010). Thus, Drew becomes agitated when he feels Nina pressuring him; he is not adept at empathic conversation, and his autonomy as a male is threatened when Nina raises her concerns. There is a confluence here of gendered cultural expectations and the reactivity of his emotional brain. For her part, Nina does not see Drew's vulnerability; she only sees his "power over" behavior, and she becomes furious when she feels shut down by her husband. Neither partner can think straight during this amygdalae avalanche. The therapist offers a bit of "neuroeducation" (Fishbane 2013) about their emotional reactivity and helps them explore their gendered expectations that contribute to it. These reflections allow Drew and Nina to step back, identify, and interrupt their own reactivity cycle. The challenge is to bring back online the thoughtfulness and perspective of the PFC so the partners are not prisoners of their own amygdala responses and can be more open to relational engagement.

Neural Dynamics of Habits and Change

We humans are creatures of habit. Circuits of neurons support our habits, and our habits recursively strengthen these circuits of neurons. The more we do something, the more likely we will do it again in the future. Drew and Nina's reactive dance has become wired into their brains; the more they enact their pattern, the more habitual it becomes. But we are not doomed to be slaves to our habits: We are also creatures of change and adaptation. The human brain is unique in its capacity to adapt to changing circumstances. Research in the last decade has found that neuroplasticity, the ability of the human brain to change, can continue throughout life. It is neuroplasticity that allows for relational plasticity; each partner's ability to change enables transformation of the relationship. There is a catch, however. In adulthood, neuroplasticity takes work and entrenched societal processes need to be challenged. New relational habits require a lot of repetition in order to become wired into the brain.

"Getting Meta": Working with the Couple's Impasse

Nina and Drew are noticeably upset at the start of a session. Drew explains that they just had a fight because he received a pay raise at work: "Nina said this boost to our income means we can have a baby. I told her for the hundredth time that I'm not ready for this responsibility." Nina follows with her reasons of why they should start trying to get pregnant. Drew interrupts to make his counterpoints. Nina, visibly upset, retorts: "If we wait for Drew, it will be too late. He'll never be ready." Nina glares at Drew, and he turns away. Fight (Nina) and flight (Drew) take over, as each partner's HPA axis and sympathetic nervous system kicks into high gear.

This gendered power conflict has catapulted both partners into an amygdalae avalanche. Their body and brain's reactive processes are linked to the dominant discourses of the partners. Nina is influenced by sociocultural messages of "women should be mothers" and "my biological clock is ticking." Drew refuses to take in her needs. His gendered power response is fueled by discourses of "I have to be the breadwinner" and "I don't have any power when she tells me what to do." Each feels threatened as their amygdala's stress-response system overpowers the cognitive functioning of the PFC. Furthermore, the amygdala, which holds old emotional memories, reactivates past hurts in the relationship, as well as painful events from childhood, in this couple's current impasse.

Nina's amygdala is reactivating old wounds from their courtship, when Drew was hesitant to commit and she felt uncherished and unchosen. Never having processed this issue together, the wound continues to fester and is retriggered now around having a child. Nina gets reactive and goes into contempt, dropping snide comments that Drew will never act like a grown-up. In response, Drew resorts to his defensive posture of stonewalling; nothing Nina says can get through to him now. Neither partner can think clearly, and they become polarized, each seeing the other as the enemy. In a soft voice, the therapist (Mona) notes that both feel alienated and alone at this moment. Mona "holds" both partners with care and respect, making room for both of their experiences. She asks them to do some deep belly breathing; the outbreath activates the parasympathetic nervous system, calming them. Commenting that both are in pain, Mona invites them to begin a dialogue of mutual understanding. She notes that their bond, while frayed, is still strong; and she offers them a safe space to let their guard down and explore their impasse. Only then can their amygdalae relax and the partners open up to each other.

Together with the therapist, Nina and Drew identify their dance of criticize/defend-withdraw, drawing their vulnerability cycle (Scheinkman and Fishbane 2004). In this process, they are able to "get meta" to their dance (Fishbane 2013), looking at it together as a team. Their PFCs are activated and amygdalae calmed. "Getting meta" often includes exploring underlying emotions or a larger relational context. The therapist asks Nina whether the feeling of not being heard, of her needs being ignored, is familiar to her from earlier in life. She tears up, saying that she never felt heard by her parents, and had to dance around everyone else's needs in her family of origin. Drew is moved by Nina's childhood pain and begins to see how his shutting her down in their impasse over the baby is activating her old wounds. The therapist then turns to Drew, asking whether his sense of being criticized by Nina is familiar from an earlier time in his life. He shares that his father abandoned the family when he was 10, leaving his mother furious and contemptuous of irresponsible men. His father's abandonment put the family in financial jeopardy. Drew resolved that when he grew up, he would protect and provide for his family.

Drew begins to see that shutting Nina out is a kind of abandonment. He shudders at the thought of being like his father, and, with the help of the therapist, sees connecting with Nina's pain as a kind of protection. Nina, feeling the loving care in her husband, starts to feel safer with him. She also realizes that her contempt has been triggering Drew's sense of inadequacy, and she makes a conscious decision not to act like his angry mother.

Relational Empowerment: Tools for Change

The therapist helps Drew and Nina identify their higher goals and values for the relationship. Both indicate that they want a relationship of greater trust, peace, and affection. They are tired of the blame game. But they are each wary, fearful that their needs would not be honored by the other. The therapist validates their concerns, noting that in a good relationship, each of them would feel affirmed and each would have voice. She operationalizes their values, identifying specific relational skills they can develop to support the mutuality they desire. These are skills for relational empowerment, "tools for your toolbox" (Fishbane 2013). They include competencies in emotion regulation and empathy, mutual respect, and cultivating compassion and care in the relationship. Drew and Nina learn and practice mindfulness techniques, which slow down their reactivity and allow them to make more thoughtful choices in their interactions. This work challenges cultural discourses of autonomy and individualism and promotes relational responsibility in both partners.

They also learn ways to speak and be heard, to "make a relational claim" (Fishbane 2013). This involves speaking one's own needs, while holding the needs of the other partner and of the relationship at the same time. Drew works to make space for Nina's voice. Nina takes "voice lessons," learning to speak up without blowing her husband out of the water. Drew is proud of his new ability to protect Nina by hanging out with her around her concerns. As these partners get the hang of the skills of relational empowerment, they are less likely to resort to "power over" tactics such as contempt or shutting down. The power struggle abates as they make room for both of their voices in the relationship. They also learn techniques for repair when they do hurt each other, so they can rebuild their connection after conflict. This process of repair after hurt builds trust in couples' relationships (Gottman 2011).

Cultivating Connection

Trust is the bedrock of a good relationship. It can become frayed when couples are distressed. Partners co-regulate—or co-dysregulate—each other, as either "vicious cycles" of reactivity or "virtuous cycles" of mutual care are enacted. A trusted partner can help the other not get upset by engaging in listening and validating practices that result in an interpersonal regulation of emotion (Beckes and Coan 2011). And if one becomes upset, the other can offer empathic connection, stimulating the release of oxytocin and promoting regulation and calm.

The therapist looks for "resources of trustworthiness" in the couple's relationship (Boszormenyi-Nagy and Ulrich 1981). While Drew and Nina are divided on the topic of having a baby, they have otherwise been quite supportive of one another. Earlier in their marriage, when Nina attended graduate school, Drew's encouragement was calming to her if she became anxious about her academic performance. Later, when Drew was unemployed, Nina helped him find ways to manage the inevitable distress of joblessness. They worked together to facilitate Drew's re-employment process as a couple, rather than Drew handling this challenge alone. He readily acknowledges that Nina's unquestioning support made it much easier to go through this challenging time. Mona encourages the couple to bring these resources of care and support to bear on the fraught topic of when to have a baby.

The Eyes Have It: Communication and Compassion

Emotions are communications to others; both brain and body are involved. The muscles of the face convey emotions, especially around the eyes. Specific neurons in the brain are dedicated to reading the emotions expressed in another's face.

We evolved for face-to-face contact, for reading each other's emotions at close range. Yet, many couples make little or no eye contact and are thus deprived of vital information. Devoting more attention to their electronic devices than to each other, they miss out on opportunities for connection. The relational therapist encourages couples to create these opportunities (including eye contact), building "micro-moments" of "positivity resonance" (Fredrickson 2013). The possibility for compassion and connection is built into our neural processes. The vagus nerve, loaded with oxytocin receptors, is central to emotions of generosity and kindness (Keltner 2009). When Drew and Nina attune to one another, their oxytocin increases, allowing them to relax and feel safe with each other. The therapist offers to teach them loving-kindness meditation and encourages them to seek opportunities for connection in the course of their day.

Facilitating Trust

Compassion and care can flourish if there is safety and trust between partners. While our society emphasizes individual rights, helping partners to also focus on relational responsibility is equally important. Intentional processes of care, gratitude, and generosity can help partners engage in the relationship responsibly. Helping both partners think about their part in couple interactions is crucial to building trust. Mona invites Drew and Nina to consider how their individual reactivity contributes to their impasse. When they pull together to take co-responsibility for the relationship, they adopt a "power with" stance, an antidote to the "power over" struggles that have plagued them. Empowered as partners, they are resisting societal patterns that work against relationship for both women and men.

The Neurobiology of Empathy

Neuroscientists have identified four components of empathy: resonance (feeling in one's body what the other feels, a subcortical automatic process); cognitive empathy (consciously putting oneself in the other's shoes); boundary between self and other; and self-regulation in the face of the other's pain (Decety and Jackson 2004). With resonance, I feel in my body what you feel. Many males are socialized not to feel vulnerable emotions; aside from anger, such men are unable to identify their own feelings. This was the case with Drew. He was stumped when it came to empathizing with Nina, partly because he never learned as a male to tune into his own feelings. The therapist works with him to identify his own body cues of emotion. As he becomes more proficient with self-attunement, he is better able to tune into Nina's feelings. Nina is better at resonance, but her cognitive empathy has become distorted because she is so hurt and angry by his shutting down conversation about having a baby. Mona helps the couple reframe Drew's concern with job security as a stance of protectiveness toward his family, not a selfish position. This softens Nina's anger as she better understands his experience. At the same time, Drew is able to be more open to her concerns.

Empathy is not an innate, static ability; it is shaped by culture and expectations. It is a skill that can be taught. Research has found that motivation affects empathic accuracy; gender differences in empathic accuracy (favoring women) are tied to motivation, not just to innate ability (Ickes et al. 2000). Men's motivation and empathic accuracy were found to increase when they were offered money for each accurate empathic observation or when they read that women find empathic men sexier (Klein and Hodges 2001; Thomas and Maio 2008). Motivating men to learn the skills of empathy challenges their gender socialization and empowers them to be relationally co-responsible partners. Framing empathy as a skill of relational empowerment is particularly appealing to males.

Mutual Empowerment: Nurturing the "We"

Respect, fairness, and the perception of equity are essential to successful relationships. A key aspect of shared power is the ability of each partner to introduce and discuss issues safely (Wilkie et al. 1998). Listening and empathy bring a spirit of generosity to the relationship that affirms the importance of partners to each other (Fowers 2001). Helping partners shift from self-protective reactivity toward more collaborative values involves moving from "an individual to relational perspective; from independence to interdependence; from competition to collaboration; from debate to dialogue" (Fishbane 2013, p. 12).

A key shift in Drew and Nina's relationship involves a greater investment in the "we," a stance adopted by happier couples (Gottman 2011). As both partners feel less threatened and more invested in connection and care, they become more adept at holding each other's concerns. This frees them to talk about the timing of having a baby in a calmer manner that makes room for both of their feelings. Nina feels relieved that Drew cares about her desire to become a mother and shares her commitment to raising a family. And Drew is able to talk more calmly about his concerns about financial stability, inviting Nina to join him in planning their fiscal future. Their power struggle eases. They still have somewhat different timelines for starting a family, but there is now room for both points of view, and their communication becomes collaborative rather than adversarial. They move from a "me-versus-you" to a "we" perspective. They are making space for both voices, for each "I" in the relationship.

The couple is shifting from blame toward mutual care and protectiveness. As Nina observes Drew struggling to take in her experience, her own empathy for Drew increases. She is visibly calmer. Mona asks Nina: "What is this like for you, Nina, to feel Drew's concern?" She quietly responds: "I think he finally hears me, that he's there for me ... and I have a little more hope." Mona: "When Drew is able to shift from being defensive and instead takes your needs into consideration, you feel that he is protecting you?" She nods. Drew reaches for Nina's hand. This tender gesture of touching activates the partners' calm-and-connection systems. The oxytocin is flowing between them.

As with Drew and Nina, a socio-neurobiologically oriented therapy helps couples create opportunities for dialogue by encouraging each partner to learn how to recognize the onset of reactivity and to choose more empowered responses of respect and care for the other. Understanding the brain's labile system of reactivity for self-protection can be liberating for partners as they bring alternative strategies to their relationship. Knowing that the PFC works slowly, yet provides the power of choice in their couple interactions, partners can become proactive in their approaches to each other rather than remain victims of "hair-trigger" reactivity.

Nurturing Relational Plasticity: Maintaining Change

As couples cultivate mutuality and shared relational responsibility, they are creating new dances that are not dictated by constraining societal assumptions about gender and relationships. And they are developing new neural networks for connection. With use, this new neural circuitry becomes more efficient and stable. But even when these new circuits are strong, the couple may have setbacks and revert to old behaviors. The brain circuits involved in reactivity do not disappear; when sick, tired, or stressed, partners may fall back to old habits, especially when they are societally reinforced. If a couple does have a slip to old ways, the therapist reminds them that this is normal and invites them to return to their practice of collaborative, reflective prefrontal conversation.

Drew and Nina are early in their process of learning how to manage reactivity, but they are discovering the benefits of empathically holding each other's experience. They are developing relational plasticity and flexibility that will support their experience of mutuality. Both partners seem pleased as they acquire skills and competencies that allow them to co-construct a more satisfying relationship. They have managed to move away from "power over" interactions and are cultivating a "power with" approach, shouldering together the responsibility for transforming and nurturing their bond.

References

Baron-Cohen, S. (2013). *The essential difference: Male and female brains and the truth about autism.* New York, NY: Basic Books.

Beckes, L., & Coan, J. A. (2011). Social baseline theory: The role of social proximity in emotion and economy of action. *Social and Personality Psychology Compass, 5*, 976–988.

Boszormenyi-Nagy, I., & Ulrich, D. (1981). Contextual family therapy. In A. S. Gurman & D. P. Kniskern (Eds.), *Handbook of family therapy* (pp. 159–186). New York, NY: Brunner/Mazel.

Chaisson, E. (1989). *The life era*. New York, NY: Norton.

Decety, J., & Jackson, P. L. (2004). The functional neuroarchitecture of human empathy. *Behavioral and Cognitive Neuroscience Reviews, 3*, 71–100.

Eliot, L. (2009). *Pink brain, blue brain: How small differences grow into troublesome gaps—and what we can do about it*. New York, NY: Houghton Mifflin Harcourt.

Fishbane, M. D. (2007). Wired to connect: Neuroscience, relationships, and therapy. *Family Process, 6*(3), 395–412.

Fishbane, M. D. (2008). "News from neuroscience": Applications to couple therapy. In M. E. Edwards (Ed.), *Neuroscience and family therapy: Integrations and applications*. Washington, DC: American Family Therapy Academy.

Fishbane, M. D. (2011). Facilitating relational empowerment in couple therapy. *Family Process, 50*, 337–352.

Fishbane, M. D. (2013). *Loving with the brain in mind: Neurobiology and couple therapy*. New York, NY: Norton.

Fowers, B. (2001). The limits of a technical concept of a good marriage: Exploring the role of virtue in communication skills. *Journal of Marital and Family Therapy, 27*, 327–340.

Fredrickson, B. (2013). *Love 2.0: Creating happiness and health in moments of connection*. New York, NY: Plume.

Gottman, J. M. (2011). *The science of trust: Emotional attunement for couples*. New York, NY: Norton.

Hines, M. (2011). Gender development and the human brain. *Annual Review of Neuroscience, 34*, 69–88.

Ickes, W., Gesn, P. R., & Graham, T. (2000). Gender differences in empathic accuracy: Differential ability or differential motivation? *Personal Relationships, 7*, 95–109.

Jordan, J. V. (2010). *Relational-cultural therapy*. Washington, DC: American Psychological Association.

Jordan, J. V., Kaplan, A. G., Miller, J. B., Stiver, I. P., & Surrey, J. L. (1991). *Women's growth in connection: Writings from the Stone Center*. New York, NY: Guilford Press.

Jordan-Young, R. M. (2010). *Brain storm: The flaws in the science of sex differences*. Cambridge, MA: Harvard University Press.

Keltner, D. (2009). *Born to be good: The science of a meaningful life*. New York, NY: Norton.

Klein, K. J. K., & Hodges, S. D. (2001). Gender differences, motivation, and empathic accuracy: When it pays to understand. *Personality and Social Psychology Bulletin, 27*, 720–730.

Knudson-Martin, C. (2012). Changing gender norms in families and society: Toward equality and complexities. In F. Walsh (Ed.), *Normal family processes* (4th ed., pp. 324–346). New York, NY: Guilford Press.

Knudson-Martin, C., & Huenergardt, D. (2010). A socio-emotional approach to couple therapy: Linking social context and couple interaction. *Family Process, 49*, 369–386.

Lips, H. M. (1991). *Women, men, and power*. Mountain View, CA: Mayfield Publishing.

Maccoby, E. E. (1999). *The two sexes: Growing up apart, coming together*. Cambridge, MA: Harvard University Press.

Panksepp, J., & Biven, L. (2012). *The archeology of mind: Neuroevolutionary origins of human emotions*. New York, NY: Norton.

Scheinkman, M., & Fishbane, M. D. (2004). The vulnerability cycle: Working with impasses in couple therapy. *Family Process, 43*, 279–299.

Siegel, D. J. (2007). *The mindful brain: Reflection and attunement in the cultivation of well-being*. New York, NY: Norton.

Taylor, S. (2003). *The tending instinct: Women, men, and the biology of relationships*. New York, NY: Holt.

Thomas, G., & Maio, G. R. (2008). Man, I feel like a woman: When and how gender-role motivation helps mind-reading. *Journal of Personality and Social Psychology, 95*, 1165–1179.

Uvnas-Moberg, K. (2003). *The oxytocin factor: Tapping the hormone of calm, love, and healing*. Cambridge, MA: Perseus.

Wilkie, J. R., Ferree, M. M., & Ratcliff, K. S. (1998). Gender and fairness: Marital satisfaction in two-earner couples. *Journal of Marriage and the Family, 60*, 577–594.

Zak, P. J. (2012). *The moral molecule: The source of love and prosperity*. New York, NY: Dutton/Penguin.

How Gender Discourses Hijack Couple Therapy—and How to Avoid It

Jessica L. ChenFeng and Aimee Galick

How do ideas about being a "woman" or a "man" influence couple therapy? Within the larger societal context, there are governing ideas about what it means to be a "man" or a "woman," which are known as discourses. Discourses that have the most power to influence us are labeled dominant (or hegemonic). In this chapter, we share what we have learned about how dominant gender discourses influence the process of couple therapy; that is, how therapists relate to each partner and how partners respond to therapists and each other. In the context of two dominant gender narratives, what discourses dominate sessions? How do we recognize them? Do they facilitate or hinder connection in therapy? These are the questions we attempted to answer with a grounded theory analysis of 23 couple therapy sessions that we conducted early in our doctoral studies. Here, we share the journey by which we became sensitized to gender discourses and how, now, not a day goes by without drawing upon these realizations in our lives and in the therapy room.

Personal Backgrounds

Both of us began our doctoral studies in marital and family therapy at Loma Linda University in 2010 and became part of the Socio-Emotional Relationship Therapy (SERT) clinical study group which met once a week for 4 hours (described in Knudson-Martin and Huenergardt, "Bridging Emotion, Societal Discourse, and Couple Interaction in Clinical Practice," 2015; Knudson-Martin et al. 2014). At the

J.L. ChenFeng (✉)
Department of Educational Psychology and Counseling, California State University, Northridge, CA, USA

A. Galick
School of Health Professions, University of Louisiana-Monroe, Monroe, LA, USA

© American Family Therapy Academy 2015
C. Knudson-Martin et al. (eds.), *Socio-Emotional Relationship Therapy*,
AFTA SpringerBriefs in Family Therapy, DOI 10.1007/978-3-319-13398-0_4

same time, we took an advanced qualitative research methods course and decided to pair up to begin this grounded theory analysis of gender discourse in couple therapy sessions, a topic we knew little about.

I (Jessica) was about to become licensed, and though I knew I was Taiwanese American, second-generation, an able-bodied heterosexual, raised in a conservative Christian environment, and female, I was not aware of how any of these identifiers played a significant part in my work as a clinician and student. In those early months as a doctoral student researcher in the SERT group, everything felt foreign and uncomfortable to me. I was challenged by how *different* I felt from people around me, and that difference resulted in my initially not knowing how to have a voice and presence in the group. With the embracing professors and colleagues of SERT as support, I began to explore those areas of discomfort: how as a younger Taiwanese American female, I did not know how to speak competently to an older European American male professor, or how in my Asian cultural heritage, I was inclined to tend to others and let them finish speaking before I felt allowed to talk.

Every week in the SERT group I had the opportunity to encounter, reflect, and be critical about my own social contextual identity while learning and helping to advance the SERT approach and applying these ideas to my clinical work. My own critical consciousness was being raised at the same time we began the grounded theory qualitative analysis. I was growing to become very familiar with my own feelings around others and my gender, race, age, ability, culture, class, and other social locations.

The impact of gender constructions on identity and relationships fascinates me (Aimee) because I think they are so powerful, yet so rarely talked about. That I had to read about gender to understand its influence on how I think, feel, and behave attests to how out of my awareness it had been. As a heterosexual Canadian woman from a middle-class family with Polish and French heritage, I have experienced much privilege. Although I benefited from White privilege, I experienced feelings of powerlessness in certain contexts, such as my family of origin in which my father's voice mattered most and had the power to organize our daily interactions. It was no secret that he desperately wanted a boy or two, but had three girls. Working with what he had, he shaped us to be more masculine than feminine. While all my same-sex friends were in dance class, I was in hunter training, being taught how to fight, and told to stand up for myself (except in relation to him, of course). I rarely experienced not having a strong voice with people other than him. In the SERT group, I had to learn to make space for other voices and express my opinions less. I also had to (and am still working on) learn to be more accommodating and allow myself to be influenced. I have found it very empowering to be more relational and to also be comfortable being an individual; however, maintaining this balance requires a great deal of deliberateness. This is why I think it is so important to help clients (of all genders) increase their range of possible behaviors.

When we began the grounded theory analysis, we had no idea what we would find because between us we knew very little about the dominant gender discourses that influence heterosexual couple interactions. It is one thing to read about how gender organizes families and couples and another to be able to see it happening in moment-to-moment therapeutic processes. Engaging in this research has literally changed the way we view self, relationships, therapy, and the world. The best way to describe it is once you see it, you cannot *not* see it anymore.

Impact of Gender Discourse on Couple Therapy

That gender influences families and therapy is not a new idea. Attention was being drawn to this in the 1970s and 1980s by feminist family therapy scholars such as Hare-Mustin (1978) and Goldner (1985), among many others. Since then, we have learned a great deal about how gender impacts families and functioning. Although there have been studies on how gender influences therapy, we could not find a study that examined in detail, as we have done, how dominant ideas about gender impact moment-to-moment processes in couple therapy.

Discourse can be defined as a "system of statements which cohere around common meanings and values" (Hollway 1983, p. 231). Dominant or hegemonic discourses related to gender are the product of societal values and inform us of appropriate ways of acting, thinking, and feeling (Hare-Mustin 1994; Knudson-Martin and Huenergardt 2010). Discourses related to gender become intricately woven into our sense of personal identity through gender socialization. Gender is constructed through interactions with others (West and Zimmerman 1987).

Through the socialization process, gender discourses often become implicit, subtle, and easily overlooked (Keeling et al. 2010; Robinson 1999). Sometimes this socialization is direct, like when little Johnny is told to "stop crying like a little girl." Other times it is indirect, as when little Sally's parents tell her she is being "selfish" for voicing her need to be alone when she is expected to play with her sister. Often these discourses are unquestioned as "the way it is," natural, and accepted as what most people think of as "normal" (West and Zimmerman 1987). It is quite the contradiction because on one level societal influences are often invisible and on another level they are experienced as extremely real, personal parts of self-identity. These are not inevitable gender prophecies; there is a lot of variation, even within one person, and the situation greatly influences which discourses may be enacted (Paechter 2006).

Some dominant gender discourses facilitate intimacy and mutuality in couple relationships and some hinder it. It is not necessarily true that feminine gender discourses facilitate relationships and male gender discourses hinder them. As we found in our analysis, it seems that when these discourses are limited to only one partner on the basis of gender, it leads to impasses and a disproportionate burden of change resting on one partner. For example, most men in American culture receive direct and indirect messages that they should be autonomous, powerful, strong, and aggressive (Doull et al. 2013). When a woman portrays these qualities, she may be considered unfeminine and even labeled with disparaging names. Instead, she is expected to be timid, other-focused, and vulnerable (Almeida et al. 2008).

Together these male and female discourses contribute to the larger discourse that women should be responsible for the couple relationship. When a woman implicitly takes on this responsibility and something goes wrong so that the couple seeks therapy, she typically becomes the one the therapist and her male partner ask for change. She is also likely to take on that role herself in many subtle ways, which we will discuss later. When it comes to heterosexual couple relationships, being socialized into stereotypical masculine and feminine roles sets couples up for inequality. When women are socialized to be other-focused and men are socialized to be autonomous, the flow of support is almost inevitably skewed in favor of men.

Therapists also bring these invisible, constricting discourses about gender into therapy (Haddock and Bowling 2001; Keeling et al. 2010), and this profoundly affects what clinicians hear and how they respond to it (Robinson 1999). Responsibility for the couple relationship, the well-being of her partner, and change often rests with the female partner (Crawford 2004; Keeling et al. 2010; Knudson-Martin 2003). We are all deeply influenced by gender ideals, so it is unlikely that therapists can just "check" them at the door. When couples seek therapy, it becomes easy to see how therapists may unintentionally place the burden of change on women. In our analysis, even some of the experienced feminist-oriented therapists inadvertently reinforced dominant ideas about gender at times.

Despite the powerful influence gender has on individual identity, there is little literature on how this influences the dynamics of couple therapy. We were able to find a few studies undertaken by scholars and therapists who identify as feminist. These studies on therapists' gender biases and differential treatment of men and women in therapy reveal how women are disproportionately blamed for couple problems (Harris et al. 2001). One study found that female clients were interrupted three times as much as male clients (Werner-Wilson et al. 1997). Another study examining therapist attributions found that long-term negative relationship outcomes were attributed to the female partner, while positive events were attributed to the male partner (Stabb et al. 1997). Studying conversational strategies, Haddock and Lyness (2002) found that therapists not self-identified as feminists challenged female clients more and gave male clients more compliments, indicating preferential treatment of male clients. In contrast, those therapists who self-identified as feminists challenged men and women to act in ways contrary to gender stereotypes. However, another study concluded that being trained in feminist practice did not necessarily prevent therapists from using sexist interventions (Leslie and Clossick 1996).

Many therapists may fail to address gender because they are unsure how to do so effectively (Haddock et al. 2000). Therapists may be concerned that if they do not appeal to the male partner's position, he may not return to therapy (Dienhart 2001; Haddock and Lyness 2002). It may also be easier to work with the female partner who is ready and willing to engage (Dienhart 2001). The literature gives us some clues as to *why* dominant gender discourses are reinforced in couple therapy, but there is still much to learn about *how* it happens, which is what we set out to find in our study.

Study Design

Our study was part of a larger participatory action research project approved by the Loma Linda University Institutional Review Board (IRB), in which marital and family therapy doctoral students and faculty studied their own practice (see Knudson-Martin et al. 2014). Self-referred couples provided consent for use of their therapy sessions as research. The sessions were recorded and transcribed by the therapist and added to a data bank managed by the primary investigator. Twenty-three transcripts were available and analyzed for this study. All were conducted at the initial phase of the larger project, prior to the development of the SERT approach summarized in the chapter "Bridging Emotion, Societal Discourse, and Couple Interaction in Clinical Practice" (Knudson-Martin and Huenergardt, 2015).

The sample included 19 heterosexual client couples and 17 therapists. Female partners' ages ranged from 27 to 65 years; male partners' ages ranged from 24 to 68 years. Cultural backgrounds included Filipino, African American, Puerto Rican, Latino, and European American (79 %). The therapists were 26–66 years of age, including advanced doctoral students working toward licensure in California and two licensed marriage and family therapy professors. Their cultural backgrounds were Korean, Taiwanese American, African American, and European American; their stated theoretical orientations ranged across narrative, solution-focused, Bowen family systems, structural therapy, and feminist approaches.

The 23 transcripts we analyzed totaled 579 pages of narrative. When we began, we were both seeking to increase our consciousness about societal, cultural, and gendered contexts and how this impacted our clinical work. Thus, we first started our analysis of the transcripts observing how gender, culture, and societal power were present in therapy sessions. In the initial open coding phase of the study, we began to see how gender discourses seemed to have an especially powerful influence on what was happening between partners in couples and between the therapist and couple. We decided that our grounded theory analysis would focus on gender, specifically examining how dominant gender discourses influenced the in-session therapeutic process.

We returned to open coding with a specific focus on how gender discourses were showing up in the therapy transcripts. As we took note of clients' and therapists' language and the process of therapy, we observed three significant gender discourses that seemed to be influencing the therapeutic process in almost all of the transcripts (these are discussed more specifically in the "Results" section). Once these three primary discourses were identified, we did more focused coding on how they influenced the process of therapy in each session. We found that there were generally two ways that therapists engaged with the gender discourses: either challenging them or reinforcing them. Through the process of constant comparative analysis (Charmaz 2006), we linked these processes across the transcripts and noticed the many surprising similarities and very few differences.

Results

Our findings are all the more compelling because we did not know what we were looking for when we started the analysis. At first, it was difficult to spot when the gender discourses were reinforced, especially through more subtle actions, because we were working through our own internalization of these dominant discourses. It was much easier to spot when the therapist was working with alternative discourses. We would have a revelation like, "Whoa, wait a minute, something really different is happening here; we need to look at this closer." We attributed this to the fact that the way these gender discourses influenced partners is what most people, including us, consider "normal." It is similar to how you become accustomed to the sounds of your house (sensory adaptation); our society is like the house, we are all used to how gender is done, and we do not really think about it. In doing this analysis, we had to sit in our house and listen very, very carefully and pay deliberate attention so we could hear what we typically did not notice.

Within the *unique* context of heterosexual couple therapy, three gender discourses appeared most often. The first was "men should be the authority." The second was "women should be responsible for relationships." The third was "women should protect men from shame." Sometimes they occurred together, interwoven into a long sequence of interaction, and sometimes they occurred alone.

In the majority of the transcripts, it seemed therapists were reinforcing these gender discourses. This appeared to be unintentional, as none of the therapists said things like, "men should do this" or "women shouldn't do that." Reinforcement was often so subtle within the therapeutic process that it is difficult to show in a short quotation. It happened in many ways, such as to whom questions were directed, who answered particular questions, whose story was followed, whose experiences and views were validated, who was asked to change, what each partner was asked to change, and how the presenting problem was defined. Here are some examples.

Reinforcing Male Privilege

We found an interesting process of men's experiences and views becoming privileged through validation from therapists and women's experiences being minimized by her partner and the therapist. For example, when the male client answered a question, therapists often unquestioningly took his view as the issue that needs to be addressed without tending to the female client's experience. This reinforced the gender discourse that men should be the authority and women should defer to them. This discourse sounds so outdated, something we were not expecting to see in this day and age. In fact, we saw it often. In one session centered on the in utero death of the couple's baby, the partners appeared to have differing agendas for the direction of the therapy session. The wife attempted to talk about the emotional experience of losing the baby, while the husband oscillated between the medical reasons it happened and blaming his wife for their current relational problems. The husband talked over his partner and cut her off numerous times. By not interjecting in this process, the therapist reinforced the gender discourse that the husband should be the authority.

Eventually, the therapist turned the conversation to the relationship by asking the couple, "How is your relationship now?" The wife answered this question—which may indicate her gendered sense of responsibility for the relationship—saying, "It's still rocky." The therapist immediately asked the husband his opinion. He responded by placing blame for relational problems on his wife's "cycle," and the therapist proceeded to expand the husband's version of the story. This therapist action reinforced both the husband's dominance and the idea that women are responsible for relational problems.

Expecting Women to Accommodate

The ease with which therapists may end up expecting women to change was demonstrated a little later in the same session. The therapist asked the husband first what he needed from his wife during this difficult time. The husband responded with, "If her perceptions change, I think that alone will pretty much take care of everything," again placing responsibility on his wife. Significantly, the therapist continued to expand the husband's opinion and help the wife figure out how she can change. Importantly, the therapist never asked the wife what she needed from her husband or validated her experience around the loss.

Protecting Men from Shame

Similarly, the gender discourse of "women should protect men from shame" showed up in a number of sessions and is connected to the idea that women are responsible for relationships. We saw therapists reinforcing this discourse when they did not address or follow up on female concerns. For example, with one couple attending therapy after the male partner's infidelity, the female partner said, "Instead of picking on him all the time, I've been trying to focus on what he's been doing right." While this woman's response can be very helpful and important, with an experience such as infidelity, it is also appropriate for the woman to feel anger or to spend some time in therapy expressing her frustrations about her partner. In this session, the therapist focused completely on what the woman was doing to improve the relationship and never made space to explore her concerns or what she needed from her male partner.

In another therapeutic dynamic, a different female partner also gave voice to the subtle discourse that women should protect men from shame, "everything is good [in the relationship] as long as I don't have any complaints." Here, the female client voiced that she feels that she is expected to always be okay and not complain. This expectation is constraining and does not attend to her underlying resentment and sadness. However, the therapist did not appear to recognize this as a deeply embedded and internalized gender discourse. Instead of validating her right to have concerns and counteracting the discourse by encouraging her to explore the issues she might wish to express, the therapist changed the subject completely, saying, "Going over your relationship history, you've been together 11 years, but you've only been married two or three." By unintentionally reinforcing the idea that women should not shame or blame men, the therapist minimized the woman's experience, privileged male experience, and colluded with the expectation that women should protect men from shame and blame, even at their own expense.

Challenging Dominant Gender Discourse

In a few therapy sessions, therapists did challenge dominant gender discourses by giving voice to and acknowledging alternative discourses, i.e., validating men for being relational and women for expressing their needs. They contextualized couples' old patterns as part of societal discourse. These therapists made the implicit explicit; one therapist named the discourse of female responsibility and contextualized it as a societal problem:

> Our society has done the two of you, as well as many others in marriages, injustice by prescribing certain roles and norms for spouses. And, oftentimes, it's expected that wives should be the ones to stabilize a relationship, move it into the future.

These therapists also encouraged couples to enact mutually supportive behaviors in the therapy session. One therapist highlighted the male partner's intentional effort to be present, rather than shutting down emotionally, when discussing a difficult issue with his wife:

> You were present, you were listening, you were attending, you were there, and as you processed your thoughts, you also gave [her] the space to process hers. At the same time, you held onto yourself. Because you could have just given up, said, "screw it," and checked out... I've seen people do that before.

Note that the therapist compared the male partner's behavior to other men in order to highlight how different he was being. Shortly after this, the therapist encouraged the female partner to voice her needs. This deliberate validating of female needs was very different from what we saw in the gender-reinforcing examples.

A key part of keeping the male partner engaged while asking him to come out of his comfort zone was validating his feelings while still asking for accountability and change. When the male partner was having difficulty expressing vulnerable emotions and requesting his wife to take over for him, the therapist said, "I think you're doing a good job. I need you to stay with it because you are taking action to allow the feeling of vulnerability and she's here with you as you do it." This therapist made the process of avoiding vulnerability explicit and encouraged him to keep trying. This discourse could have been reinforced had the therapist let the wife take over for him.

The pervasive nature of the gender discourses seemed to make adopting alternative discourses difficult for clients. Gender discourses needed to be worked with consistently throughout the entire session. This makes sense because people are so used to doing things a certain way that it becomes taken for granted. Starting new patterns of interaction that move beyond the limitations of dominant gender discourses took persistent effort, and therapists who did not reinforce stereotypic gender discourse seemed aware of this.

What Do We Do Now That We Know?

It has been nearly four years since we first began this qualitative study. The influence of gender discourses on our perception of relationships, ourselves and others, can be so subtle that it took multiple re-reads of the transcripts for us to really begin to see the impact. We are now both faculty members in family therapy programs. Our heightened consciousness about gender discourses has significantly impacted our clinical, teaching, and supervisory work. In this part of the chapter, we want to share what we have seen can happen when we address gender discourses in therapy and suggest some practical ways to apply this awareness to our work as therapists.

New Possibilities

When we put forth effort to prevent gender discourses from hijacking couple therapy, new relational options are possible.

Empowering both women and men. People might wrongly assume that knowing about gender discourses is more about empowering women. Though this certainly happens, it is not the only positive outcome. As SERT therapists, we see that in tending to how gender discourses impact all of us, we empower both women and men. The binary gender discourses we internalize from our social context rob both women and men of the fullness of who we can be. As we recognize and tend to gender discourses in therapy, we give women and men permission to be something different from what they thought they were expected to be.

Equality and mutuality. As women become comfortable with sharing relational responsibility with their male partners and men feel okay sharing authority and power with their female partners, both get to experience more equality and mutuality in the relationship. This becomes a natural outcome when light is shed on how gender discourses can restrain us and when both partners in a heterosexual relationship challenge themselves to new ways of being.

Consciousness of marginalized experiences. One of the gifts we received in the process of this research is seeing how embedded our own assumptions and beliefs about gender are. It has opened our hearts and minds to being more attentive to how we have internalized other discourses about race, class, sexuality, religion, and so many other contextual issues. Though we see this process as unfolding over our lifetimes, we experience this expanded consciousness as making us more embracing of the marginalized realities of our clients.

Practical Applications

As clinicians. It is helpful to become aware of our own subtle biases toward privileging men's perceptions of the problem. Even as we become aware of this, it is not an easy task to challenge this, as attempts to do so can result in the male partner trying to provide more "evidence" to convince therapists what is "really" going on. It takes courage to interrupt male power and to support male clients in becoming aware of and taking responsibility for their power. However, we have found that clients experience freedom from shame and being stuck when they learn how discourses so powerfully influence behaviors, thoughts, and feelings. Bringing this into awareness gives clients permission to consider new ways of being in relationship with themselves, each other, and their context. Sometimes we do this work more implicitly by:

- Suspending our judgment/assessment of "what's really going on" until we have heard the perspectives of both partners,
- Remembering that "what really happened" may not be as important as how partners relate to one another in relation to that event,
- Paying attention to who speaks first and who speaks over others,
- Noting our own privileging of male ways of being, such as trying to get clients to be more logical, rational, less emotional, and less dependent on others.

Or we can do it more explicitly by inviting conversations and providing education about societal gender discourses. Some things to say might be:

- How do you think you learned to be _____ as a man/woman?
- I wonder if there are expectations from our society that say _____ about being a woman/man in intimate relationships.
- What did your mother/father teach or show you about what it means to be a man/woman?
- Do you both ever notice who is listened to most in session? I wonder why that is.

Supervision and teaching. Because of our own experience with this study, we believe it is valuable for supervisors and professors to encourage their students to review their own transcripts of clinical work, identify gender discourses, and explore how these might be influencing the therapeutic process. In transcribing and analyzing transcripts, the process of learning from our own therapy is slowed down to a pace that permits observation of the subtle influences of gender discourses. This process can also take place when reviewing video recordings of sessions. Supervisors can walk supervisees through their video recordings and help them recognize when gender discourses are presenting in session and what it looks like to clinically reinforce or challenge such discourses.

Closing and Personal Reflections

We cannot imagine what our personal and professional lives would be like without having engaged in this grounded theory qualitative study. Gaining awareness about gender discourses has not only given us tools to apply to our clinical work, but has also brought each of us liberation from the ways we have been constrained by the gender discourses absorbed from our social contexts.

References

Almeida, R. V., Dolan-Del Vecchio, K., & Parker, L. (2008). *Transformative family therapy: Just families in a just society*. Boston, MA: Pearson Education.

Charmaz, K. (2006). *Constructing grounded theory: A practical guide to qualitative analysis*. Thousand Oaks, CA: Sage.

Crawford, M. (2004). Mars and Venus collide: A discursive analysis of marital self-help psychology. *Feminism and Psychology, 14*(1), 63–79. doi:10.1177/0959-353504040305.

Dienhart, A. (2001). Engaging men in family therapy: Does the gender of the therapist make a difference? *Journal of Family Therapy, 23*(1), 21–45. doi:10.1111/1467-6427.00167.

Doull, M., Oliffe, J., Knight, R., & Shoveller, J. A. (2013). Sex and straight young men: Challenging and endorsing hegemonic masculinities and gender regimes. *Men and Masculinities, 16*(3), 329–346.

Goldner, V. (1985). Generation and gender: Normative and covert hierarchies. *Family Process, 27*, 17–31.

Haddock, S. A., & Bowling, S. W. (2001). Therapists' approaches to the normative challenges of dual-earner couples: Negotiating outdated societal ideologies. *Journal of Feminist Family Therapy An International Forum, 13*(2–3), 91–120.

Haddock, S. A., & Lyness, K. P. (2002). Three aspects of the therapeutic conversation in couples therapy: Does gender make a difference? *Journal of Couple and Relationship Therapy, 1*(1), 5–23. doi:10.1300/J398v01n01_02.

Haddock, S. A., Zimmerman, T. S., & MacPhee, D. (2000). The power equity guide: Attending to gender in family therapy. *Journal of Marital and Family Therapy, 26*(2), 153–170.

Hare-Mustin, R. (1978). A feminist approach to family therapy. *Family Process, 17*, 181–194.

Hare-Mustin, R. T. (1994). Discourses in the mirrored room: A postmodern analysis of therapy. *Family Process, 33*(1), 19–35.

Harris, T., Moret, L. B., Gale, J., & Kampmeyer, K. L. (2001). Therapists' gender assumptions and how these assumptions influence therapy. *Journal of Feminist Family Therapy, 12*(2–3), 33–59. doi:10.1300/J086v12n02_02.

Hollway, W. (1983). Heterosexual sex: Power and desire for the other. In S. Cartledge & J. Ryan (Eds.), *Sex and love: New thoughts on old contradictions*. London: Women's Press.

Keeling, M. L., Butler, J., Green, N., Kraus, V., & Palit, M. (2010). The gender discourse in therapy questionnaire: A tool for training in feminist-informed therapy. *Journal of Feminist Family Therapy International Forum, 22*(2), 153–169. doi:10.1080/08952831003787883.

Knudson-Martin, C. (2003). How to avoid gender bias in mental health treatment. *Journal of Family Psychotherapy, 14*(3), 45–66. doi:10.1300/J085v14n03_04.

Knudson-Martin, C., & Huenergardt, D. (2010). A socio-emotional approach to couple therapy: Linking social context and couple interaction. *Family Process, 49*(3), 369–384. doi:10.1111/j.1545-5300.2010.01328.x.

Knudson-Martin, C., & Huenergardt, D. (2015). Bridging emotion, societal discourse, and couple interaction in clinical practice. In C. Knudson-Martin, M. A. Wells, & S. K. Samman (Eds.) *Socio-emotional relationship therapy: Bridging emotion, societal context, and couple interaction* (pp. 1–13). New York, NY: Springer.

Knudson-Martin, C., Huenergardt, D., Lafontant, K., Bishop, L., Schaepper, J., & Wells, M. (2014). Competencies for addressing gender and power in couple therapy: A socio-emotional approach. *Journal of Marital and Family Therapy*. Advance online publication. doi: 10.1111/jmft.12068.

Leslie, L. A., & Clossick, M. L. (1996). Sexism in family therapy: Does training in gender make a difference? *Journal of Marital and Family Therapy, 22*(2), 253–269. doi:10.1111/j.1752-0606.1996.tb00202.x.

Paechter, C. (2006). Masculine femininities/feminine masculinities: Power, identities and gender. *Gender and Education, 18*(3), 253–263. doi:10.1080/09540250600667785.

Robinson, T. L. (1999). The intersections of dominant discourses across race, gender, and other identities. *Journal of Counseling and Development, 77*(1), 73–79.

Stabb, S. D., Cox, D. L., & Harber, J. L. (1997). Gender-related therapist attributions in couples therapy: A preliminary multiple case study investigation. *Journal of Marital and Family Therapy, 23*(3), 335–346. doi:10.1111/j.1752-0606.1997.tb01041.x.

Werner-Wilson, R. J., Price, S. J., Zimmerman, T. S., & Murphy, M. J. (1997). Client gender as a process variable in marriage and family therapy: Are women clients interrupted more than men clients? *Journal of Family Psychology, 11*(3), 373–377.

West, C., & Zimmerman, D. (1987). Doing gender. *Gender and Society, 1*(2), 125–151. doi:10.2307/189945.

Expanding the Lens: How SERT Therapists Develop Interventions that Address the Larger Context

Julie Estrella, Veronica P. Kuhn, Cassidy J. Freitas and Melissa A. Wells

Men and women who are flexible regarding gender norms and achieve a relatively equal distribution of power in their couple relationships have an increased ability to tolerate stress, respond to change, and enhance one another's health and well-being (Gerson 2010; Knudson-Martin 2013). In the context of two dominant societal narratives, guiding scripts for gender originate from a variety of sociocultural sources—culture, religion, family members and peers, the media, etc. These sociocultural contextual discourses influence men and women regarding how they should perform in couple relationships. The processes of power and privilege embedded in these dominant discourses are taken for granted and tend to go unnoticed in heterosexual relationship dynamics (Hildebrand and Markovic 2007). Couple and family therapists (CFTs) are challenged to recognize these processes when people seek help with relationship distress.

As therapists new to dealing with gender and power issues, we decided to study how other CFTs conceptualize and attend to the effects of sociocultural context on their client couples. We use a definition of contextual consciousness initially coined by Esmiol et al. (2012) to expand on critical consciousness that includes three components: (1) consciousness about the inherent power differentials in a person's social context, (2) sensitivity to clients' unique experiences within these

J. Estrella (✉) · V.P. Kuhn · C.J. Freitas
Department of Counseling and Family Sciences, Loma Linda University,
Loma Linda, CA, USA

M.A. Wells
Department of Counseling and Family Sciences, Loma Linda University,
Loma Linda, CA, USA

M.A. Wells
Marital and Family Therapy Intern, Mt. Vision Family Therapy, Redlands, CA, USA

© American Family Therapy Academy 2015
C. Knudson-Martin et al. (eds.), *Socio-Emotional Relationship Therapy*,
AFTA SpringerBriefs in Family Therapy, DOI 10.1007/978-3-319-13398-0_5

different contexts, and (3) attention to the intersection of the larger context with clients' relational processes and presenting issues (p. 573).

In this chapter, we summarize our qualitative research on what informs CFTs as they apply the Socio-Emotional Relationship Therapy (SERT) (Knudson-Martin and Huenergardt 2010) contextual lens with their couple clients. We started this study because we had unique access to verbatim transcripts of SERT therapists discussing couple therapy sessions in live supervision and debriefings with as many as nine other team members. Our goal was to understand how these therapists conceptualize, apply, and critique their process of developing contextually conscious approaches in their work with heterosexual couples. We present our study findings on how these therapists identified and attended to invisible power imbalances between partners through the use of case examples. We also share our personal reflections on what we learned through this study process.

Author Backgrounds and Theoretical Lenses

We are CFT doctoral students at Loma Linda University who are actively integrating a critical social constructionist perspective into our practice. Julie, Veronica, and Melissa have participated in the ongoing development of the SERT model, which addresses power differentials between partners while promoting mutually supportive relationships by addressing the effects of the larger societal context on couples (Knudson-Martin and Huenergardt 2010). Cassidy joined the project to continue developing her critical consciousness and to provide a lens from outside of the SERT clinical group. We are also informed by research looking specifically at how therapists can develop contextual consciousness and greater awareness of how couple relationships are impacted by societal discourses (Esmiol et al. 2012). This research helped us focus our study on bridging the gap in how critical contextual awareness translates into practice.

Study Design and Method

We used a qualitative analysis with a grounded theory design (Daly 2007) in order to understand how contextually conscious therapists develop clinical approaches when working with couples. We selected our sample from a database of verbatim transcripts of the SERT clinical group from 2009 to the present. These notes include pre- and post-session discussions. We chose to use theoretical sampling (Charmaz 2006) and specifically studied the 2009 transcripts, since they offered rich detail on how therapists in the early stages of developing the SERT model learned how to recognize critical contextual issues in therapy and considered how to sensitively address them. See "Bridging Emotion, Societal Discourse, and

Couple Interaction in Clinical Practice" (Knudson-Martin and Huenergardt 2015) and Knudson-Martin et al. (2014) for more information about the SERT clinical study group.

We followed a process of open and focused coding and theory development (Charmaz 2006) and wrote reflective journals and analytic memos to account for how our own experiences impacted the final theory as it developed (Daly 2007). At the end of our analysis, we created a grounded theory that identified what informed this sample of therapists as they created interventions designed to address how socio-contextual processes impact couples' relational dynamics and promote equitable, mutually supportive relationships.

Making the Invisible Visible: How to Work with Power

Though we originally set out to understand in a broad sense what informed our sample of therapists as they created and implemented critical contextual interventions, it became clear that something important consistently happened throughout this process. Unlike other therapeutic approaches that do not specifically address issues of power and privilege between partners, these therapists were organizing their entire approach from the first point of contact until termination around shifting the power dynamic between the partners. Our grounded theory explaining their process is illustrated in Fig. 1.

For each session, the therapists focused discussion on at least one of the three basic clinical goals: (a) identifying power imbalances, (b) disrupting the flow of power, and (c) generating alternative experiences of shared power. These three clinical goals occurred in a recursive manner throughout therapy. For example, in one case therapists identified a gender imbalance initially and used their own non-neutral position of leadership to disrupt the flow of gendered power. They then realized that another critical aspect of the couple's identity—their cultural context—was also impacting the power dynamic. They therefore attuned to each partner's culturally contextual experience as a way to generate transformative experiences of shared power.

Our findings also showed that when considering how to address these power process goals, the therapists drew upon three guiding perspectives to inform their clinical approaches: (a) a contextual lens or theory, (b) the client's experiences of sociocultural context, and (c) the therapist's experiences of sociocultural context. Each of these guiding perspectives was instrumental in helping the therapists consider how to approach the unique clinical goals for each couple's shift toward a more mutually supportive relationship.

Finally, we observed the importance of professional consultation for developing contextually conscious therapeutic approaches, as a sort of sounding board. In this sample, professional consultation involved a clinical research group composed of two doctoral-faculty supervisors and eleven doctoral-student therapists. Two student therapists typically conducted the couple sessions live, while the rest observed

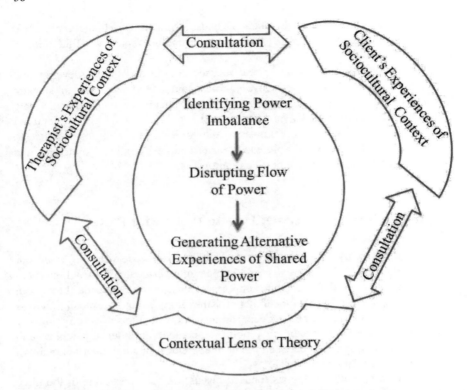

Fig. 1 How therapists develop interventions that address powerful larger contexts

behind a two-way mirror. The reflections and support of the clinical research group made it possible for the session therapists to expand their own lens and see beyond potential blind spots. Through the use of this supportive consultation and the three guiding perspectives, session therapists were able to create contextually conscious approaches centered on addressing power dynamics with their couple clients.

Transforming Couple Power Processes

Identifying Power Imbalance

From the beginning of therapy, the therapists in the SERT group actively engaged a contextual lens that oriented them toward identifying the power processes at play in the relationship and how these relational dynamics were related to the sociocultural context of partners.

Contextual lens or theory. During the initial stage of therapy, SERT therapists focused on how larger social contexts impacted the balance of power in the couple relationship. As they listened to the couple, they drew on extensive awareness from critical theory and feminist literature as a way to view what was happening between partners in session as well as to understand the ways the partners approached one another with regard to gender and cultural socialization. This can be challenging, since power processes are so embedded in gender among heterosexual couple processes (Lips 1991). In other words, what looks like gender performances can actually be the mechanisms of power.

In the case of a heterosexual Puerto Rican couple, the group was trying to understand competing beliefs described by the husband (i.e., being deeply religious while working in a profession in which infidelity was common). A therapist raised the issue of connecting larger contexts to deeper emotions for both partners:

> What are some of the underlying sociocultural issues? If we're trying to imagine what the sociocultural emotion is in these cases, what would be the first step of recognizing it and figuring out how to work with it? Understanding their experience through that lens of culture and gender, what does she feel? What does he feel? What's it like for her to be in this place as a Puerto Rican woman?

In this example, the therapists used theory as a guiding lens that reframed the case from an individual to a more collective experience that could help open up alternative possibilities as therapy progressed.

Client's experiences of sociocultural context. Below is an example of how this guiding perspective informed the SERT therapists as they socioculturally attuned to the Puerto Rican couple's power dynamics by paying close attention to each partner's felt experience of his and her sociocultural context. A member of the research group observed how the husband's behavior was causing him to lose his connection with his wife and raised questions about the possibility of his experience of guilt and shame associated with his masculine gender socialization versus the actual unwanted behavior getting in the way of this connection between the couple. In this early stage of therapy, the team identified his withdrawing behavior as a way of maintaining power in the couple relationship while also blocking his ability to connect with his wife. Understanding the behavior of withdrawal as a tactic to gain power is useful in identifying the power imbalance, but the therapists also attempted to understand how underlying emotions, such as shame, are linked to contextual cultural messages the man received about lusting being "wrong" and how this perhaps contributed to his desire to isolate from his partner. When he experienced shame, he did not see himself as the more powerful partner or how his pulling away affected their relationship. It is as if the larger discourses and shame hijacked any chance of connection (ChenFeng and Galick, "How Gender Discourses Hijack Couple Therapy—and How to Avoid It," 2015).

Therapist   He loses her in that moment because he says, "I can only think about myself and my own guilt, my own shame." ... Shame [in relation to societal expectations] is so pervasive. ... it could be the bigger issue that has him withdrawing.

Therapist's experiences of sociocultural context. At times, the SERT therapists would explore their own experiences and roles, i.e., as a wife, husband, mother, and father. In the following example, two male clinicians reflect on the gender processes that appear in their own marriages as they tried to understand the experience of their male client and why he may be disengaging:

Therapist 1   My wife and I deal with this all the time ... all the issues of gender and power and initiative.

Therapist 2   I felt the same sort of thing [describes his confusion as a man], because I learned as a man to fix things, yet was told that wasn't what she needed ... So, what do I do?

As they related back to their own experiences as men in relationships, they were able to develop hypotheses that informed the way they intervened in the next session.

Gender and power in action. The following example of work with a heterosexual couple illuminates how therapists combined these guiding perspectives to identify and reframe the power imbalance from the first session. Tim, African-American, and Margaret, European American, both business professionals in their mid-40s entered therapy because of marital problems related to Tim's habit of staring at other women's physical attributes. Tim was quite embarrassed about this behavior and had previously sought individual therapy. He reported that this helped somewhat, yet did not change this disruptive habit. Margaret became increasingly frustrated and drew the line, saying that she would not stay in the marriage if Tim did not change his behavior.

The SERT team puzzled over how to best frame the couple's challenges. One way to view the problem was from a perspective of sexual addiction. Another more systemic perspective was that circular causality between the partners occurred. When Tim stared at another woman, Margaret became irate and communicated her feelings to Tim, and then, his anxious response fueled more staring. The group considered how to work with these ideas, but grappled more with how gender and power were at work in this particular problem. How did Tim's gender socialization empower his inclination to stare? How did this affect Margaret's sense of her ability to keep the relationship working well? This is a discourse that influences many women. The group deliberated how to address these issues without adding weight to the societal message that puts responsibility on the female partner to maintain the relationship. Ultimately, the couple's experiences of sociocultural context, as seen through a critical contextual lens, helped the therapists determine which aspects of the couple's power dynamic needed to be disrupted in order to generate a shared alternative experience of power.

Disrupting the Flow of Power

During this phase of therapy, the therapists actively looked for ways to provide leadership in the session by positioning themselves to challenge the existing relational power dynamics, that is, making the invisible visible.

Therapist's experience of sociocultural context. The use of the therapist's personal experience through consultation allowed the therapist to give voice to and link larger social discourses to the emotions either showing up or not showing up in the room with the clients. In the following excerpt, the therapists were able to address their own emotions that reflected common societal sentiments that the woman should do something to make the relationship work. They then applied their awareness of this discourse to postulate an alternative approach of relating that afforded the husband the chance to experience a new way of connecting with his wife:

Therapist 1   I feel so sad. I've been fighting back tears. I feel so sad for her. It really feels like she has to do something different. He's not. I'm angry. How can you not be? He seems to be taking over the session and rationalizing everything.

Therapist 2   As he leaves his emotional experience, we're asking him to hold onto that hot wire and he's jiggling from the shock. We need to help him be grounded. You're coaching him through it … by saying, "This is important; stretch for her. She needs to know that you know what she's feeling. Try it again."

Consultation. The sounding board of consultation was used frequently during this time to help therapists create clarity about the use of interventions and also aided in examining the potential impact of alternative interventions to address the power imbalance. The SERT therapists looked to one another to make sure they were not being blinded by their own experiences of larger societal discourses. Conversations within the group challenged therapists' taken-for-granted realities, reflected on therapeutic processes, expanded the view of how power imbalances impact the couple interactions, and created clarity and intentionality about proposed interventions:

Therapist 1   He talked about being a man. If you were him, how are you feeling?
Therapist 2   There seems to be a lot of shame and guilt.
Therapist 3   How are those things related to the larger sociocultural context?
Therapist 2   His ideas of how a husband is supposed to be in a relationship are influencing him. He talked about, "It's not how husbands are supposed to be or treat a wife or not being a good husband." Those are some ideas about what it means to be in relationship with someone.
Therapist 1   About being good; where might those messages be coming from? What questions do you have if you don't know? Frame it as capturing his experience of the struggle as opposed to thinking of it as an inconsistency.

As this excerpt illustrates, the consultation process was useful in identifying gender discourses, emotional experiences of the couple, and in challenging the therapist to name influential relational discourses that impacted the way interventions were chosen.

Contextual lens or theory. Referencing a contextual lens helped move therapist interventions toward attuning to the powerful partner enough to keep him engaged without reinforcing the position of power, all the while raising awareness of the need to challenge power. For example, by emphasizing stereotypic gender interactions, the therapist could draw on the larger collective human experience to normalize and deconstruct challenging emotions, such as shame, anger, and hurt, in a way that provided the couple space to rethink the role and influence of these emotions in their relationship.

Generating Alternative Experiences of Shared Power

During the progression of therapy, couples became more aware of larger societal discourses, and as a result, the conversation became more explicit about how these discourses were impacting the couple relationship. The goal of therapy shifted to allow the couple to experience new ways of interacting with mutual influence and flexibility.

Contextual lens and theory. Prior to a final session with Tim and Margaret, a group member used the contextual and theoretical lens to reflect on the couple's move toward a more equal relationship and how to sustain the change over time. This excerpt shows how the group also integrated a contextually conscious lens with a variety of therapeutic theories, for example, narrative therapy:

> You have laid seeds throughout the sessions, but he managed to open it up now so that it is no longer about looking at women's physiques. It's about committing on both their sides … this is the phase that they work through what an equal relationship looks like and deal with difficult issues and sustain that over time … In narrative, this is the stage of sharing the good news. You don't change these habits and images of yourself all alone.

Client's experiences of sociocultural context. During a post-session wrap-up, a group member used the client's experience to help punctuate the issue of safety for the wife during the session. This also offered an alternative way for the husband to understand why his being vulnerable is so critical in shifting the couple's power dynamic and why this matters to the well-being of their relationship.

> I felt like he really opened up, and you acknowledged what he'd just said. Next time I would want to reach to him, because here's a man that will acknowledge the fear that he will be left … We get to help him link how his stepping out and making it safe for her makes it safe for him, too. If she feels safe, then she won't leave. Yet when he withdraws or closes down, she is left with very few options.

Therapist's experience of sociocultural context. The SERT therapists often reflected on their own personal experience of the change in the couple. They tended to privilege examples or reflections that spotlighted the couple's progress: in this case, the ability to mutually influence one another for the benefit of the relationship. The following excerpt is from a post-session wrap-up after another couple spoke about how they wanted to be with one another and discussed what happened during the therapy that contributed to the new experience of mutual vulnerability:

> Therapist 1 … when describing what they would create: being able to deal with difficult issues in a safe context, I liked the way you labeled it as a societal discourse and moved the focus away from him alone to men in general. It opened up possibilities for both of them.

Therapist 2 You were authentic.

Therapist 3 You validated [the husband] as a man.

Therapist 1 Women really need to get that. It's not an easy thing, and the idea that "I might look weak as a man when I'm vulnerable" is really hard ... If we think about it as his concern as to how she responds, as part of the discourse, we could pursue his experience in terms of "how have people responded to this when you have shown you were weak?" Then ask for exceptions to that, and ask [wife] about how it is for her to experience him in this new way.

Consultation. To highlight the magnitude of the shifts in the couple dynamic, the members of the consultation group joined a session to bring in multiple voices to talk about the change and open up alternative ways to connect and create safety within the new experience. The consultation group brought life to the room, spotlighting a larger collective experience that could possibly open up something for the couple as they continued to determine how they would like to relate to one another in a mutually supportive way.

Clinical Implications

Interestingly, the three clinical goals revealed in this study resonate closely with the seven identified core competencies that emerged later as this group attempted to codify a framework that eventually became known as SERT (see Knudson-Martin and Huenergardt, "Bridging Emotion, Societal Discourse, and Couple Interaction in Clinical Practice," 2015; Knudson-Martin et al. 2014). The first goal, coded as identifying the power imbalance, would be best described as encompassing the following competencies: (1) facilitate relational safety, (2) identify relational power dynamics, and (3) attune to underlying sociocultural emotions. The second goal, disrupting the flow of power, would seem to be supported by the following two SERT competencies: (4) identify enactments of cultural discourse and (5) foster mutual attunement. The last goal, generating an alternative experience of shared power, aligns with the following two SERT competencies: (6) create a relationship model based on equality and (7) facilitate shared relational responsibility. Together these seven competencies serve as clinical guides for therapists as they fine-tune implementation of contextually conscious interventions and study how these relate to important clinical processes and outcomes.

Influence of Research on Authors

These findings regarding how to integrate critical contextual consciousness into practice have significantly impacted our own professional growth.

Julie, MPH, MFTI

As a Swiss American, female, married, heterosexual middle-class relatively new marital and family therapy intern, this study has directly influenced the development of my practice. Working predominantly with families enrolled in Department of Housing and Urban Development (HUD) programs, I now see how important it is to tune into my own sociocultural lenses and biases. I must quiet down the collective societal discourses impacting this population—e.g., beliefs about families living in poverty, unmarried mothers, and work ethics—that can get in the way of connecting with the clients' perceived experience. I can now apply t heoretical lenses that help me contextualize and identify the power dynamics from the first point of contact. I use my own experience as an emotional thermometer and am intentional about framing and connecting their experiences to one another's shared experiences or to larger societal discourses. My focus then is on finding ways to disrupt the flow of power such that the couple or family can begin to "share power, nurture one another, have full expression of emotions, emotional openness and vulnerability ... recognize humanity in their partner, and value others" (Almeida et al. 2008, p. 73).

In practice, transforming power imbalances can be tricky. Throughout this study, I have been introduced to ways people with less power organize around or pay careful attention to the more powerful partner and am surprised to see how we as therapists often do the same thing. Whether it is organizing around a co-therapist, trying to please a supervisor, or privileging our theoretical lens, we are unable to escape the invisible lines of power that shape how we engage others relationally. And like the first SERT therapists in our sample, I am learning that being authentic and transparent about my own experience can help disrupt the flow of power in a way that sets our consultation network up for an alternative experience of shared power. While we may not be able to escape the impact of larger societal discourses, we are able to create the same kind of mutually supportive relationships that our clients seek to experience with one another, and our own breakthroughs directly influence theirs.

Veronica, LMFT

Prior to pursuing my doctoral education, I worked in a variety of mental health settings. And, while all these sites required some sort of cultural competency training, ideas of power and privilege were rarely discussed in clinical supervision/consultation even as I worked with marginalized and underserved populations, most of whom experienced significant oppression due to various contextual factors. I remember being told in training that culturally conscious interventions meant taking into account education and literacy levels of the client. While these are very important considerations, they were only the tip of the iceberg.

Through my involvement in SERT and this qualitative research process, I am beginning to appreciate the complexity of developing contextually conscious interventions and, more importantly, the role that consultation can play in facilitating their development. I learned that it is not enough to look at the client's experience, but to also consider my own experience of privilege and oppression and how these might influence the therapeutic process. An example of this occurred when I shared a video during consultation of a couple engaged in an enactment attempting to resolve differences in parenting approaches. I had felt the session had gone well and the couple was beginning to make movement toward an alternative discourse of shared power. While the group agreed there was significant movement toward shared power, they also pointed out how I may have privileged a masculine-dominated discourse that, had it been interrupted, may have provided more room for the less powerful partner's ideas on parenting. The reflections from the consultation group not only raised my awareness of gender discourses for future reference, but also informed my next session with the couple.

Cassidy, MFTI

As I have become more familiar with my social position and its clinical and personal implications, I have seen the impact that power imbalances, oppressive experiences, and larger contextual discourses have on my clients. I have struggled with how to turn this awareness, now unavoidable in all of my work, into clinical practice and interventions. As the sole researcher who is not a regular part of the SERT group, intimacy with the data in this study provided a framework from which to intentionally develop my contextually conscious lens which I apply through a critical, feminist-informed narrative approach.

My participation in this study has highlighted the importance in attuning to a client's experience and opened doors from which I may use my own experiences to inform my clinical decisions. I have found that when working to shift power imbalances, it is critical that I attune to the client's experience-near narrative and language that they use to describe the problem. Privileging the clients' experiences, similar to the three guiding perspectives found within the transcripts, provides an opening for me to connect invisible power dynamics to larger societal discourses. In addition, I have seen how useful drawing upon my own experiences with power and privilege can be. I used to believe I had to leave myself outside the door when entering the therapy room. Instead, my participation in this study has shown me how contextually conscious therapists are able to use their own experiences to deepen their therapeutic understanding and inform the clinical decisions that they make. None of this can be done adequately without consultation, which has led me to seek out other clinicians with whom I may consult when working with these sensitive issues.

Melissa, MFTI

Being a part of the SERT clinical group has added sophisticated insight to my smoldering indignation when witnessing social injustice. From an early age, I was intuitively aware of the unfairness and disadvantages embedded in the gender power relations of my social environment. I questioned that the females in my circle of family and friends were regarded as "wayward" or, worse yet, "mentally ill" by the husbands whose wives balked at the power differentials in their marriages. I have since discovered that these "patriarchs" were rigidly adhering to their standards for male gender socialization of that time, not all that long ago (1950s–1960s in the USA). The collective price of self-sacrifice paid by these women to maintain their marriages was costly (e.g., unwanted abortions, sterilization without knowledge or consent while under general anesthesia, forced abandonment of career, even denial of her religion). Yet, these women were tenacious.

Now in my work with couples, engaging in therapeutic conversations about their experiences of sociocultural context seems to create a bridge for a positive emotional alliance. We gain a sense of trust so that, even though I am a European American, middle-class, heterosexual, middle-aged, able-bodied, formally educated female, men and women of various races and ethnicities permit me to join them in their worlds tinged by sexism, racism, classism, etc. I find that I can still become indignant about power inequities, but processing the intricacies of my feminist, social constructionist worldview in consultation with my trusted clinical mentors helps me examine my biases and challenge my own authority. Tenacity with heart worked for the women of my youth. I try to bring this spirit to my clinical endeavors with my clients as we join forces to transform injustice in their lives and relationships.

Conclusion

Through this study, we see that in order to make invisible power dynamics visible in therapy, we first need to focus on power, keeping that lens central and always returning to it. No matter what therapeutic approach is being used to guide treatment, power must be given a primary role. We need to recognize that there are three revolving clinical goals that must be approached from a non-neutral position, intent on (1) identifying the power imbalances, (2) disrupting the flow of power, and (3) generating an alternative experience of shared power. We need to be present to three important sources of information: (1) contextual lens or theory, (2) the client's experiences of sociocultural context, and (3) the therapist's experiences of sociocultural context.

We also highly recommend developing a consulting network, whether with peers, supervisors, or groups such as the SERT clinical group, when practicing from a critical contextually conscious orientation. We noticed that regular checking in with colleagues as a sounding board supports contextually conscious therapists to (1) reveal any unspoken beliefs, discourses, or taken-for-granted contextual realities or biases; (2) provide professional accountability for therapists in order to keep their own power and privilege in check; and (3) create interventions that foster mutual support and vulnerability.

References

Almeida, R. V., Dolan-Del, V., & Parker, L. (2008). *Transformative family therapy: Just families in a just society*. Boston, MA: Pearson Education.

Charmaz, K. (2006). *Constructing grounded theory: A practical guide to qualitative analysis*. Thousand Oaks, CA: Sage.

ChenFeng, J. L., & Galick, A. (2015). How gender discourses hijack couple therapy and how to avoid it. In C. Knudson-Martin, M. A. Wells, & S. K. Samman (Eds.), *Socio-emotional relationship therapy: Bridging emotion, societal context, and couple interaction* (pp. 41–52). New York, NY: Springer.

Daly, K. J. (2007). *Qualitative methods for family studies and human development*. Thousand Oaks, CA: Sage.

Esmiol, E. E., Knudson-Martin, C., & Delgado, S. (2012). Developing a contextual consciousness: Learning to address gender, societal power, and culture in clinical practice. *Journal of Marital and Family Therapy, 38*, 573–588.

Gerson, K. (2010). *The unfinished revolution: How a new generation is reshaping family, work, and gender in America*. New York, NY: Oxford University Press.

Hildebrand, J., & Markovic, D. (2007). Systemic therapists' experience of powerlessness. *Australian and New Zealand Journal of Family Therapy, 28*, 191–199.

Knudson-Martin, C. (2013). Why power matters: Creating a foundation of mutual support in couples relationships. *Family Process, 52*(1), 5–18.

Knudson-Martin, C., & Huenergardt, D. (2010). A socio-emotional approach to couple therapy: Linking social context and couple interaction. *Family Process, 49*, 369–384.

Knudson-Martin, C., & Huenergardt, D. (2015). Bridging emotion, societal discourse, and couple interaction in clinical practice. In C. Knudson-Martin, M. A. Wells, & S. K. Samman (Eds.), *Socio-emotional relationship therapy: Bridging emotion, societal context, and couple interaction*. (pp. 1–13). New York, NY: Springer.

Knudson-Martin, C., Huenergardt, D., Lafontant, K., Bishop, L., Schaepper, Wells, M. (2014). Competencies for addressing gender and power in couple therapy: A socio-emotional approach. *Journal of Marital and Family Therapy*, Advance online publication. doi:10.1111/jmft.12068

Lips, H. M. (1991). *Women, men, and power*. Toronto: Mayfield Publishing.

SERT Therapists' Experience of Practicing Sociocultural Attunement

Mayuri (Mia) Pandit, Jessica L. ChenFeng and Young Joo Kang

This chapter is a revised version of Pandit, M., ChenFeng, J. L., & Kang, Y. J., Knudson-Martin, C., & Huenergardt, D. (2014). Practicing socio-cultural attunement: A study of couple therapists. Journal of Contemporary Family Therapy, 36, 518–528.

Because larger societal dynamics influence individual relationships, therapists need to be mindful of cultural and social injustices (Knudson-Martin and Mahoney 2009; Zimmerman et al. 2001). To understand more about this process, we have been part of an ongoing action research project focused on developing Socio-Emotional Relationship Therapy (SERT), an approach that involves attention to larger societal dynamics being played out within couple relationships (Knudson-Martin and Huenergardt 2010). Previous research from this group found that attunement to the client's unique social, cultural, and emotional experience was a foundational competency (Knudson-Martin et al. 2014; Williams et al. 2012). However, there has been no clear consensus in the field on how to practically include sociocultural context in clinical work (Owen et al. 2011; Sperry 2010).

M. (Mia) Pandit (✉)
Loma Linda University Behavioral Medicine Center, Outpatient Services,
Redlands, CA, USA

J.L. ChenFeng
Department of Educational Psychology and Counseling, California State University,
Northridge, CA, USA

Y.J. Kang
Department of Counseling and Family Sciences, Loma Linda University,
Loma Linda, CA, USA

© American Family Therapy Academy 2015
C. Knudson-Martin et al. (eds.), *Socio-Emotional Relationship Therapy*,
AFTA SpringerBriefs in Family Therapy, DOI 10.1007/978-3-319-13398-0_6

Development of a Model

We are middle-class Christian women of Asian descent who work with a very diverse population. Mayuri (Mia) is an Asian Indian immigrant born in India and raised in the United States. Jessica is a second generation Taiwanese American raised in the greater Los Angeles area. Young is a South Korean citizen born and raised in South Korea. In our work with couples, we quickly realized that although we acknowledged the importance of sociocultural attunement (SCA), we did not know what it actually looks like in practice. So we set out to identify a model of how we socioculturally attune to our client couples in therapy.

In a previous paper summarizing SERT (Knudson-Martin and Huenergardt 2010), SCA was defined as the ability to "tune into each client such that we are able to resonate with that person's sociocultural experience on an affective level" (p. 370). This definition expands upon Siegel's (2007) definition of interpersonal attunement, i.e., pausing to reflect on another's "being," emotions and intentions, focusing on understanding, empathizing, and resonating with the other emotionally as well as physiologically. Based on discussions with the SERT study group (Knudson-Martin and Huenergardt, "Bridging Emotion, Societal Discourse, and Couple Interaction in Clinical Practice," 2015; Knudson-Martin et al. 2014), we concluded that one could emotionally attune, but not be socioculturally attuned, if we focused only on the clients' emotions without considering the larger social context that influences relationship processes. Thus, we assumed that SCA goes beyond understanding and awareness to opening oneself fully to another's emotional experience within their unique societal contexts.

To study therapists' experiences of SCA, we engaged other members of the SERT research team. Our project thus involved a diverse group of ten women and three men practicing SERT. Eleven were in various stages of doctoral study in couple and family therapy; two were faculty. Four were licensed MFTs.

Drawing on action research principles (Chenail 2005; Mendenhall and Doherty 2005), we used a cyclical process of observing our own clinical work with couples, analysis, theory development, and observation of more clinical work in order to collect information about what SCA looks like in session and to improve our practice of it. In particular, we asked open-ended questions of therapists conducting therapy in front of a one-way mirror (*in-session team*) and therapists who were observing behind the one-way mirror (*observing team*). Mia was one of the therapists on the in-session team in front of the mirror, and Jessica and Young were therapists on the observing team.

Some of the open-ended questions we asked ourselves were: In this session, how do you distinguish between emotional and sociocultural attunement? Which indicators told you [*observing team*] that the therapist(s) achieved sociocultural attunement? Do you feel that you [*in-session team*] achieved SCA with clients overall? How did you know? In addition to our written answers to these questions, the SERT team discussed each other's experiences and ideas related to SCA in the observed sessions. At the end of each session, we checked with clients about what the session had been like for them in order to inform our understanding of SCA.

Following each group discussion, Mia and Young, and eventually Jessica, met to code and further analyze the sessions and therapists' experience of them and then brought our evolving grounded theory back to the larger group for further discussion and development. We participated in this process for four months, meeting with the large group for four hours each week. Within that time, we focused on five heterosexual couple cases and 25 sessions.

We found that therapists experienced themselves creating SCA through three recursive processes. These were present concurrently and interacted with one another. The first process involved the therapist's guiding lens, e.g., the contextual lens the therapist used to view clients and their relational processes. The second process consisted of the therapist's sociocultural interpretation, e.g., what sociocultural information the client gave the therapist and what the therapist reflected back to the clients. The third process entailed client resonance, e.g., whether clients appeared to resonate with the therapist's sociocultural reflections (see Table 1). Additional details about this study are also available in Pandit et al. (2014).

Table 1 Processes involved in therapists' SCA

Process	Involves
Therapists' guiding lens	*Therapist asks self*
The lens therapists use to view clients and their sociocultural processes	1. What messages about self in relation to others are perpetuated by client's position in societal context?
	2. In what kinds of contexts is the client embedded? How have they changed over time?
	3. What messages about gender has the client internalized?
	4. How do socioeconomic status and economic situation impact constructions of self and relationships?
	5. How does the client's relationship with legal structures (immigration, justice system, and so on) impact constructions of self and relationships?
	6. How do the client's religion, age, race, ethnicity, and disabilities impact constructions of self and relationships?
	7. How much personal, interpersonal, and institutional power does the client experience as a result of his or her societal position? (Silverstein et al. 2006, p. 399)
Sociocultural interpretation	*Therapist's inner dialogue*
The sociocultural information the client imparts to the therapist and what the therapist reflects back to the clients	1. Listening for social discourses
	2. Linking emotions and behaviors to discourses and power
	3. Awareness of personal experience
	Therapist's observable actions
	1. Questioning
	2. Validating
	3. Naming

(continued)

Table 1 (continued)

Process	Involves
Client resonance	*Clients resonating when they*
Clients appear to connect with the therapist's sociocultural reflections	1. Expand their level of disclosure
	2. Show more emotion
	3. Become more relational in conversation
	4. Nod, maintain eye contact with therapist, lean forward
	Clients not resonating when they
	1. Avoid eye contact
	2. Disagree with therapist's assessment
	3. Look blank or confused
	4. Do not follow therapist's direction in conversation and change the subject
	5. Tell the same story again and again

Therapist's Guiding Lens

The first aspect of being socioculturally attuned—utilizing a socio-contextual lens—quickly became apparent. For example, in response to the question of whether she thought she was socioculturally attuning to the clients that session, Aimee answered, "Most of the time; I felt attuned in my mind, used that to guide my interventions and comments."

After much discussion regarding the group's experiences of sociocultural attunement, we concluded that SCA begins with a guiding lens. In other words, knowledge and training regarding how to recognize possible social discourses and the importance of social context to clients' identities and processes appear vital to SCA (see Esmiol et al. 2012). Social discourses are shared ideas and messages about how to think, act, and feel in various circumstances (Gergen 2009), i.e., "I should not cry at work because men don't cry and I am a man." (See ChenFeng and Galick, "How Gender Discourses Hijack Couple Therapy—and How to Avoid It," 2015, for a study of gender discourses in couple therapy.)

We also agreed that awareness of how the social context is important and influential in relational dynamics was the key to utilizing a sociocultural conceptual framework. For example, one of our observing team members, Carmen, knew that the in-session therapists were socioculturally attuning because "the therapists seemed to know what each [client] was feeling and used knowledge of gender and culture discourses to frame expectations of each client." We found it was important for us to have a baseline theoretical understanding of the connections between sociocultural issues and discourses within the clients' experiences and that this awareness prompted us to want to understand more.

Since we never knew for sure what particular social discourses were being played out in our clients' lives, we noticed ourselves engaging the clients in conversation surrounding social context. We used our general understanding of the clients' sociocultural status when we initiated such conversation or simply asked clients about their understanding of their social contexts. For example, one observing therapist, Hans, reported that the in-session therapists, Mia and Aimee, would socioculturally attune "by exploring [the wife's] ideal [of] a good wife."

Although knowledge and training regarding probable cultural discourses were helpful, we concluded that it was possible to socioculturally attune without prior knowledge of specific discourses likely to influence a particular client. We began by understanding that there is a link between social context and emotion, behavior, and relational patterns and then engaged clients in conversation that explored those links. Seven specific questions outlined by Silverstein et al. (2006) were particularly helpful and are included in Table 1.

Sociocultural Interpretation

We found that we intentionally drew on our contextual lens to inform a sociocultural interpretation of client experiences. This involved a circular process of inner dialogues and observable actions of the therapist. In other words, during this process, whatever interaction the therapist observed in the therapy room was viewed through the guiding social context lens and then reflected back to the client through that lens. For example, Kirstee and Doug had been conducting therapy with a conservative Christian couple in front of the one-way mirror. The wife frequently discussed her conflict between accommodating her husband's desire for her to solely focus on raising their children and her own desire to work from home as a consultant while taking care of their children. During the course of therapy, Kirstee and Doug specifically listened for sociocultural content and cues and viewed those ideas through a social context lens (inner dialogue). This internal process led them to make an intentional verbal reflection back to the client (observable action), e.g., "You [to the wife] seem to be struggling to reconcile your idea of being a good Christian wife who takes care of her children and obeys her husband with your heartfelt desire to work as a consultant."

Therapist Inner Dialogue

We concluded that three specific internal processes occurred when we observed clients through a sociocultural lens. First, we started to listen for social discourses based on the couple's relationship dynamics and power balances. Second, we linked emotions and behaviors to discourses and power. Third, we also noticed our own personal awareness and reaction to being socioculturally attuned to our clients.

Listening for social discourses. Since we anticipated that social context impacts emotions and behaviors, we found that we approached each couple with intentional curiosity regarding their own view of their context. For instance, in the example mentioned above, when the wife discussed the conflict between her husband's desires, the church's views, and her own desires, Kirstee and Doug began to wonder about how conservative Christian cultural discourses may be influencing the husband and the wife. Specifically, they wondered whether the idea that men should be the "priests" and leaders in the household and women should be "the homemakers and focus on child-rearing" contributed to the wife's internalized discourse. Maybe she had received ideas in her religious network that being a "good Christian woman" meant doing what her husband wanted, whereas focusing on her career and her family meant she was acting in a selfish "non-Christian way."

Kirstee described her inner dialogue of identifying social discourses in this way: "I felt like I could reflect [in my mind] what I thought her expression was or what discourses were motivating her behavior or emotional experience and then ask her if that was what it was like for her." As a team, we reflected that when we began wondering about particular messages the clients are receiving from their social context regarding how they were acting, thinking, or feeling, we had already begun to identify social discourses. Focusing on "shoulds" and "musts" helped to uncover emotionally salient discourses, e.g., what does it mean to be a "good man? What should he be saying, doing?"

Linking emotions and behaviors to discourses and power. We also noticed that societal discourses gave rise to emotions and behaviors. We found that understanding emotions and behaviors related to social discourse was a very important part of SCA. One of our main goals was to understand how clients' underlying emotions connected to sociocultural experience and to help them understand their partner's emotions in this context as well. For example, when we worked with unemployed men, it was common for them to receive the message in their societal context that they should be making money to support their family; otherwise, they are not good, competent men. They would express emotions such as frustration and shame connected with not making money and being the financial provider.

Aimee reflected on what it was like for her to socioculturally attune to a Latino Catholic male client who was unemployed. She wondered whether he was receiving messages from his social context that he was a man only if he was making money. His gendered, religious, and ethnic context might have been influencing his internalized discourse that his worth and identity as a man rested on his monetary success. She reported that it made sense to her that this man's depression and isolation were partly influenced by the discourse he had internalized that he has no worth or identity if he is not working. She noted that creating this link in her mind was part of her initial process of socioculturally attuning to him.

On the other hand, Mia noted that she knew she was not socioculturally attuned when she could not link possible discourses to apparent emotion or behavior: "I may sense or acknowledge or name the emotion, but if I don't know what discourses the emotions are stemming from, I am not socioculturally attuned yet." In addition, "[I could not socioculturally attune] as easily [because] I [didn't] know what ... motivates his behavior."

Young, an observing team member, sometimes wished the therapists in front of the one-way mirror could have spent more time to really get at how discourses were being linked to behavior, to "explore more about [husband's] side (such as being a male)." In one of the cases in which a husband had cheated on his wife by texting inappropriately with another woman, it was difficult to get a sense of his emotional experience as well as the social discourses linked to it. On one hand, he expressed that one of the reasons he did not like to talk about the affair was to protect his wife from her pain, yet at the same time, we wondered about there being more we could have explored in terms of how his feelings as a man may have affected his not knowing how to take responsibility for the influence of his behavior on the relationship and his wife's responses.

Awareness of personal experience. We also concluded that we knew we demonstrated SCA, not only when we were linking emotions and behaviors to discourses and power, but also from the reaction we felt toward our clients, a profoundly visceral sense of attunement. We realized that we resonated and sensed connection when the clients seemed to feel "felt" (Siegel 2007) and our sense of SCA included an emotional as well as physiological component. For example, Doug spoke of his own reaction in the therapy room. He said, "I felt a resonance personally and culturally, a feeling of connection. I was oblivious [to anything else around me]. I felt it viscerally."

Therapist's Observable Actions

Our internal dialogues about how societal discourses influence emotion, behavior, and power dynamics, as well as our personal awarenesses, were enacted through three observable processes—questioning, validating, and naming—that seemed to facilitate our SCA with clients.

Questioning. We discovered that when we wondered about societal discourses and their possible links to emotion and behavior, we would inevitably question the clients to get a better basis for understanding discourses. We would do this to make sure we truly understood the clients' experiences, as opposed to what we thought or assumed the clients' experiences were. For example, Hans noted that he knew the therapists were seeking SCA because they were "asking questions regarding [how the wife was] different from [a] typical Mexican American female." Another observing team member, Les, knew the therapists were attuning socioculturally because they asked about "general rules, expectations both in the couple and from their cultural background."

Validating. We also noticed that we would frequently validate the emotional experience of what we sensed, hypothesized, and felt was happening for clients, i.e., underlying emotions, relationship patterns, experiences, and motivations that we linked to sociocultural context. In a session in which a European American man was having a hard time expressing emotions, Hans noted that he knew the therapist was socioculturally attuned because he was "validating [the man's] experience as a 'typical guy,'" e.g., "I can understand that talking about your feelings is hard because as men we don't often talk about or express emotions." Another observing team member, Carmen, knew the therapist was demonstrating SCA because the therapist "acknowledged how it must be for him as a man and encouraged vulnerability."

Naming. We also found that we would name emotions, experiences, and processes that are influenced by sociocultural context. Jessica noted that the beginning of SCA is when the therapist is "looking for language connecting [client's] experience to larger societal contexts." Kirstee knew the therapist was socioculturally attuned because she was "naming emotions connected to discourses." For example,

> It makes sense that you would feel frustrated with your wife's expectation that you tell her all your thoughts and feelings. It's frustrating to feel like she wants more from you as a man than all that you already do for her. Stereotypically a man's role in the home isn't often portrayed as being in touch with his feelings and emotions. I wonder what ideas you have learned are a "man's role?"

Client Resonance

We found that for SCA to occur, clients must resonate with our feedback. We determined that clients must acknowledge that we have "gotten" their experience and in turn we must feel connected to the clients. Jessica reflected that

> If clients don't agree, then it's not really attunement … For example, when tuning a guitar, if the tuning isn't right on pitch, then it's not tuned. Both the guitar and the tuning fork must be on the same note. In the same way, both the therapist and the clients must mutually resonate.

We also concluded that SCA not only attends to overt emotions but also explores underlying emotions and motives influenced by social discourses. Carmen noted, "Therapists took the time to reflect and expand what clients said [and] in doing so addressed nuance and contradiction around feelings/issues that they [clients] at first [did not recognize]." For example, a male client had not considered that he learned he should not express vulnerable emotions and that not reflecting those emotions was getting in the way of his marriage. When we talked about a man's role with him, he agreed that showing vulnerable emotions was not part of what he had learned was "manly." He went on to discuss what he had learned a man's role included. He resonated with our reflections, validation, naming, and questioning.

We noted that we knew clients were resonating with our feedback when clients expanded their level of disclosure, showed more emotion, became more relational in conversation, and used body language to connect with therapists, i.e., nodding, maintaining eye contact, and leaning forward. We knew clients were not resonating with our feedback when they avoided eye contact, disagreed with the therapist's assessment, looked blank or confused, did not follow the therapist's direction in conversation and changed the subject, or told the same story again and again.

Our team concluded that clients resonate with the therapist on a continuum from highly or quite a bit to not much at all. We observed that when clients highly resonated, we continued providing reflections and questions that further expanded the experience. SCA was a cyclical process. For example, Aimee and Mia were attempting to socioculturally attune to a Latina woman who found out her husband had been unfaithful to her. During the course of therapy, it became clear that it was important for the wife to be able to express her emotions and have her husband hear and validate her right to feel as if she cannot trust him. However, the wife seemed to be having difficulty verbally expressing that she was upset and hurt and that she could not trust her husband anymore. After discussing gendered and cultural messages associated with being a "good wife," Aimee asked a question based on her attunement to complex feelings associated with those messages and a sense that the woman felt she was not allowed to have those feelings because of her social discourses of being a "good wife."

Aimee: … and is there some feeling of, like, guilt that you don't trust him?
Woman: Yes! (head nodding) Yes, there is because I always tell him, that's what I've been telling him a lot lately. I feel bad that I can't trust him because I want to trust him…

In this brief example, the client expressed high resonance through her enthusiastic verbal and nonverbal responses and was able to expand her level of disclosure, discussing her feelings of guilt, hurt, and frustration, not only with her husband but also with herself for not being a "good wife." The experience of expressing her conflicted emotions to her therapist as well as her husband seemed to help create a mutual sense of connectedness in the couple's relationship. Through the process of sociocultural attunement, the couple not only appeared to feel understood, but also became aware of and addressed key socio-emotional aspects of their relationship.

Conclusion

This study provided direction for us, as we were interested in developing our capacity to attune to clients' socio-contextual experiences. These findings move SCA from an abstract concept to concrete processes that can be applied in therapeutic settings. Though we all still feel the need for additional experience and growth, members of our SERT team found that the process of defining and outlining how to be socioculturally attuned has influenced our clinical work and increased our sense of competency when working with social context. We feel particularly grateful for the diversity within our SERT team that allowed for multiple perspectives to be heard and integrated into our understanding of sociocultural attunement. We now seem to naturally ask ourselves about the impact of social context on our clients' experiences and use this information to guide our therapy. We are also more aware of sociocultural experience in our personal lives.

Clinical Implications

Our study adds to a small but emerging body of literature that helps therapists translate awareness of the importance of larger contextual issues to the moment-by-moment practice of couple and family therapy (e.g., Aniciete and Soloski 2011; Vargas and Wilson 2011). The practice of SCA moves attention to the larger societal context from the periphery of therapy to the center. We suggest three practices for making societal contexts an integral part of therapy rather than an add-on (e.g., McGoldrick and Ashton 2012).

1. **Cultivate an intentional contextual lens**. The therapists in this study maintained an internal contextual lens throughout the therapy session. The lens made us curious about how the feelings, behaviors, and relationship patterns expressed by clients in relation to the current clinical issues were linked to their sociocultural context, which prompted questions that would expand understanding of them.
2. **Listen for societal discourses embedded in clients' stories**. We used the notion of societal discourse to help link clients' personal experience with their sociocultural context. When clients expressed particular behaviors or feelings and spoke of experiences that were meaningful to them, we asked ourselves what larger societal discourses were being expressed, for example, ideas that women should not get angry or that "sleeping" with other women is normal for men. Listening for societal discourses helped us move from an individualistic interpretation to a contextual one that is less pathologizing.
3. **Focus on emotion associated with sociocultural identities and expectations**. Seeking SCA encouraged the therapists in this study to not only cognitively identify contextual influences, but to emotionally resonate with what it feels like in this context. Reflecting this emotional sense back to clients furthered the clinical process. When successful, sociocultural resonance helped expand therapist–client engagement and enabled the therapy to focus on emotionally salient issues likely to provide the impetus for transformation (Fosha 2009). Client expressions of emotion provide a good starting place to probe for salient sociocultural meanings and experience. In this way, we follow client input rather than seeming to impose a sociocultural lens.

Implications for Training

Learning to utilize a contextual lens can be challenging. Trainees are often puzzled about how to raise contextual issues in session. Attempts that are general and abstract (i.e., how does your culture affect you?) may not generate in depth or nuanced responses. The model for SCA identified here offers a useful teaching tool that breaks down the process into its component parts and encourages therapists to stay close to the clients' unique experience by formulating questions that explore which cultural contexts underlie particular emotions or actions expressed by clients.

Previous research (Esmiol et al. 2012) found that awareness was not sufficient. Developing a contextual lens typically required a period of self-reflection and challenge as the contextual lens intersected with other organizing clinical frameworks. Having positive client experience as a result of addressing contextual issues—for example, as a result of SCA as described here—encouraged therapists to become more intentional and committed to application of a contextual lens. Because the sociocultural context is often difficult to recognize in session, we also recommend that therapists of any level of experience engage in focused reflection about their practice, such as we did in this clinical project. Thus, our study provides a basis of understanding SCA from which clinical practice can grow and develop.

References

Aniciete, D., & Soloski, K. (2011). The social construction of marriage and a narrative approach to treatment of intra-relationship diversity. *Journal of Feminist Family Therapy, 23*(2), 103–126.

Chenail, R. J. (2005). Future directions for qualitative methods. In D. H. Sprenkle & F. P. Piercy (Eds.), *Research methods in family therapy* (pp. 100–118). New York, NY: Guilford Press.

ChenFeng, J. L., & Galick, A. (2015). How gender discourses hijack couple therapy—and how to avoid it. In C. Knudson-Martin, M. A. Wells, & S. K. Samman (Eds.), *Socio-emotional relationship therapy: Bridging emotion, societal context, and couple interaction.* (pp. 41–52). New York, NY: Springer.

Esmiol, E. E., Knudson-Martin, C., & Delgado, S. (2012). Developing a contextual consciousness: Learning to address gender, societal power, and culture in clinical practice. *Journal of Marital and Family Therapy, 38*(4), 573–588.

Fosha, D. (2009). Emotion and recognition at work: Energy, vitality, pleasure, truth, desire, and the emergent phenomenology of transformational experience. In D. Fosha, D. J. Siegel, & M. F. Solomon (Eds.), *The healing power of emotion: Affective neuroscience, development & clinical practice* (pp. 172–203). New York, NY: Norton.

Gergen, K. L. (2009). *An invitation to social construction* (2nd ed.). Los Angeles, CA: Sage.

Knudson-Martin, C., & Huenergardt, D. (2010). A socio-emotional approach to couple therapy: Linking social context and couple interaction. *Family Process, 49*(3), 369–384.

Knudson-Martin, C., & Huenergardt, D. (2015). Bridging emotion, societal discourse, and couple interaction in clinical practice. In C. Knudson-Martin, M. A. Wells, & S. K. Samman (Eds.), *Socio-emotional relationship therapy: Bridging emotion, societal context, and couple interaction.* (pp. 1–13). New York, NY: Springer.

Knudson-Martin, C., & Mahoney, A. R. (Eds.). (2009). *Couples, gender, and power: Creating change in intimate relationships.* New York, NY: Springer Publishing Company.

Knudson-Martin, C., Huenergardt, D., Lafontant, K., Bishop, L., Schaepper, J., & Wells, M. (2014). Competencies for addressing gender and power in couple therapy: A socio-emotional approach. *Journal of Marital and Family Therapy*, Advance online publication. doi: 10.1111/jmft.12068

McGoldrick, M., & Ashton, D. (2012). Culture: A challenge to concepts of normality. In F. Walsh (Ed.), *Normal family processes: Growing diversity and complexity* (pp. 249–272). New York, NY: Guilford Press.

Mendenhall, T. J., & Doherty, W. J. (2005). Action research methods in family therapy. In D. H. Sprenkle & F. P. Piercy (Eds.), *Research methods in family therapy* (pp. 100–118). New York, NY: Guilford Press.

Owen, J., Leach, M. M., Wampold, B., & Rodolfa, E. (2011). Multicultural approaches in psychotherapy: A rejoinder. *Journal of Counseling Psychology, 58*(1), 22–26.

Pandit, M., ChenFeng, J., Kang, Y. J., Knudson-Martin, C., & Huenergardt, D. (2014) Practicing socio-cultural attunement: A study of couple therapists. *Contemporary Family Therapy, 36,* 518–528.

Siegel, D. J. (2007). *The mindful brain: Reflection and attunement in the cultivation of well-being.* New York, NY: Norton.

Silverstein, R., Bass, L., Tuttle, A., Knudson-Martin, C., & Huenergardt, D. (2006). What does it mean to be relational? A framework for assessment and practice. *Family Process, 45*(4), 391–405.

Sperry, L. (2010). Culture, personality, health, and family dynamics: Cultural competence in the selection of culturally sensitive treatments. *Family Journal: Counseling and Therapy for Couples and Families, 18*(3), 316–320.

Vargas, H. L., & Wilson, C. M. (2011). Managing worldview influences: Self-awareness and self-supervision in a cross-cultural therapeutic relationship. *Journal of Family Psychotherapy, 22,* 97–113.

Williams, K., Galick, A., Knudson-Martin, C., & Huenergardt, D. (2012). Toward mutual support: A task analysis of the relational justice approach to infidelity. *Journal of Marital and Family Therapy, 39*(3), 285–298. doi:10.1111/j.1752-0606.2012.00324.x.

Zimmerman, T. S., Haddock, S. A., Ziemba, S., & Rust, A. (2001). Family organizational labor: Who's calling the plays? *Journal of Feminist Family Therapy, 13*(2–3), 65–90.

Relational Engagement in Heterosexual Couple Therapy: Helping Men Move from "I" to "We"

Sarah K. Samman and Carmen Knudson-Martin

Therapists often find it difficult to engage men in couple therapy (Sherpard and Harway 2012). Attention to the intersection of gender and power adds another layer of complexity, especially when mutual support is a relationship goal (Knudson-Martin 2013). As part of the team developing Socio-Emotional Relationship Therapy (SERT; see Knudson-Martin and Huenergardt 2010, "Bridging Emotion, Societal Discourse, and Couple Interaction in Clinical Practice," 2015), we found that our ability to relationally engage powerful men is critically important to the success of heterosexual couple therapy (Williams et al. 2013). We define relational engagement as the ability to demonstrate commitment to one's relationships and actively participate in the therapeutic process through exploring, acknowledging, and intentionally attending to their female partner's experiences. This contrasts with a common pattern we have seen of men tending to focus primarily on their own issues and experiences in session.

Our Interests in Relational Processes

As female therapists, we confront gender and power issues daily, both in our practice and in our personal lives. Though the actions of both partners are important and reciprocally tied to the other, for this project, we decided to zero in on how we could better help men engage in these relational processes.

S.K. Samman (✉)
Department of Counseling and Family Sciences, Loma Linda University,
Loma Linda, CA, USA

C. Knudson-Martin
Counseling Psychology Department, Lewis & Clark College, Portland, OR, USA

© American Family Therapy Academy 2015
C. Knudson-Martin et al. (eds.), *Socio-Emotional Relationship Therapy*,
AFTA SpringerBriefs in Family Therapy, DOI 10.1007/978-3-319-13398-0_7

Sarah

As a Muslim Arab and European American able-bodied married heterosexual woman raised in Saudi Arabia and pursuing a doctoral degree in the USA, I feel blessed to speak two languages fluently. This has allowed me to recognize the nuanced ways in which larger social contexts such as language and culture, particularly gender and power discourses, work against both women and men in relationships. As I struggle to challenge gender and power inequalities in my own life, I have also become keenly aware of how difficult it can be to resist the influences of gender and power in my clinical work. Because of these daily struggles, I worked with a group of fellow doctoral students—Isolina Ixcaragua, Brittney France, and Golnoush Yektafar—to explore the ways in which men do and do not engage with their female partners in couple therapy sessions. Since we were not yet well trained in how to address gender and power issues, we were especially interested in what therapists do to influence these relational processes.

Carmen

I am a married, heterosexual, able-bodied woman of Scandinavian heritage who grew up in the USA during the women's movement of the 1960s. Though I have been researching, writing, and teaching about gender and power issues in couple relationships for many years (e.g., Knudson-Martin 1997, 2013), I remain struck and somewhat surprised by how tenacious gendered power imbalances can be (see Knudson-Martin, "When Therapy Challenges Patriarchy: Undoing Gendered Power in Heterosexual Couple Relationships," 2015). The men I see almost universally say they do not want to dominate their female partners and, instead, say they want a two-way relationship. Yet they are stuck in gendered relational processes that limit their ability to attain these goals (Knudson-Martin and Mahoney 2009), leaving each partner frustrated, angry, and in pain. When I began to help Sarah study this issue, I was fascinated. I, too, wanted to know how I can be more effective in relationally engaging men and how I can better prepare the students that I teach for this challenging work.

Male Engagement in Therapy

In their research, Grove and Burnaugh (2002) reported that men were often withdrawn in their relationships and participated in sessions by discussing their own feelings or experiences (see also Dickerson 2013). This style of communication is directly related to how men are socialized to assert their own needs and avoid a one-down position, while women commonly learn to accommodate and orient toward the needs of others (Knudson-Martin and Mahoney 2009).

Men also report fewer help-seeking behaviors (McKelley 2007; Oliver et al. 2005). According to Evans (2013), roughly three-quarters of individuals seeking counseling were women. Berger et al. (2008) found that men were also less likely to pursue help when recommended by their female partners compared to a physician or psychotherapist. This suggests that masculine norms not only play a role in men's resistance to mental health services, but also limit men's openness to influence from their female partners.

Power Impacts Relationships

Couple distress often stems from power disparities in couple relationships (Almeida et al. 2008; Dickerson 2013; Haddock et al. 2000; Knudson-Martin and Huenergardt 2010). These inequities are typically a result of larger social contexts, such as patriarchy, that impact genders differently and implicitly lead to power disparities (McGoldrick 2011; McKelley 2007). However, power differences tend to be invisible and taken for granted by society, couples, and therapists alike (see Knudson-Martin, "When Therapy Challenges Patriarchy: Undoing Gendered Power in Heterosexual Couple Relationships," 2015). They are perpetuated by the more powerful partner's lack of awareness of their own power or inattentiveness to the needs and concerns of their partners (Dickerson 2013; Parker 2009). As men tend to automatically prioritize their own experiences, women are left carrying the responsibility for the well-being of their relationships (ChenFeng and Galick, "How Gender Discourses Hijack Couple Therapy—and How to Avoid It," 2015; Doss et al. 2003).

Male Engagement Cultivates Relationships

Researchers have described male engagement in many forms, i.e., spousal social support or reciprocity (Acitelli and Antonucci 1994), mutual support (Knudson-Martin and Huenergardt 2010), intimacy (Real 2003), attunement (Jonathan 2009), and responsivity (Matta and Knudson-Martin 2006). Grove and Burnaugh (2002) reported that men's involvement with their partners often led to marked improvement in couple satisfaction. Wives' marital satisfaction has been shown to increase with reciprocity and the perception of social support from their partners (Acitelli and Antonucci 1994).

In related work, Jonathan and Knudson-Martin (2012) noted positive relational experiences when men were more responsive to their spouses' and children's needs. Knudson-Martin (2013) reported similar results when couples shared relational responsibility, i.e., when both partners were "sensitive and accountable for the effect of their actions on others and taking an active interest in doing what is necessary to maintain their relationship" (p. 6). These studies suggest that helping powerful men relationally engage is an important aspect of clinical change in couple therapy and that when men orient toward their relationship, overall partner and relational satisfaction are likely enhanced (Knudson-Martin and Mahoney 2009; Williams et al. 2013).

Gender and Power in Couple Therapy

Engaging men relationally is an ongoing clinical challenge because gender and power inherent in social structures commonly impede these relational orientations in heterosexual couple relationships (see Knudson-Martin, "Undoing Gendered Power in Heterosexual Couple Relationships," 2015). Therapists need to devise clinical strategies that intentionally counteract taken-for-granted social norms that maintain power imbalances and invisible privileges (Jordan 2009; Knudson-Martin 2013); however, there are few guidelines for clinicians (Williams and Knudson-Martin 2013). Our purpose in this study was to develop a grounded theory about how therapeutic interventions can invite and sustain male relational engagement based on observations of therapists utilizing the SERT model.

Method: Our Grounded Theory Process

Participants and Sample Selection

The sample consisted of 28 couple therapy sessions with 11 heterosexual couples conducted by nine licensed and pre-licensed marriage and family therapy (MFT) doctoral students and two faculty supervisors utilizing the SERT model. All couples provided consent to videotape and transcribe sessions and to utilize data for research that advances clinical practice. The couples included in the study reported high levels of distress as well as male partner relational disengagement. We selected sessions to comprise various ages, ethnicities, and educational levels.

Male clients' ages ranged from 32 to 49 and the female clients' ages ranged from 26 to 44. Couples' ethnicities varied but were predominantly European American; however, other couples were from African American, Asian, East Asian, and Latin American backgrounds. Members of the couples were from an array of religious backgrounds, including agnostic, atheist, Catholic, Christian, Jewish, Muslim, and Seventh-day Adventists.

There were 7 male and 11 female therapists in the SERT clinical research group, which consisted of therapists in session and observers who sometimes briefly joined sessions to make comments (see Knudson-Martin et al. 2014). Their ages ranged from 28 to 63, and they came from a variety of ethnic backgrounds, including African American, Arab American, Asian American, European American, Latin American, and East Indian. Sometimes, observers from the SERT clinical research group briefly joined sessions to share reflections or questions that might help move the session forward with a focus on gender and power.

Grounded Theory Analysis

We approached the analysis without preconceived theoretical ideas or expectations (Charmaz 2006), remaining open to all possibilities emerging from the data. We began with line-by-line coding to identify relevant components of the therapy session. For example, when a male participant stated, "I get nervous ... but in the end, I feel better ... because I know she feels better," this was coded as "positive experience of attending to wife's comfort." Another example included the therapist encouraging the male partner in session by saying, "Ask her how she's feeling." This was coded as "suggests male connects with female partner."

Next, we developed axial codes and repeatedly modified them based on new information (Charmaz 2006). We revisited transcripts focusing on when and how men spoke about their relationships and if and when they recognized and acknowledged the impact of their behaviors on their partners. We also examined other factors, such as level of couple distress, therapist interventions, and partner responses, and compared them with instances when men did and did not appear to relationally engage. We repeated this process through constant comparative analysis until no new themes emerged (Charmaz 2006). We also performed member checks with the observing SERT group in order to receive feedback to promote further understanding.

Results: How Therapists Influence Male Relational Engagement

We found five therapist interventions that consistently worked together to rebalance power in the relationship by influencing disengaged men's ability to relationally engage with their partners. The following cumulative order of interventions was necessary to facilitate and sustain each successful event: (1) attend to male's sociocultural context, (2) validate male's relational intent, followed immediately with, (3) highlight the impact of male's behavior on the female partner, (4) punctuate alternative relational interactions, and (5) demonstrate persistent therapist leadership. These are illustrated in Fig. 1.

Attend to Sociocultural Context

In each successful change event therapists had attended to and sought to understand the impact of larger dominant social discourses on men's abilities to relationally engage with their female partners. As also found in a study by Williams et al. (2013), attending to sociocultural context seemed to be foundational to the rest of the engagement process and was demonstrated over time. In the

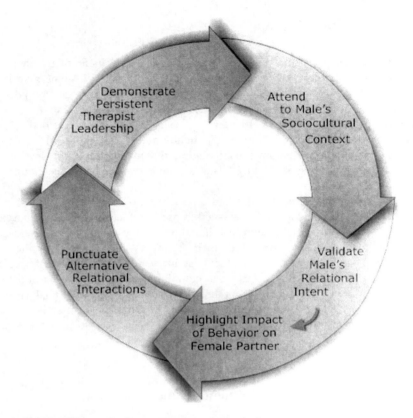

Fig. 1 Relationally engaging heterosexual men in couple therapy

following example, the therapist is working with a couple who has been together for 10 years. Jessica, a European American woman, reported feeling let down in her relationship with Michael, an African American man. The therapist has previously attended to the sociocultural experiences of each partner, bringing these contexts front and center in multiple couple sessions. In the following excerpt, the therapist inquires about what Michael has learned as a man in response to his sociocultural experiences. Note that Michael highlights how he has learned to disengage:

Therapist   I'm curious about what you've learned about yourself in response to society and in relation to your partner.

Michael   Well, whoever I become, including this person who detaches, is in response to this world in which I live. Being aware of it is helpful and recognizing sometimes the fact that I'm doing it. I see how it might have [harmed as well as] benefited me [as a Black male] at times.

Validate Male's Relational Intent and Highlight Impact of Behavior on Female

The second and third key factors in facilitating men's relational engagement included validating their relational intent followed *immediately* with highlighting the impact of their behavior on their partners. If the therapist only validated the male's relational intent, this served to engage males in the session but did not appear to encourage them to engage relationally with their partners. For example, here, the therapist is working with a Christian couple in substance abuse recovery struggling with "trust issues" in their relationship. The therapist first attends to how Randy, a European American working-class male in his late forties, experienced conflict and marginalization in his sociocultural context, then follows this by emphasizing Randy's desire to have a non-conflictive relationship with his partner Samantha, a European American unemployed female in her mid-forties.

Therapist   It seems like you've been hurt so much [by how people viewed his disabled single mother] that you ... in many ways, haven't experienced what it's like not to be in conflict.

Randy   Conflict in our home was normal.

Therapist   I can imagine how difficult that was for you ... It makes sense that you would enter a relationship expecting conflict ... I can also imagine you'd like things to be different with Samantha.

Randy   Yeah, I do. But ... you don't see how she really is. You don't know how hard it is to be with *her*.

Note that Randy follows this intervention validating his relational intent by focusing on his experiences of Samantha's shortcomings. In this case, the therapist did not follow up with interest in the impact of Randy's behavior on Samantha.

Men tended to relationally engage with their partners more readily when therapists both validated their relational intent *and* highlighted the impact of their behaviors on their partners. For example, Nicole and Howard, a retired Jewish European American couple in their sixties who met while in recovery from substance abuse, sought therapy to address their "communication styles" regarding Nicole's struggles with chronic illness and his responsibilities as her caregiver. In the following excerpt, the therapist validates Howard's relational intent:

Therapist   I really get that she's important to you and that you feel compelled to stay in charge because you love her and want her to get the best treatment and be healthy.

Howard   Yeah, I do want her to be around longer. Much longer.

The therapist follows this with questions about the impact of Howard's behavior on his partner:

Therapist   I can also understand that you're used to being in charge and I'm wondering how you think being in charge of her treatment impacts her?

Howard [to Nicole]	When you get scared, I get scared and I think you struggle with my way of doing things.
Therapist	What do you think she needs from you right now?
Howard [to Nicole]	I think you need to have a voice in your treatment.

By focusing on his commitment to Nicole as well as recognizing the negative impact of his usual approach to her care, the therapist was then able to move the conversation beyond a focus on his own experience to recognizing and acknowledging her needs.

Punctuate Alternative Interactions

In Nicole and Howard's example above, the therapist continued to explore ways Howard could approach their relationship differently and punctuated successful alternative interactions:

Therapist	So how would you engage her differently knowing that's what she needs from you?
Howard	I need to be able to calm my own fears instead of taking control. I don't want her to feel alone in all this.
Therapist	You answered that pretty quickly. Are there times when you've been able to not automatically take control of her treatment?
Howard	Yeah, there have been. [laughs]
Therapist	And how has Nicole responded?
Howard	Pretty good actually. She seems happier, less isolated and depressed.

Below is another example in which the therapist worked with Mary, a European American female, married to Mathew, an African American male, both in their thirties and biological parents of three children. Mary sought therapy for issues with "insecurities" with her weight and in her relationship with Mathew, who worked with "beautiful women." In the following excerpt, the therapist highlights a time Mathew was able to move beyond feelings of shame and defensiveness when Mary questioned him about his workday, and instead actively listened to Mary's fears and desires for reassurance.

Therapist	So, the way you [Mary] enter the dialogue with your husband is to be honest, and [Mathew], you responded to her honesty with active listening … [Looking at Mary] Would it be right to assume you felt heard?
Mary	Absolutely. I did actually. It felt really good. I felt valued.
Therapist	So, while eating puts a wedge between the two of you, it no longer completely severs your ability as a couple to connect. Dialogue is possible and your commitment is reestablished.
Couple responds in unison	Yeah!
Mathew	I hadn't thought about that. Yeah, we did pretty good, didn't we?

Demonstrate Persistent Therapist Leadership

Persistent therapist leadership in session was a key factor in creating a cumulative effect sustaining men's relational engagement. Therapists positioned themselves against larger societal influences that appeared to otherwise dominate couple interactions and to perpetuate the expectation that women attend to men, but not the reverse (see ChenFeng and Galick, "How Gender Discourses Hijack Couple Therapy—and How to Avoid It," 2015). In the example below, the therapist persists in her attempts to engage Miguel, a Latino in his late twenties, and highlights the ways he relates to his spouse of seven years, Lena, a Latina in her early twenties:

Therapist	How do you view yourself interacting with your wife? How do you think you're supposed to act as her husband?
Miguel	When I go back home I have to take on a leadership role, not boss her around or anything, [but] meet my obligation to pay my bills and take care of my family financially and emotionally ... Basically, I emulate my father.
Therapist	Those are a lot of responsibilities. I'm curious though, I haven't heard about relating to Lena at an emotional level.
Miguel	I'm not relating on an emotional level right now. But I would like to act differently. I want to.
Therapist	What would that look like?
Miguel	Not talking from my head all the time.
Therapist	What would that feel like?
Miguel	It would feel real, more connected. I want to connect with her more.

As we can see, the therapist consistently built upon each intervention. She inquired about how Miguel related to his wife based on expectations as a husband and moved back to attend to his sociocultural contexts and expectations as a husband. Then, she highlighted how this may impede his actual intentions and deep desire to connect and relate emotionally to Lena. In the end, Miguel appeared to engage more readily in therapy and with Lena as a result of the therapist's persistent supportive leadership in this session and others.

Summary

The results of this study offer guidance on how to conceptualize male relational engagement and what therapists can do to make a difference.

Conceptualizing Relational Engagement

Male relational engagement is a multifaceted process that works to overcome two aspects of the US gender context that emphasizes individualism and autonomy (e.g., Loscocco and Walzer 2013). First, we found that when therapists focused on men, these conversations tended to stay individually focused on their own thoughts and feelings. Men did not automatically move to a more relational focus (see Silverstein et al. 2006). Second, even when men in the study acknowledged their partners' emotions and experiences, they usually did not also attend to her or take responsibility for the impact of their behaviors on her. Perhaps because of our criteria for selecting cases to study, this process seemed to apply to all the men, regardless of their age, abilities, parenting status, socioeconomic level, or ethnic background.

We did not see this individualistic focus as a personal failing of the men, but rather as a societal gender pattern that is challenging to overcome. Therapists in this study played an important part in helping men move from an individualistic "I" focus to a "we" focus that takes into account the relationship as a whole and is accountable to their partner's well-being as well as their own, that is, taking relational responsibility (see Knudson-Martin and Huenergardt, "Bridging Emotion, Societal Discourse, and Couple Interaction in Clinical Practice," 2015).

What Therapists Do Matters

The video and transcript segments reviewed in this study were selected because male partners appeared particularly stuck in an individualistic mindset. In therapy sessions that successfully helped men overcome this pattern, therapists followed a specific set of interventions. All of them were necessary to initially engage men relationally and build a cumulative effect over time; all required multiple efforts to sustain their engagement with their female partners.

1. **Attend to men's sociocultural context**. Therapists in the successful sessions focused on the impact of larger social contexts on the construction of men's identities. By showing awareness of this context with compassion, empathy, and without blame (see Pandit, ChenFeng, and Kang, "Expanding the Lens: How SERT Therapists Develop Interventions That Address the Larger Context," this volume), the men in this study were more able to gain compassion for self as well as acknowledge their impact on their female partners and the relationship in subsequent interventions.

2 and 3. **Validate men's relational intent and highlight impact on partner**. Male validation without also highlighting the behavioral impact on his partner tended to reinforce the one-down position of the female partner. The most successful interventions were when men experienced personal and relational validation while also being able to recognize and take accountability for the impact of their behaviors on their partners. When these happened together, this effectively encouraged shared relational responsibility without reinforcing male privilege in session.

4. **Punctuate alternative relational interactions**. When therapists acknowledged and validated the positive effects of successful relational engagement strategies by highlighting alternatives to stereotypically gendered relationship patterns, couples were more able to solidify these ways of relating and reflect on their successes.

5. **Demonstrate persistent leadership**. Therapists needed to recognize and address gender and power issues over and over again (see ChenFeng and Galick, "How Gender Discourses Hijack Couple Therapy—and How to Avoid It," 2015; Ward and Knudson-Martin 2012). This did not mean that the therapists maintained an expert role, as though they know clients better than they know themselves. Rather, therapists utilized their knowledge of the impact of larger social discourses and inequities to help the couple reflect on their experiences and persistently supported a relational focus in therapy.

Future Research and Clinical Practice

This study focused only on men. We are curious to also see how female partners' responses are part of the process and plan to study that next. However, we have already found that intentionally applying this grounded theory model has helped us more successfully relationally engage heterosexual men in couple therapy. This is a key component of SERT (e.g., Knudson-Martin et al. 2014) and is likely to be relevant in other clinical approaches as well.

References

Acitelli, L. K., & Antonucci, T. C. (1994). Gender differences in the link between marital support and satisfaction in older couples. *Journal of Personality and Social Psychology, 67*(4), 688–698.

Almeida, R.V., Dolan-Del Vecchio, K., & Parker, L. (2008). *Transformative family therapy: Just families for a just society*. Boston, MA: Pearson Education.

Berger, J. L., Addis, M. E., Green, J. D., Mackowiak, C., & Goldberg, V. (2008). Men's reactions to mental health labels, forms of help-seeking, and sources of help-seeking advice. *Psychology of Men and Masculinity, 14*(4), 433–443.

Charmaz, K. (2006). *Constructing grounded theory*. Thousand Oaks, CA: Sage.

ChenFeng, J. L. & Galick, A. (2015). How gender discourses hijack couple therapy—and how to avoid it. In C. Knudson-Martin, M. A. Wells, & S. K. Samman (Eds.), *Socio-emotional relationship therapy: Bridging emotion, societal context, and couple interaction*. (pp. 41–52). New York, NY: Springer.

Dickerson, V. (2013). Patriarchy, power, and privilege: A narrative/poststructural view of work with couples. *Family Process, 52*(1), 102–114. doi:10.1111/famp.12018.

Doss, B. D., Atkins, D. C., & Christensen, A. (2003). Who's dragging their feet? Husbands and wives seeking marital therapy. *Journal of Marital and Family Therapy, 29*(2), 165–177.

Evans, M. P. (2013). Men in counseling: A content analysis of the journal of counseling & development and counselor education and supervision 1981–2011. *Journal of Counseling and Development, 91*(4), 467–474.

Grove, D. R., & Burnaugh, R. (2002). *Invisible men: Finding, engaging and inspiring men in therapy*. Pheonix, AZ: Zeig, Tucker & Theisen.

Haddock, S. A., Zimmerman, T. S., & MacPhee, D. (2000). The power equity guide: Attending to gender in family therapy. *Journal of Marital and Family Therapy, 26*(2), 153–164.

Jonathan, N. (2009). Carrying equal weight: Relational responsibility and attunement among same-sex couples. In C. Knudson-Martin & A. Mahoney (Eds.), *Couples, gender, and power: Creating change in intimate relationships* (pp. 79–103). New York, NY: Springer Publishing Company.

Jonathan, N., & Knudson-Martin, C. (2012). Building connection: Attunement and gender equality in heterosexual relationships. *Journal of Couple and Relationship Therapy, 11*, 95–111.

Jordan, J. (2009). *Relational-cultural therapy*. Washington, DC: American Psychological Association.

Knudson-Martin, C. (1997). The politics of gender in family therapy. *Journal of Marital and Family Therapy, 23*, 431–447.

Knudson-Martin, C. (2013). Why power matters: Creating a foundation of mutual support in couple relationships. *Family Process, 52*(1), 5–18. doi:10.1111/famp.12011.

Knudson-Martin, C., & Huenergardt, D. (2010). A socio-emotional approach to couple therapy: Linking social context and couple interaction. *Family Process, 49*, 369–386.

Knudson-Martin, C., Huenergardt, D., Lafontant, K., Bishop, L., Schaepper, J., & Wells, M. (2014). Competencies for addressing gender and power in couple therapy: A socio-emotional approach. *Journal of Marital and Family Therapy.* doi:10.1111/jmft.12068. Advance online publication.

Knudson-Martin, C., & Mahoney, A. (Eds.). (2009). *Couples, gender, and power: Creating change in intimate relationships*. New York, NY: Springer Publishing Company.

Knudson-Martin, C. (2015). When therapy challenges patriarchy: Undoing gendered power in heterosexual couple relationships. In C. Knudson-Martin, M. A. Wells, & S. K. Samman (Eds.), *Socio-emotional relationship therapy: Bridging emotion, societal context, and couple interaction.* (pp. 15–26). New York, NY: Springer.

Knudson-Martin, C., & Huenergardt, D. (2015). Bridging emotion, societal discourse, and couple interaction in clinical practice. In C. Knudson-Martin, M. A. Wells, & S. K. Samman (Eds.), *Socio-emotional relationship therapy: Bridging emotion, societal context, and couple interaction.* (pp. 1–13). New York, NY: Springer.

Loscocco, K., & Walzer, S. (2013). Gender and the culture of heterosexual marriage in the United States. *Journal of Family Theory and Review, 5*, 1–14.

Matta, D. S., & Knudson-Martin, C. (2006). Father responsivity: Couple processes and the coconstruction of fatherhood. *Family Process, 45*, 19–37.

McGoldrick, M. (2011). Becoming a couple. In M. McGoldrick, B. Carter, & N. Garcia-Preto (Eds.), *The expanded family life cycle: Individual, family, and social perspectives* (pp. 193–210). New York, NY: Allyn & Bacon.

McKelley, R. A. (2007). Men's resistance to seeking help: Using individual psychology to understand counseling-reluctant men. *Journal of Individual Psychology, 63*(1), 48–58.

Oliver, M. I., Pearson, N., Coe, N., & Gunnell, D. (2005). Help-seeking behavior in men and women with common mental health problems: Cross-sectional study. *British Journal of Psychiatry, 186*, 297–301. doi:10.1192/bjp.186.4.297.

Parker, L. (2009). Disrupting power and privilege in couples therapy. *Clinical Social Work Journal, 37*, 248–255.

Pandit, M., ChenFeng, J. L., & Kang, Y. J. (2015). Becoming socioculturally attuned: A study of therapist experience. In C. Knudson-Martin, M. A. Wells, & S. K. Samman (Eds.), *Socio-emotional relationship therapy: Bridging emotion, societal context, and couple interaction.* (pp. 67–78). New York, NY: Springer.

Real, T. (2003). *How can I get through to you? Closing the intimacy gap between men and women*. New York, NY: Scribner.

Sherpard, D. S., & Harway, M. (2012). *Engaging men in couples therapy*. New York, NY: Routledge.

Silverstein, R., Bass, L. B., Tuttle, A. R., Knudson-Martin, C., & Huenergardt, D. (2006). What does it mean to be relational? A framework for assessment and practice. *Family Process, 45*, 391–405.

Ward, A., & Knudson-Martin, C. (2012). The impact of therapist actions on the balance of power within the couple system: A qualitative analysis of therapy sessions. *Journal of Couple and Relationship Therapy, 11*(3), 221–237.

Williams, K., Galick, A., Knudson-Martin, C., & Huenergardt, D. (2013). Toward mutual support: A task analysis of the relational justice approach to infidelity. *Journal of Marital and Family Therapy, 39*(3), 285–298. doi:10.1111/j.1752-0606.2012.00324.x.

Williams, K., & Knudson-Martin, C. (2013a). Do therapists address gender and power in infidelity? A feminist analysis of the treatment literature. *Journal of Marital and Family Therapy, 39*(3), 271–284. doi:10.1111/j.1752-0606.2012.00303.x.

Williams, K., & Knudson-Martin, C. (2013b). Do therapists address gender and power in infidelity? A feminist analysis of the treatment literature. *Journal of Marital and Family Therapy, 39*(3), 271–284. doi:10.1111/j.1752-0606.2012.00303.x.

Building a Circle of Care in Same-Sex Couple Relationships: A Socio-Emotional Relational Approach

Jason C. Richards, Naveen Jonathan and Lana Kim

Imbalances of power are harmful to intimate relationships. They tend to exacerbate problem areas, such as increasing depression and anxiety, while invalidating personal identity (e.g., Beck and Clark 2010; Collett 2010). Power imbalances may also limit many factors which we know increase relationship satisfaction, such as emotional attunement, vulnerability, trust, mutual responsiveness, communal focus, and shared investment (e.g., Beck and Clark 2010; Collett 2010). Relationship distress and dissatisfaction are a likely result (DeMaris 2007).

Although same-sex couples tend to be more egalitarian than their heterosexual counterparts, power differences still matter. With heterosexual couples, differences in power between genders tend to be accepted because they feel "natural" as a product of social norms, with little discussion or intentional negotiation of the unequal relationship patterns present (Knudson-Martin 2013; Knudson-Martin and Mahoney 2005). In contrast, taken-for-granted societal gender norms do not exist for same-sex couples, since gender differences are not present (Jonathan 2009). This means potential power differences may be somewhat easier to see.

As practitioners of Socio-Emotional Relationship Therapy (SERT; Knudson-Martin and Huenergardt 2010, "Bridging Emotion, Societal Discourse, and Couple Interaction in Clinical Practice," 2015), and as gay men (Jason and Naveen) and an

J.C. Richards (✉)
Department of Counseling and Family Sciences, Loma Linda University,
Loma Linda, CA, USA
e-mail: jcrichards@llu.edu

N. Jonathan
Frances Smith Center for Individual and Family Therapy,
Crean College of Health and Behavioral Sciences Chapman University,
Orange, CA, USA

L. Kim
Marriage and Family Therapy Department, Valdosta State University, Valdosta, GA, USA

© American Family Therapy Academy 2015
C. Knudson-Martin et al. (eds.), *Socio-Emotional Relationship Therapy*,
AFTA SpringerBriefs in Family Therapy, DOI 10.1007/978-3-319-13398-0_8

ally (Lana) ourselves, it was important to us that conditions of equality be studied in same-sex couples. To accomplish this, we looked at the many studies that have been done with respect to same-sex couples using the mutuality processes defined in SERT's Circle of Care: mutual influence, shared vulnerability, shared relational responsibility, and mutual attunement. Comparison studies have long found that same-sex partners maintain more equal relationships than their heterosexual counterparts, largely because they do not divide roles and responsibilities based on gender (e.g., Connolly 2005; Gottman 2011). In fact, both gay men (Shechory and Ziv 2007) and lesbian women (e.g., Hardtke et al. 2010) have been shown to be more aware of and attentive to equality issues in their relationships than heterosexual couples. In this chapter, we present our understanding of the dynamics of power and equality in same-sex relationships and consider how these may apply to SERT clinicians.

The Jonathan Study (2009): Mutual Attunement Explored

In their study of heterosexual couples, Knudson-Martin and Mahoney (2005) discovered that despite couples' stated desire for relationship equality, their relationships were often organized by prescribed societal gender patterns instead, leaving them open to harmful power differences. Through conversations with Knudson-Martin about the study, Naveen became fascinated to discover how same-sex couples organize and handle issues of power and equality, given that gender differences do not exist in their relationships, and decided to interview same-sex couples in committed relationships.

Participants and Methods

Interviews with same-sex couples (20 female couples and 20 male couples) were analyzed using grounded theory methodology. These couples had been together for an average of 14 years. The three main patterns that emerged were attuned equality, attuned inequality, and unattuned inequality. More specific information is contained in a previous article about the study (Jonathan 2009).

Results

Nearly all of the couples interviewed appeared to share responsibility for the relationship in some way. Further analysis revealed how this equality among the participants is a reflection of attunement to each other's needs and interests, attention to fairness, and conscious relationship strategies. These processes appeared similar for both male and female couples, with only minor differences in communication style, and helped the couples deal with power imbalances in their relationships. In the few cases in which sustained power imbalances did exist, partners were less attuned to each other and also less likely to share responsibility in the relationship.

Attuned Equality Couples: Fairness and Strategy. In this study, relational responsibility was expressed primarily through a focus on and interest in the current state of one's partner and the relationship. Participants' shared commitment to understanding each other and concern for each other's needs seemed to be the basis upon which most of the couples in this study (30 out of 40) organized their relationships. This attunement appears to be at the heart of participants' ability to maintain relationship equality.

Couples with attuned equality also appeared to use fairness as an organizing factor. Both male and female couples engaged in conversations about fairness, helping to define what would be fair for each member, and thus promoting equality. Ensuring that partners were "heard" was a common emphasis in this type of conversation. While some couples went on to describe fairness in terms of both partners carrying equal responsibility, each couple organized themselves in a unique way with fairness always at the heart of the conversation.

In order to develop and maintain equality in the relationship, couples engaged in several intentional strategies. These strategies included the following: (a) regular relationship evaluation—setting aside time to check in on where the relationship is and where the couple would like it to go; (b) conscious decision-making—having conversations in which both partners are heard before a decision is made; (c) negotiation of labor—consciously paying attention to fairness in the division of household labor; (d) direct conflict management—incorporating efforts to understand the position of each partner in attempting to resolve conflict; and (e) attention to fairness—consciously attempting to carry equal weight in the relationship.

Attuned Inequality Couples: Paying Attention to Issues of Power. Even though same-sex couples do not have to deal with "gendered" power differences, they are not immune to power differences of other types. For example, six couples in this study (four male; two female) dealt with power imbalances resulting from unequal sharing of childcare or household labor due to a job or financial situation. Couples in this category still organized around fairness and awareness of needs by acknowledging this inequality and making attempts to maintain reciprocal give and take when they could. In these cases, acknowledging the inequality appeared to maintain a sense of mutuality and fairness because the inequality was being voiced and the benefitting partners expressed awareness of their partner's experience and concern about the consequences of the imbalance. Couples also attempted to maintain reciprocity and balance the relationship by emphasizing times when job/financial burdens did not exist or by balancing roles in another area of the relationship.

Unattuned Inequality Couples: Acknowledged and Unacknowledged Power. There were very few couples in this study (two male; two female) in which inequality existed without efforts to compensate through attunement. However, there were times when power differences were acknowledged and proved to be a source of conflict in the relationship. Other times, power differences existed but were not acknowledged or discussed, with one partner merely accommodating the other in order to stay in the relationship.

Acknowledged issues of power emerged when one partner was "out" and one was not. While these couples acknowledged this issue, social inability to be public about themselves and their relationship created much tension and distress in the relationship. In these instances, both partners had to accommodate to the other, but the experience sometimes tended to be viewed as an unwanted sacrifice by one of the partners. Here, couples tended to feel "expectation" rather than acknowledgment, or even a "take it or leave it" stance from the other. This lack of attunement and acknowledgment left partners feeling isolated and disconnected from each other, and when the accommodation was not equal, this created power imbalances.

SERT's Circle of Care: Mutuality Processes in Same-Sex Relationships

In this section, we examine how the components of the Circle of Care—mutual attunement, mutual influence, shared vulnerability, and shared relational responsibility—appear to shape the experience of equal power between partners in same-sex relationships.

Mutual Attunement

Mutual attunement involves "each partner being aware of and interested in the needs of the other. This type of awareness contributes to the other partner's experience of feeling important and supported in the relationship" (Knudson-Martin 2013, p. 11). Studies suggest that lesbian couples are more likely than heterosexual couples to value intimacy, closeness to one another, and to use effective communication skills in their relationships to try to understand each partner's needs (Eldridge and Gilbert 1990; Reilly and Lynch 1990). Similarly, gay men report nonconformity to gender roles in this area and are thus often able to nurture and develop connections with one another, allowing them to engage in partner attachment just as successfully as female couples (Gaines and Henderson 2002; Kurdek 2004). In fact, gay men have been found to be particularly adept at sensing when their partners are disturbed about something (Solomon et al. 2005).

Mutual attunement appears to be at the heart of same-sex couples' ability to maintain relatively equal relationships. Jonathan's (2009) interviews are full of examples of how they seek to attune and resonate with each other. According to Lisa, "The ability for me to understand what is going on with Judy and being able to respond to her needs makes me feel like we are in tune together." Judy agreed: "I appreciate that we have built our relationship on mutually understanding each other." Ron and Reid reported that they "had to learn each other's cues" and "make sure that they are on the same page with each other" or else conflict followed. These couples all learned that recognizing what each member is going through emotionally is a key to relationship success.

Promoting Mutual Attunement: Regular Relationship Evaluation. In the Jonathan study (2009), both male and female "attuned equality" couples regularly evaluated their relationships. Rick: "Every 6 months or so, we ask how things are going in the relationship … we figure out what we can do to improve things or keep them the same way." Scott added: "I like this a lot and it makes me feel like I can evaluate things every now and then" (p. 87).

A key aspect of the evaluation process is a shared focus and attention on the needs and experience of each partner. Sean said:

> I enjoy our weekly date night because we can talk about where our relationship is and where we want to go. It's been a thing that we have done from the beginning of our relationship and I think it brings us together in that we are open and converse about the good things and the bad things that have happened in our relationship and what we want to do about them together.

Chad liked that they deliberately set aside time each week to process their concerns with each other: "In our relationship, we often wait to bring things up during our weekly check-in time. This is something we have done for the last 7 years. It works for us." Sue described a similar pattern with her partner Heather: "We go out every Friday night as a couple and examine our relationship over the past week" (p. 87).

Mutual Influence

Mutual influence involves being able to "permit one's partner to make an impression on and have an impact on one's thoughts, feelings, and actions" (Knudson-Martin 2013, p. 11). This includes maintaining fairness in the relationship in all its forms, an area in which same-sex couples seem to excel. In fact, sexual orientation has been found to be a better predictor of an egalitarian division of labor than income, a predictor with a rather large effect size (Solomon et al. 2005).

Research shows that lesbian couples demonstrate an "ethic of equality" (Kurdek 1994) and are more likely than heterosexual couples to be aware of issues regarding power and equality (Eldridge and Gilbert 1990; Reilly and Lynch 1990). They prioritize equality in both real and ideal terms and, contrary to myth, are not typically locked into roles or power differentials that contribute to inequalities (Peplau 1991). Lesbian couples place value on attributes that encourage mutual influence, such as independence, equality, and equitable distribution of labor (Jonathan 2009). As a result, lesbian partners have been found to demonstrate high levels of both autonomy and cohesion that coexist with equality (e.g., Kurdek 2004).

Similarly, gay men consciously strive for equality in their relationships (Peplau and Fingerhut 2007). Since social norms do not dictate that one partner should have more power than the other, the norm of reciprocity seems to guide them instead. As a result, they tend to be aware of power issues and attempt to negotiate them (Jonathan 2009).

Difference in Outness: A Risk to Mutual Influence. Although same-sex couples' reports of equality may mask some differences in their actual contributions, it is well documented that they are likely to actively seek equality in their relationships (Carrington 1999; Jonathan 2009). However, there seems to be an exception. How "out" each partner is has the potential to be a difficult power issue for same-sex couples. Other literature has identified threatening to out a partner as a potential form of power and control (Almeida et al. 2007).

Among the committed long-term same-sex couples in Jonathan's study (2009), partners wanting to remain closeted appeared to have the power to limit their partner's decision-making options. With a closeted lesbian couple, for instance, this was troubling for Esther, since Wilma was not willing to accommodate Esther's desire for public acknowledgment:

> Esther: Wilma and I have been together for 4 years and although it's no one's business that we are together, it almost makes me feel like our relationship does not exist. I would be willing to be more out, but Wilma is not ready for that.
> Wilma: Well, as you said it's no one's business. I'm comfortable the way we are. Why do we have to come out, just because it suits you?
> Esther: It's not that I want to force us to come out, but I really feel that it would give our relationship more value and make it feel as if it was real if others knew (Jonathan 2009, pp. 93–94).

Promoting Mutual Influence. Two factors are commonly used by same-sex couples to promote mutual influence in their relationships. These include attention to fairness and direct conflict management (Jonathan 2009).

With regard to attention to fairness, both male and female "attuned equality" couples spoke directly about fairness. This helped them define what equality means to them and determine what they expect for each other. This meant that they carry equal weight. Michael: "We're both equal. We take turns doing things around the house." Eric and Simon spoke of equality in similar terms. Eric: "I'd say that we're equal in that we carry the same weight around the house." Ensuring that each partner is "heard" was a common aspect of fairness. Tim said: "I know we're equal in that we each allow the other person to be heard" (Jonathan 2009, p. 86).

Female couples also focused on household responsibilities, mutual respect, and access to resources. Heather: "If one is giving more into the relationship than the other, then that would be an indication that things were not equal." Sara: "If you respect someone then you will be in an equal relationship with them. It goes hand in hand." Erica described a commitment to equality even though their financial situations are not the same: "Everything is equal for us … bank account and everything." Her partner Nicole responded, "Yes, and I'm happy with that. It really matters to me that we can have a decent relationship and not worry about who makes the most money" (p. 86).

With regard to direct conflict management, attention to both persons' perspectives meant there would sometimes be disagreements. In these situations, both male and female "attuned equality" couples in the Jonathan study (2009) reported that they address conflict directly so that both partners' views can be heard. Rachel: "We sit down and talk when there is conflict in the relationship." Men reported the same focused attention to addressing signs of conflict. Richard: "When something comes up, we're quick to drop everything and say what is going on here?" Partners said that they talk about conflict directly because they are each invested in maintaining the relationship and expect that each partner has an equal role in resolving the problem. Both male and female couples reported a desire to resolve conflicts and not allow them to go for a prolonged time. Lisa: "I like that we try to resolve everything up front." Erica agreed: "We don't go for weeks with the same conflict."

Shared Vulnerability

Shared vulnerability involves bringing a "spirit of openness, curiosity, and self-honesty" to the partnership so that "each partner can experience the other in a flexible, adaptive way that permits space for admitting one's own mistakes while still being accepted and worthy of love" (Knudson-Martin 2013, p. 10). This can be an area of difficulty for some same-sex couples. For example, lesbian partners may have trouble with emotional fusion that prevents them from stating their specific wants and needs (e.g., Hardtke et al. 2010; Spencer and Brown 2007). That is, rather than opening themselves up and addressing controversial issues, lesbian women may expect their partners to intuit their feelings and needs (Hardtke et al. 2010; Kurdek 1994), which in turn can cause confusion and conflict (Hardtke et al. 2010). Internalized homophobia, a distaste for oneself that can result from negative societal messages, may also cause lesbian women to close off to their partners (Spencer and Brown 2007).

Similarly, some gay men may become over-attached or fused, as a result of experiences with societal rejection (e.g., Drescher 1998). However, gay men can also be prone to having difficulty maintaining relational commitments because of a high value men tend to place on independence (Greenan and Tunnell 2003) and an inability to open up and achieve emotional closeness due to anxiety (e.g., Oringher and Samuelson 2011). Thus, in working with same-sex couples, the practitioner should be aware of an increased probability of shared vulnerability issues, which in turn might stand in the way of creating the mutuality that SERT uses to facilitate positive relationship change (Knudson-Martin and Huenergardt 2010). A therapist can help same-sex couples by creating an environment of therapeutic safety, giving each individual a chance to share his or her thoughts and feelings without fear, thereby promoting shared vulnerability.

Shared Relational Responsibility

"Shared relational responsibility involves both partners being sensitive to and accountable for the effects of their actions on others and taking an active interest in doing what is necessary to maintain their relationship" (Knudson-Martin 2013, p. 10). In contrast to many heterosexual couples (e.g., Knudson-Martin and Mahoney 2005), Jonathan's (2009) study of long-term same-sex couples found that none of the couples reported that relationship roles and patterns just automatically fell into place. Nearly all described intentional efforts to make the relationship work for both partners. Jonathan surmised that such conscious attention to the relationship made sense given the social obstacles that many same-sex couples must overcome in order to have a relationship. This interaction also mirrors what equal and collaborative heterosexual partners do (Cowdery and Knudson-Martin 2006; Knudson-Martin and Mahoney 2005).

In general, both gay men and lesbian women report a high degree of shared relational responsibility in their relationships compared to heterosexual couples. Specifically, they accomplish this through less frequent use of demand/withdraw communications, more openness, and better skill at conflict resolution (Kurdek 2004). However, it appears that even within same-sex couples, women may be better at this than men. In contrast to male couples, females tend to use more emotionally expressive communication techniques and try to spend more time with their partners (Hardtke et al. 2010). Research suggests that this is because women are socialized to be relationship-oriented and to engage in caretaking skills and the nurturing of one another (Eldridge and Gilbert 1990; Hardtke et al. 2010; Reilly and Lynch 1990).

Promoting Shared Relational Responsibility. Two factors are commonly used by same-sex couples to promote shared relational responsibility in their relationships. These include conscious decision-making and negotiation of labor (Jonathan 2009).

Concerning conscious decision-making, "attuned equality" male and female couples in the Jonathan study (2009) communicated extensively when making decisions, with a concern for making sure that each partner feels understood and involved. Lynn: "In our decision-making, both of our thoughts and ideas are heard. No one has privilege over the other." Mutual engagement in decision-making helped partners feel emotionally connected and supported. For example, Ellen emphasized the validation she feels: "With decision-making, raising our children, all of that, we both have our say and therefore I feel as if my voice is validated."

Conscious attention to both voices contributed to feeling that they have equal influence and responsibility. Mary: "The Saturday morning powwow is when we discuss important decisions. Both sides are heard and we try to come out with an amicable way of tackling what is going on." Arthur said, "We tend to talk about our decisions over a meal." Rich responded, "I like the way that each of our ideas are heard…that makes me feel like my opinion matters" (pp. 87–88).

With negotiation of labor, arriving at an equitable division of labor tends to begin with who *wants* to do what. In fact, most of the male couples in the Jonathan study (2009) said they hire outside help for some household tasks. Scott said, "We are so busy in our jobs. Thank God we have a maid that helps us keep the place clean" (p. 88). Female couples were more likely to describe interest in at least some domestic responsibilities and tended to negotiate around these interests. For example, when Ellen said, "I love the outside and so I feel like that's my domain," her partner Anna responded, "See, I hate yard work! So I tell Ellen, go for it. It's all yours. I love cleaning and dusting and having a spotless bathroom" (p. 88).

Money management was also often divided on skill and preference. Rick: "I run away from the finances at work and home. I'm glad that Scott does them." Scott appeared to agree: "I like to do the finances." Laura took over finances because "it drives [Ellen] crazy" (p. 88).

Implications for Same-Sex Couple Therapy

Although men and women may use somewhat different tactics to influence their partners and struggle with different kinds of problems, research consistently finds no difference between heterosexual, lesbian, and gay relationships on standardized measures of love, satisfaction, and relationship adjustment—all of which are predictors of relationship quality (Kurdek 2004; Peplau and Fingerhut 2007). However, when it comes to the equality-promoting conditions in SERT's Circle of Care, most same-sex couples tend to function well in the areas of shared relational responsibility, mutual influence, and mutual attunement, but may experience more difficulty with shared vulnerability, primarily because of needing to negotiate their relationships in discriminatory societal contexts. As in other distressed relationships, some same-sex partners are not equally attentive and supportive of the other (Williams 2011).

In order to develop and maintain equality in their relationships, healthy same-sex couples engage in several intentional strategies, such as regularly evaluating the relationship, shared decision-making, negotiating division of labor, managing conflict directly, and attending to fairness between partners. All of these strategies promote mutuality in same-sex relationships as identified within the SERT Circle of Care. More importantly, each strategy is an activity with which the therapist can engage same-sex couples during therapy. For example, a therapist could facilitate negotiation of household labor or help the couple evaluate their relationship by checking in with each other emotionally.

Sharing vulnerability remains a challenge for many same-sex couples and can interfere with the other aspects of the Circle of Care. Whether the cause be internalized homophobia (Spencer and Brown 2007) or anxiety (e.g., Oringher and Samuelson 2011) from living in a heteronormative world, emotional fusion resulting from experiences of societal rejection (e.g., Hardtke et al. 2010), or a high value placed on independence (Greenan and Tunnell 2003), same-sex couples seem to have a particular need for a safe space to express their emotions. By focusing on creating therapeutic safety, therapists can facilitate shared vulnerability and mutual support by helping create a context for same-sex couples to renegotiate the ways in which covert power processes may operate in the relationship (Knudson-Martin and Huenergardt, "Bridging Emotion, Societal Discourse, and Couple Interaction in Clinical Practice," 2015). In order to do this, therapists must first learn to recognize and name power imbalances, begin to conceptualize what sociocultural discourses may be contributing to the power differential, and help couples consciously negotiate unequal relationship patterns (Knudson-Martin et al. 2014; Knudson-Martin and Huenergardt, "Bridging Emotion, Societal Discourse, and Couple Interaction in Clinical Practice," 2015).

For example, Lana worked with a lesbian couple[1] that came into therapy after one of the partners, Arlene, stated she was feeling depressed. Arlene explained that six months ago, she had hit a wall in her previous career as a dental hygienist and had since been uncertain about which direction to pursue next in life. The longer that time passed and Arlene could not find clarity about her personal goals and decisions, she started to doubt herself and began to think she could not do anything "right" on her own. Therefore, she decided that at the very least, she needed to move out of the couple's apartment in order to regain a sense of independence. Arlene's partner, Susie, feared that this was Arlene's way of leaving the relationship, and she was struggling to understand the motivation for this. Arlene and Susie had been dating for six months. They had met shortly after Arlene had lost her job, and Arlene moved in with Susie relatively soon afterward. Because Arlene was unemployed during that time, she had to rely on Susie for financial support. Susie was financially stable, and she did not indicate that the couple's financial responsibilities were a burden. However, in a society in which independence and self-sufficiency are privileged, relying on another person can be considered a sign of weakness. Therefore, Arlene felt apologetic for needing to depend on Susie financially.

Not only was there a difference between the partners' financial status, there was also a difference between the length of time that each woman had been living as an "out" lesbian. While Susie had been "out" for many years, had a strong social support network that accepted her after coming out, and had dated several women in the past, this was Arlene's first relationship with a woman and she lacked the social support that Susie experienced. Thus, in addition to relying on Susie as her provider, Arlene also looked to her as her main source of social support, adding to the power imbalance.

Similar to many of the lesbian couples described in Jonathan's (2009) study, Susie and Arlene demonstrated a high degree of mutual attunement—they were emotionally attentive to one another and both strived to be supportive partners. Susie tried to help Arlene curb feelings of depression by offering encouragement and taking initiative with planning and problem-solving. Her efforts to be "helpful" were intended to show that she cared, and she believed that Arlene experienced it in this way. However, Susie's task-oriented, caretaking approach combined with her financial support inadvertently placed Arlene in a one-down position, creating a situation of attuned inequality (Jonathan 2009). In fact, Arlene eventually stated in therapy that she felt "smaller and more helpless" as time went on. However, Arlene could read Susie's heart and knew that Susie was simply trying to be a good partner. Therefore, in a way, her ability to recognize the

---

[1] Case details have been modified, and pseudonyms have been used to protect the confidentiality of the clients.

emotional undercurrent of Susie's intent is also what constrained her and made her feel unable to tell Susie that her efforts to help, in fact, made her feel weak.

The more that Susie tried to "help," the more Arlene felt she needed space from the relationship. In contrast, when Arlene tried to offer Susie "help" with making difficult decisions and getting through stressful situations, Susie would reject this and claim she could do things on her own, further maintaining Arlene's one-down position. When Susie seemed stressed, Arlene would tiptoe around her moods. This imbalance maintained the assumption that Arlene needed Susie's help, but had nothing valuable to offer Susie in return.

To shift the couple's balance of power, a context of therapeutic safety had to be created to allow greater shared vulnerability on the part of both partners. Both Arlene and Susie feared that they would hurt one another's feelings, and this stance of emotional caretaking kept them from being transparent about their individual experiences in the relationship. To help create a safe context for increased shared vulnerability, Lana started by validating Susie's need for relationship and affirming the positive relational intentions of each partner and the ways they were both willing to focus on their partner's needs above their own. She also explicitly brought in a sociocultural lens to help the couple deconstruct the ways in which ideas about being a "good" partner and a "good" woman shaped and limited the range of ways that Arlene and Susie might approach each other.

Therapy focused on renegotiating a more equal partnership—one based on shared vulnerability and enabling mutual influence and support. This is illustrated by how the couple shifted their process of decision-making from one for which Susie made decisions for both of them to a "we" centered process in which Susie, as the more powerful person, learned how to listen to and value Arlene's active participation (see also Samman and Knudson-Martin, "Relational Engagement in Heterosexual Couple Therapy: Helping Men Move from "I" to "We"," 2015). Each partner learned that it was important to authentically express their points of view and state what was unspoken, rather than expecting their partner to intuit their feelings or staying silent around delicate issues for fear of hurting one another. The final decision they made before terminating from therapy involved where Susie should enroll in medical school. She had been accepted by two schools—one in Iowa and the other in New Zealand. By learning to allow disagreement and engage in difficult conversations, Arlene became able to shift from stating that she simply wanted Susie to choose the place that would make her happiest to asserting her opinion, and Susie started to take Arlene's perspectives to heart. In the end, the couple made a shared decision based on what would allow Susie to pursue her medical training while also keeping employment opportunities alive for Arlene.

This case example illustrates that even when the gender binary does not serve as a main organizing principle in a relationship, sociocultural scripts and other societal inequities still actively shape how partners orient to one another and how power manifests. Just as focusing on self-sufficiency and autonomy does not invite relationship, emotional caretaking in the absence of being able to directly communicate one's needs reinforces power differences and also limits relational possibilities. In order for mutual connection and partnership to develop, each person must feel that their partner sees their worth and value and the relationship must support each partner to honor their own sense of self. This is the foundation of equality.

By creating a safe space of acceptance and communication, a therapist can facilitate an environment in which each partner can experience the other in a flexible, adaptive way that permits space for admitting one's own mistakes while still being accepted and worthy of love—a feeling which society has long denied same-sex couples.

References

Almeida, R., Dolan-Del Vecchio, K., & Parker, L. (2007). Foundation concepts for social justice-based therapy: Critical consciousness, accountability, and empowerment. In E. Aldarondo (Ed.), *Advancing social justice through clinical practice*. Mahwah, NJ: Lawrence Erlbaum Associates.

Beck, L., & Clark, M. S. (2010). What constitutes a healthy communal marriage and why relationship stage matters? *Journal of Family Theory and Review, 2*, 299–315.

Carrington, C. (1999). *No place like home: Relationships and family life among lesbians and gay men*. Chicago, IL: University of Chicago Press.

Collett, J. L. (2010). Integrating theory, enhancing understanding: The potential contributions of recent experimental research in social exchange for studying intimate relationships. *Journal of Family Theory and Review, 2*, 280–298.

Connolly, C. (2005). A qualitative exploration of resilience in long-term lesbian couples. *Family Journal, 13*, 266–280.

Cowdery, R. S., & Knudson-Martin, C. (2006). The construction of motherhood: Tasks, relational connection, and gender equality. *Family Relations, 54*, 335–345.

DeMaris, A. (2007). The role of relationship inequality in marital disruption. *Journal of Social and Personal Relationships, 24*, 177–195.

Drescher, J. (1998). Contemporary psychoanalytic psychotherapy with gay men with a commentary on reparative therapy of homosexuality. *Journal of Gay and Lesbian Psychotherapy, 2*(4), 51–74.

Eldridge, N. S., & Gilbert, L. A. (1990). Correlates of relationship satisfaction in lesbian couples. *Psychology of Women Quarterly, 14*, 43–62.

Gaines, S. O., & Henderson, M. C. (2002). Impact of attachment style on responses to accommodative dilemmas among same-sex couples. *Personal Relationships, 9*, 89–93.

Gottman, J. M. (2011). *The science of trust: Emotional attunement for couples*. New York, NY: Guilford Press.

Greenan, D. E., & Tunnell, G. (2003). *Couple therapy with gay men*. New York, NY: Guilford Press.

Hardtke, K. K., Armstrong, M., & Johnson, S. (2010). Emotionally focused couple therapy: A full-treatment model well-suited to the specific needs of lesbian couples. *Journal of Couple and Relationship Therapy, 9*(4), 312–326.

Jonathan, N. (2009). Carrying equal weight: Relational responsibility and attunement among same-sex couples. In C. Knudson-Martin & A. R. Mahoney (Eds.), *Couples, gender and power: Creating change in intimate relationships* (pp. 79–103). New York, NY: Springer.

Knudson-Martin, C. (2013). Why power matters: Creating a foundation of mutual support in couple relationships. *Family Process, 52*, 5–18.

Knudson-Martin, C., & Huenergardt, D. (2010). A socio-emotional approach to couple therapy: Linking societal context and couple interaction. *Family Process, 49*, 369–384.

Knudson-Martin, C., & Huenergardt, D. (2015). Bridging emotion, societal discourse, and couple interaction in clinical practice. In C. Knudson-Martin, M. A. Wells, & S. K. Samman (Eds.), *Socio-emotional relationship therapy: Bridging emotion, societal context, and couple interaction* (pp. 1–13). New York, NY: Springer.

Knudson-Martin, C., Huenergardt, D., Lafontant, K., Bishop, L., Shaepper, J., & Wells, M. (2014). Competencies for addressing gender and power in couple therapy: A socio-emotional approach. *Journal of Marital and Family Therapy, Advance online publication*. doi:10.1111/jmft.12068.

Knudson-Martin, C., & Mahoney, A. (2005). Moving beyond gender: Processes that create relationship equality. *Journal of Marital and Family Therapy, 31*, 235–246.

Kurdek, L. A. (1994). Lesbian and gay couples. In A. R. D'Augelli & C. J. Patterson (Eds.), *Lesbian and gay identities over the lifespan: Psychological perspectives on personal, relational and community processes* (pp. 243–261). New York, NY: Oxford University Press.

Kurdek, L. A. (2004). Are gay and lesbian cohabiting couples really different from heterosexual married couples? *Journal of Marriage and Family, 66*, 880–900.

Oringher, J., & Samuelson, K. W. (2011). Intimate partner violence and the role of masculinity in male same-sex relationships. *Traumatology, 17*(2), 68–74.

Peplau, L. A. (1991). Lesbian and gay relationships. In J. C. Ronsiorek & J. D. Weinrich (Eds.), *Homosexuality: Research implications for public policy* (pp. 177–196). Newbury Park, CA: Sage.

Peplau, L. A., & Fingerhut, A. W. (2007). The close relationships of lesbians and gay men. *Annual Review of Psychology, 58*, 405–424.

Reilly, M. E., & Lynch, J. M. (1990). Power-sharing in lesbian partnerships. *Journal of Homosexuality, 19*(3), 1–30.

Samman, S. K., & Knudson-Martin, C. (2015). Relational engagement in heterosexual couple therapy: Helping men move from "I" to "We." In C. Knudson-Martin, M. A. Wells, & S. K. Samman (Eds.), *Socio-emotional relationship therapy: Bridging emotion, societal context, and couple interaction* (pp. 79–91). New York, NY: Springer.

Shechory, M., & Ziv, R. (2007). Relationships between gender role attitudes, role division, and perception of equity among heterosexual, gay and lesbian couples. *Sex Roles, 56*, 629–638.

Solomon, S. E., Rothblum, E. D., & Balsam, K. F. (2005). Money, housework, sex, and conflict: Same-sex couples in civil unions, those not in civil unions, and heterosexual married siblings. *Sex Roles, 52*, 561–575.

Spencer, B., & Brown, J. (2007). Fusion or internalized homophobia? A pilot study of Bowen's differentiation of self hypothesis with lesbian couples. *Family Process, 46*(2), 257–268.

Williams, K. (2011). A socio-emotional relational framework for infidelity: The relational justice approach. *Family Process, 50*(4), 516–528. doi:10.1111/j.1545-5300.2011.01374.x.

Couple Therapy with Adult Survivors of Child Abuse: Gender, Power, and Trust

Melissa A. Wells and Veronica P. Kuhn

The session with the heterosexual couple was not going well. The tension between the partners, who were both attorneys, intensified as the Asian wife heatedly articulated why she was angry with her European American husband. While both partners were accustomed to a great deal of power in their careers, the husband seemed to hold more power in this relationship as he displayed a disinclination to consider his wife's concerns and expressed views that something must be wrong with her for getting so emotional. Then the wife tearfully told her husband he was treating her as abusively as her father had during her youth. New to her work with couples, the therapist (Melissa) naively followed this thread to understand the wife's experience of childhood abuse. Although the wife disclosed her painful memories, her husband did not respond sensitively. Instead, he saw her story as further validation of his wife's "out-of-control" emotions. By this time, the wife seemed too vulnerable, too powerless, and too unable to proceed in therapy. The couple never did return. Melissa agonized over needing to find a better way to work with the gendered power dynamics and emotional morass of adult-survivor couples such as this one.

Case details throughout the chapter have been modified and pseudonyms have been used to protect the confidentiality of clients.

M.A. Wells (✉)
Department of Counseling and Family Sciences,
Loma Linda University, Loma Linda, CA, USA
e-mail: mewells@llu.edu

M.A. Wells
Marital and Family Therapy Intern,
Mt. Vision Family Therapy, Redlands, CA, USA

V.P. Kuhn
Department of Counseling and Family Sciences,
Loma Linda University, Loma Linda, CA, USA

© American Family Therapy Academy 2015
C. Knudson-Martin et al. (eds.), *Socio-Emotional Relationship Therapy*,
AFTA SpringerBriefs in Family Therapy, DOI 10.1007/978-3-319-13398-0_9

In this chapter, we present the relational trust theory, which we are developing to address the particular relational stresses that affect couples in which one or both partners experienced abuse in childhood (Wells, in press). We both have been members of the Socio-Emotional Relationship Therapy (SERT) clinical research team during our doctoral studies (see Knudson-Martin and Huenergardt 2010, "Bridging Emotion, Societal Discourse, and Couple Interaction in Clinical Practice," 2015). Melissa is a European American woman who raised her two young-adult children as a single mother, now enjoys a remarkable couple relationship, and has recently embarked on a mid-life career change from journalist to couple and family therapist. Veronica, a European Mexican woman, and her European American husband are transitioning to parenthood with the recent arrival of their daughter. We identify as feminists who are sensitive to issues of social justice in the problems confronting our clients and in our clinical approaches. We have been studying the unique relational needs of adult-survivor couples as part of Melissa's dissertation research. Our feminist stance informs our view that, in the context of two-gender dominant discourses, gender and power relations contribute to couple problems and that it is critical to advance goals to diminish power inequities between partners (Knudson-Martin 2013; Leslie and Southard 2009; Lips 1991).

Throughout her clinical training, Melissa has applied this theoretical framework with both a lesbian couple and numerous heterosexual adult-survivor couples. We have found that not all adult survivors suffer relational distress (Himelein and McElrath 1996). Nonetheless, it is important to assess for the impact of childhood maltreatment, since it is common and its effects can range along a continuum of "a remote, almost irrelevant event for some survivors and a central, continually potent experience for others" (Millwood 2011, p. 342). We illustrate the theoretical constructs of relational trust theory through the use of case examples.

Relational Trust Theory

Couple therapy can be demanding for the most skilled clinicians, but the interpersonal challenges of adult-survivor couples add another layer of complexity to clinical efforts to support partners in fostering a mutually supportive relationship. Notably, in our work with adult-survivor couples, we have observed a dual influence of power in their interactions. One influence is gendered power dynamics between partners; the other is an emotional power response of adult survivors. The intertwining of these dual power influences can quickly break down relational processes, most observably in the form of distrustful emotional reactions from the adult survivor. However, the clinical processes of relational trust theory can guide clinicians in helping adult survivors and their partners transform these dual influences of power and thereby experience more trust in their couple relationship (Wells, in press). As described in detail in the chapter "When Therapy Challenges Patriarchy: Undoing Gendered Power in Heterosexual Couple Relationships," (Knudson-Martin, 2015), we define power as relational; it is evidenced in the ways each partner can influence the other to respond to her or his priorities, interests, and needs. While mutually supportive relationships have been found to promote well-being for each partner, power imbalances between partners can result in relational distress (Knudson-Martin 2013). Similarly, we view relational trust as being shaped when each partner can be relied upon to notice and respond to the other's needs now and in the future (Boszormenyi-Nagy and Krasner 1986; Wieselquist 2009). The components of SERT's Circle of Care (Knudson-Martin and Huenergardt 2010, "Bridging Emotion, Societal Discourse, and Couple Interaction in Clinical Practice," 2015)—shared relational responsibility, mutual influence, shared attunement, and mutual vulnerability—provide a concrete approach to help partners engage in processes of mutuality that also link to the elements of trustworthiness (Hargrave and Pfitzer 2011). Trustworthiness involves a sense of safety and security due to the reliability of partners (shared relational responsibility), give-and-take between partners (mutual influence), hopefulness resulting from each partner's attentiveness to the other's needs (shared attunement), and openness and authenticity with one another (mutual vulnerability).

Intertwining Influences of Power

Central to relational trust theory is awareness of how adult survivors engage in intimate relationships (Wells, in press). For instance, the deleterious interpersonal effects of a history of childhood abuse have been noted as enduring and pervasive (Savla et al. 2013). One of the most frequently noted stressors for adult survivors is difficulty with trusting their intimate partner (e.g., MacIntosh and Johnson 2008), as well as heightened need for comfort and reassurance (Brown et al. 2012; Dalton et al. 2013). Additionally, a tendency of adult survivors to experience shame, isolation, outbursts of anger, and sexual anxiety can contribute to conflict in their couple relationships (Nelson and Wampler 2002). Ornduff (2000) found that some adult survivors view their intimate relationships as destructive and painful. Not surprisingly, therefore, adult survivors can approach intimate relationships with caution and hair-trigger reactivity to their partners in ways that are influenced by their childhood experiences of neglect and abuse (Wells, in press).

Gender and Power

Liem et al. (1992) found that adult survivors tend to be keenly aware of power in their intimate relationships. The need for control over the partner and fear of the partner's power are common. Conversely, some adult survivors relinquish control and power to their partners (Blumer et al. 2013). We view this sensitivity to power by adult survivors as significantly impacting the emotional climate of their intimate relationships. To further complicate matters, when adult-survivor couples approach their relationships in gender-stereotypical fashion, inherent power imbalances between partners are embedded in social discourses of how to "be" a man and woman. In the context of these stereotypic gender binaries, gendered power becomes covert and invisible as men and women strive to meet societal expectations for how to perform in their intimate relationships (Knudson-Martin, "When Therapy Challenges Patriarchy: Undoing Gendered Power in Heterosexual Couple Relationships," 2015). Adhering to these societal norms, inherent power inequities in couple interactions can trigger the adult survivor's "allergic" reactions.

Understanding the ways in which gender and power structure intimate relationships is crucial when working with adult-survivor couples. The relationship between gender and power can be difficult to discern. Oftentimes, apparent gender differences are power differences (Lips 1991). Furthermore, power inequities erode trust between partners (Gottman 2011; Knudson-Martin 2013), which is a key concern for adult survivors who may already be leery about the trustworthiness of their partner.

For instance, Joseph, a Mexican American financial executive, and Michelle, a European American woman who placed her career as a pharmacist on hold to care for their two young children, came to therapy in a last-ditch effort to save their marriage. Michelle experienced childhood abuse from the age of 10, when her father left her mother for another woman and Michelle's mother started drinking heavily. Michelle's drunken mother often emotionally and physically punished her for little or no reason. To make matters worse, Michelle's father ignored her pleas for help because he was too busy with his new family. In the couple relationship, a sore topic for Joseph and Michelle is how he responds to her requests for help with the children. When he dismisses her because that is "her job," he is using his power as the male to define whose needs have priority in the relationship. Joseph unintentionally evokes that familiar sense of futility in Michelle harkening back to her childhood. Viewing him as untrustworthy, just as she had come to see her parents' treatment of her, an emotional response of distrust displayed by Michelle as anger and reactivity toward Joseph further exacerbates the tension between the partners. As these gendered power interactions between the partners entangle with Michelle's childhood coping strategy of negative emotional reactivity, the result is an inordinate amount of distress for the couple (Wells, in press).

Adult-Survivor Power Responses

In light of the adult survivor's perceived vulnerability in intimate relationships, when lack of mutuality prevails in couple interactions, many adult survivors react through power responses that can further diminish already compromised relational processes of the couple. Adult-survivor power responses emanate from not only the "external physical experience of abuse," but also the "internal emotional states" evoked by such experiences (Lisak 1995, p. 261). These emotions are tied to the various power responses used by the adult survivor, who may assume a "me first" position as a reaction to the perception of the partner as untrustworthy. Silverstein et al. (2009) have defined this individualistic orientation as position directed, in which the person is organized around being one-down or one-up in the relationship. Working to change the one-down position or to maintain a one-up position underlies that person's ways of relating in couple interactions. This self-focus often leads to limited empathy and struggles for power to protect one's own interests by controlling the other partner (Wells, in press).

We have observed that many contexts link to the distrust that triggers a power response from adult survivors, such as social environment, gender socialization, neurobiological processes, and, primarily, fear for one's position in the relationship and the perception of safety.

Social environment and gender socialization. Much of what adult survivors draw upon in gender power relations has been learned in their family of origin, which intergenerationally transmits understandings about how to perform power in intimate relationships (Lips 1991). But there are many other influences, such as peers, religious and academic authority figures, and cultural media. Lisak (1995) described gender socialization as bifurcating the emotional and lived experience of men and women. In the context of two genders, masculinity embodies independence, control, competitiveness, toughness, and denial of vulnerability (Lisak 1995; Mejia 2005), whereas femininity symbolizes passivity, dependence, vulnerability, and self-sacrifice (Krause and Roth 2011; Lisak 1995). We regard gender socialization of men as foundational to challenges they may have with restricted emotions and difficulty communicating feelings (Mejia 2005). The conundrum for male adult survivors is that the emotions associated with child abuse—fear, shame, vulnerability—must be repressed in order to appear masculine (Lisak 1995). For female adult survivors, power displays of anger and control contradict society's images of femininity (Lips 1991). These gender incongruities can contribute to significant emotional pressure for adult survivors when they perceive that they do not "measure up" to societal norms, which can then also negatively affect their couple interactions.

Trust and neurobiology. Neurobiological research can be helpful to understanding emotional processes in adult-survivor intimate relationships (Fishbane 2013; Fishbane and Wells, "Toward Relational Empowerment: Interpersonal Neurobiology, Couples, and the Societal Context," 2015). Whenever Michelle perceives Joseph as untrustworthy, her brain's amygdala snaps into action. As a result, reactive emotional responses of fight, flight, or freeze instantly override the higher cognitive processes of Michelle's prefrontal cortex. We regard the adult survivor's power responses as "under the influence" of these neurobiological processes.

Fight, flight, or freeze power responses. We use the metaphor of the amygdala's activity to categorize adult-survivor power responses as self-protective (fight), marginalizing the needs of the other partner (flight from the relationship), or self-abnegation (freeze of one's own sense of power, usually expressed as overly accommodating the other partner or as a feeling of internalized helplessness). While many adult survivors tend to draw on one or the other of these categories of power responses, we have observed that they can vacillate in their coping style. For instance, when Michelle asks Joseph whether he can leave the office early to drive their son to baseball practice and he refuses and blames her for not planning her schedule better, she at first responds in a conciliatory fashion of not pressing the issue. By using this self-abnegation power response, Michelle accommodates his needs while denying her own. The next time Michelle makes a similar request, however, she meets Joseph's dismissal with anger and accusations that the needs of their children do not matter to him, a self-protective power response. When that approach does not influence him, Michelle then marginalizes Joseph's needs in the relationship by refusing his sexual advances.

These power responses of distrust consistently contribute to relational distress for the adult survivor and, oftentimes, the partner. While emotional power responses may occur in all couples to some degree, the difference from persons with no history of childhood abuse is that adult survivors may more automatically and rigidly adhere to these positional strategies because of intrinsic challenges of trusting an intimate partner who holds the power to treat them well or badly. Adult survivors are all too familiar with being treated badly by a trusted other in power, and they have long since built their automatic responses to these unfair experiences.

The dual influences of power can easily confound relational processes between partners. For instance, how can Joseph, as the one-up male partner who has limited experience at attuning to Michelle's needs, become sensitized to her adult-survivor response of self-abnegation? Noticing and disentangling these dual influences of power can help partners alter their relational processes. Since gendered power interactions between partners appear to function as triggers for adult-survivor power responses, we consider it essential to initially focus on gendered power dynamics of the couple. Supporting Joseph in attuning to Michelle's needs could help him become more responsive, which would support her perception of Joseph as more trustworthy. Transforming gendered power inequities may be a necessary precedent to establishing greater possibility for trust and helping the couple resolve any enduring interpersonal challenges linked to a history of childhood abuse.

Survivor Power Responses and Gender

While gendered power can be difficult to discern in couple processes (Knudson-Martin 2013, "When Therapy Challenges Patriarchy: Undoing Gendered Power in Heterosexual Couple Relationships," 2015), survivor power responses can easily be misconstrued as a pathological problem of the adult survivor. We view the experience of powerlessness associated with a history of childhood abuse as systemically tied to challenges in the couple's relationship, rather than regarding this as a deficit in the adult survivor (Brown 2004). As adult survivors engage with their partners through the use of power responses, we have observed gendered nuances as follows:

Self-protective power responses. These responses of anger and reactivity, control, and suspicion are explicit and overt. Indeed, they can seem overwhelming for partners and therapists alike. We have seen both genders make frequent use of self-protective strategies in their intimate relationships. The attorney wife in the case example at the start of this chapter utilized a self-protective power response of anger and reactivity. Drawing upon rage as a coping mechanism can be inherently conflictual for women because the larger social context considers it inappropriate for women to express anger. Meanwhile, this is the only emotion that society permits males as a way of expressing hurt (Lisak 1995). Distrust expressed as reactive anger, control, or suspicion fosters an atmosphere of isolation and feeling devalued, which diminishes intimacy (Millwood 2011). Considering the context in which self-protective responses were learned, the therapist is better equipped to help the couple identify the effects of distrust between partners and to make sense of the compelling emotions at work in their interactions. A concerted effort by the therapist to join with the adult survivor, who oftentimes is both partners, is essential.

Marginalizing the partner's needs. This power response appears gendered when men employ this emotional coping strategy. But women may also use this approach, which seems incongruent, considering that our society places the onus on women to care for others and maintain relationships (Hare-Mustin 1989). Regardless of gender, this coping strategy makes sense when we consider that the adult survivor's needs were marginalized earlier in life. This became Michelle's approach in response to repeated denials by Joseph to help with the children. It played a significant role in the couple being on the brink of separation. Indeed, when a perception of the other partner as untrustworthy leads adult survivors to ignore the effects of their actions on their spouse, the relationship enters a "red zone" for inflicting tremendous hurt between partners (Wells, in press).

Self-abnegation power responses. Not having a voice in one's intimate relationship can underscore the survivor's silence in childhood about injustices that occurred due to the survivor's sense of shame, self-blame, anxiety about more abuse, or fear of disbelief by those who could possibly help (McGregor et al. 2010). Accordingly, self-abnegation power responses tend to be indirect and introvert, making them more challenging to identify. However, when adult survivors express that they have no voice or that they feel helpless to influence their partner, this is a clear indicator of a self-abnegation coping strategy. Such a response is not unusual in the experience of the less powerful partner and often occurs with women in gender-traditional heterosexual relationships. But this effect is magnified for the adult survivor due to the experience of powerlessness in the abusive circumstances of childhood (Wells, in press).

We have noticed that women more frequently employ self-abnegation power responses. Nonetheless, some men also utilize this approach, which can be confusing for male survivors who are barraged with disparate influences of working to hold the power in their intimate heterosexual relationships while relying upon disempowering self-abnegation approaches learned in childhood. The dissonance between the vulnerability, helplessness, and powerlessness of childhood abuse and the male survivor's expectations to meet society's definitions of masculinity (Banyard et al. 2004) can lead to resentment at his partner and unrelenting self-loathing. Indeed, the price paid by male survivors in their gender socialization is "separation from their emotional experience, and from the capacity for intimate connection" (Lisak 1995, p. 260), which can weaken empathy for their intimate partner and diminish their own positive self-regard.

Lucas, an African American man who experienced child physical and emotional abuse from his father over many years, drew upon a self-abnegation power response of internalized helplessness and would shut down when Bianca, his Latina wife, became angry with him. He was not stonewalling, but seemed to be waiting for the intensity to pass. We have noticed that this often occurs when a child has had a dominating parent, as was the case with Lucas. Bianca, who had experienced child sexual abuse, responded to Lucas with a self-protective power response of anger and control. The more remote he became, the more frustration and anger Bianca expressed, and both partners became all the more embroiled in their emotional morass. As with this couple, when both partners are adult survivors, we have observed that their power responses can clash and further fuel conflict.

Fostering Relational Trust

We draw upon several clinical practices in our work with adult-survivor couples to disentangle power influences. These are establishing relational safety, examining the relational ledger, and shifting gendered power imbalances between partners.

Establishing Relational Safety

Gendered power disparities affect the perception of safety in the relationship, and without safety, trust between partners is compromised (Gottman 2011). Establishing and maintaining relational safety is paramount, and the therapist needs to attend to this from the outset. This involves the therapist helping the couple engage in safe relational processes through mutual accountability and emotional vulnerability (Keeling 2007; Knudson-Martin et al. 2014). We also view the impact of neurobiological influences on each partner as an integral aspect of their shared emotions, and work to help adult-survivor couples understand the neurobiology involved in their interactions (Fishbane and Wells, "Toward Relational Empowerment: Interpersonal Neurobiology, Couples, and the Societal

Context," 2015). A primary goal is to help the couple manage anxiety responses in order to maintain calm for reflective processing in session.

Neurobiology and emotional power. Reactivity occurs frequently with some adult-survivor couples. When this happens, we slow down the pace and temporarily shift gears to allow for more emotional calm so that each partner's neural pathways and neurotransmitters can re-equilibrate prefrontal control for enhanced reflectivity during the session (Fishbane 2013). This requires sensitivity to gendered power interactions, however, as occurred when the therapist supported Michelle in voicing her strong emotions to Joseph when he had ignored her requests for his involvement with their children. Making space for her voice as the one-down partner is a way to counteract power imbalances (Ward and Knudson-Martin 2012).

Safe clinical context. We observe how couples engage in power processes. When one partner lets the other person carry more of the responsibility for making the relationship work, this is an indication of a power imbalance. Other indicators are who makes decisions, who prioritizes topics of conversation, and whose interests are more important (Knudson-Martin and Mahoney 2005). When gendered power imbalances are evident, the processing of emotions linked to childhood abusive experiences is best delayed until the more powerful partner has developed the capacity to sensitively support the vulnerable partner, particularly when the adult survivor is the less powerful partner. This is a valuable lesson we learned in the case of the professional couple in our opening example.

Examining the Relational Ledger

We initially assess strengths in the relationship and gauge the power processes and emotional climate between partners in order to understand how trust issues link to the couple's problems. In examining the relational ledger with Lucas and Bianca, who had both been abused as youths, they became aware of how they each engaged through their own self-abnegation or self-protective power response. Both agreed that these distrustful reactions were hurtful to the relationship, and they expressed the desire for a better approach. In order to achieve this goal, it became necessary to focus on how gendered power interactions triggered these distrustful emotional responses and derailed their connection.

Sociocultural attunement. To understand gendered power processes of the couple, we examine the impact of the societal discourses that inform each partner's identity and patterns of relating, and how acting on these discourses affects the couple's dynamics. This aspect of assessing the relational ledger helps the couple recognize the link of larger societal influences to problems in their relationship (Knudson-Martin et al. 2014). When our clients feel that we "get" and can resonate with their gendered and cultural experiences, a sense of safety supports their accountability for how they meet their relational needs (Keeling 2007; Pandit et al. in press, "SERT Therapists' Experience of Practicing Sociocultural

Attunement," 2015). For instance, as the therapist socioculturally attuned with Lucas, she felt his burden of the societal, cultural, and personal pressures that he internalized in order to be the "manliest man" struggling to prove himself in a racist work environment. The therapist then helped the couple explore how his male socialization also affected his ways of relating to Bianca. Both partners could then evaluate the gender discourses operating in their relationship and collaborate on alternate approaches (Dickerson 2013).

Shifting Gendered Power Imbalances

We strive to address power inequities between partners in such a way that both feel validated. Utilizing SERT approaches, our goal is to help adult-survivor couples experience mutuality by generating in-session moments of connection through the Circle of Care, namely shared attunement, mutual vulnerability, shared relational responsibility, and mutual influence (Knudson-Martin and Huenergardt, "Bridging Emotion, Societal Discourse, and Couple Interaction in Clinical Practice," 2015). To address the socio-emotional power processes that spurred trust challenges between Joseph and Michelle (whose alcoholic mother emotionally and physically abused her as an adolescent), we supported Joseph to become vulnerable by attuning to Michelle's needs and more responsive to the pain she felt when he dismissed her. Surprisingly, as he made her needs a greater priority, she did not know how to respond. This experience was so new that she said it felt awkward. Learning to engage with Joseph in ways beyond habitual adult-survivor power responses became a new challenge for Michelle. "It often takes time before the person in the one-down position—usually the female in heterosexual relationships—feels safe to risk the reciprocal vulnerability inherent in increased connection" (Knudson-Martin and Huenergardt 2010, p. 377).

Survivor power responses and SERT's Circle of Care. The Circle of Care can guide the disentangling of gendered power imbalances between partners from the distrustful reactions of the adult survivor. When Lucas uses a self-abnegation power response of internalized helplessness, we work with Bianca to attune to how her approach affects him and to explore alternative ways to raise issues with him beyond anger. Conversely, when Bianca draws upon a self-protective power response of control, we work with both partners to accept one another's influence so that they can develop a dialogical process of give-and-take when addressing challenging issues. When Michelle withholds sexual relations from Joseph as her adult-survivor coping strategy of marginalizing his needs, we work to increase shared relational responsibility by helping Joseph identify ways in which he can support Michelle in parenting processes. We also process how Joseph's greater involvement affects Michelle's perception of feeling that her needs matter to him and that she can trust him. In all of these instances, as the partners shift gendered power dynamics, a sense of trustworthiness can replace distrustful adult-survivor power responses.

Empowering Mutuality and Fairness

Relational skills of mutuality become evident as both partners feel safe to express their needs and each accommodates the needs of the other (Knudson-Martin and Mahoney 2005). As Lucas and Bianca advanced in their relational skills of mutuality, they remarked how they had become intentional about sharing power. If either one slipped back into gendered power behaviors, the other would call him or her on it, most often through the use of humor. They agreed that by taking a more egalitarian approach to their relationship, it was much easier to trust one another because both partners now demonstrated reliability and worked together to pursue their interests.

Final Thoughts

From our experience, we have learned that when working with adult-survivor couples, clinicians can be challenged to recognize and attend to the intermingling influences of gendered power dynamics between partners and the emotional power responses of the adult survivor evoked by power imbalances in couple interactions. Viewing gendered power imbalances in couple interactions as triggering distrustful emotional responses from the adult survivor, which is a key aspect of relational trust theory, we work to help the couple engage in the emotionally and relationally safe interactions of a trusting "we" approach. The mutuality processes in SERT's Circle of Care can provide an excellent guide for fostering relational connection. Our practices, while presented in a linear format, are not followed in step-wise fashion, but are recursive and typically involve:

- Establishing relational safety through attending to ways in which gendered power inequities can lead to emotional reactivity and other distrustful responses of the adult survivor.
- Assessing gendered power disparities in the relationship by socioculturally attuning with each partner.
- Identifying adult-survivor power responses and how they affect each partner.
- Maintaining awareness of the timing of processing vulnerable emotions with the less powerful partner until the more powerful partner can sensitively support this person.
- Making space for the voice of the less powerful partner as a way to counteract gendered power imbalances of the couple, which is especially essential when this person is the adult survivor.
- Helping the more powerful partner learn how to engage with the other partner through emotional vulnerability, attunement, and accountability.
- Facilitating in-session moments of connection in order to support the couple in transforming gendered power inequities.

From our experience, we have observed that when processes of mutuality begin to occur between partners, the distrustful emotional power responses of adult-survivor partners tend to diminish. As the burden of distrust lifts from couple interactions, both partners can benefit from their commitment to engage in more mutually supportive practices of caring connection that nurture and sustain love and trust.

References

Banyard, V. L., Williams, L. M., & Siegel, J. A. (2004). Childhood sexual abuse: A gender perspective on context and consequences. *Child Maltreatment, 9*(3), 223–238.

Blumer, M. L., Papaj, A. K., & Erolin, K. S. (2013). Feminist family therapy for treating female survivors of childhood sexual abuse. *Journal of Feminist Family Therapy, 25*(2), 65–79.

Boszormenyi-Nagy, L., & Krasner, B. R. (1986). *Between give and take: A clinical guide to contextual therapy.* New York, NY: Brunner/Mazel.

Brown, L. S. (2004). Toward a radical understanding of trauma and trauma work. *Violence Against Women, 9*, 1293–1317.

Brown, M., Banford, A., Mansfield, T., Smith, D., Whiting, J., & Ivey, D. (2012). Posttraumatic stress symptoms and perceived relationship safety as predictors of dyadic adjustment: A test of mediation and moderation. *The American Journal of Family Therapy, 40*(4), 349–362.

Dalton, E. J., Greenman, P. S., Classen, C. C., & Johnson, S. M. (2013). Nurturing connections in the aftermath of childhood trauma: A randomized controlled trial of emotionally focused therapy for female survivors of childhood abuse. *Couple and Family Psychology: Research and Practice, 2*(3), 209–221.

Dickerson, V. (2013). Patriarchy, power, and privilege: A narrative/poststructural view of work with couples. *Family Process, 52*(1), 102–114.

Fishbane, M. D. (2013). *Loving with the brain in mind: Neurobiology and couple therapy.* New York, NY: Norton.

Fishbane, M. D., & Wells, M. A. (2015). Toward relational empowerment: Interpersonal neurobiology, couples, and the societal context. In C. Knudson-Martin, M. A. Wells & S. K. Samman (Eds.), *Socio-emotional relationship therapy: Bridging emotion, societal context, and couple interaction* (pages of chapter). (pp. 27–40). New York, NY: Springer.

Gottman, J. M. (2011). *The science of trust: Emotional attunement for couples.* New York, NY: Norton.

Hare-Mustin, R. T. (1989). The problem of gender in family therapy theory. In M. McGoldrick, C. M. Anderson, & F. Walsh (Eds.), *Women in families: A framework for family therapy* (pp. 61–77). New York, NY: Norton.

Hargrave, T. D., & Pfitzer, F. (2011). *Restoration therapy: Understanding and guiding healing in marriage and family therapy.* New York, NY: Routledge.

Himelein, M. J., & McElrath, J. V. (1996). Resilient child sexual abuse survivors: Cognitive coping and illusion. *Child Abuse and Neglect, 8*, 747–758.

Keeling, M. L. (2007). A female therapist's dilemma: Alliance versus accommodation in feminist-informed couple therapy. *Journal of Feminist Family Therapy, 19*(4), 43–70.

Knudson-Martin, C. (2013). Why power matters: Creating a foundation of mutual support in couple relationships. *Family Process, 52*(1), 5–18.

Knudson-Martin, C. (2015). When therapy challenges patriarchy: Undoing gendered power in heterosexual couple relationships. In C. Knudson-Martin, M. A. Wells & S. K. Samman (Eds.), *Socio-emotional relationship therapy: Bridging emotion, societal context, and couple interaction* (pp. 15–26). New York, NY: Springer.

Knudson-Martin, C., & Huenergardt, D. (2010). A socio-emotional approach to couple therapy: Linking social context and couple interaction. *Family Process, 52*(1), 5–18.

Knudson-Martin, C., & Huenergardt, D. (2015). Bridging emotion, societal discourse, and couple interaction in clinical practice. In C. Knudson-Martin, M. A. Wells & S. K. Samman (Eds.), *Socio-emotional relationship therapy: Bridging emotion, societal context, and couple interaction* (pp. 1–13). New York, NY: Springer.

Knudson-Martin, C., Huenergardt, D., Lafontant, K., Bishop, L., Schaepper, J. & Wells, M. (2014). Competencies for addressing gender and power in couple therapy: A socio-emotional approach. *Journal of Marital and Family Therapy.* Advance online publication. doi: 10.1111/jmft.12068.

Knudson-Martin, C., & Mahoney, A. (2005). Moving beyond gender: Processes that create relationship equality. *Journal of Marital and Family Therapy, 31,* 235–246.

Krause, E. D., & Roth, S. (2011). Child sexual abuse history and feminine gender-role identity. *Sex Roles, 64,* 32–42.

Leslie, L. A., & Southard, A. L. (2009). Thirty years of feminist family therapy. In S. A. Lloyd, A. L. Few, & K. R. Allen (Eds.), *Handbook of feminist family studies* (pp. 328–339). Los Angeles, CA: Sage.

Liem, J. H., O'Toole, J. G., & James, J. B. (1992). The need for power in women who were sexually abused as children: An exploratory study. *Psychology of Women Quarterly, 16,* 467–480.

Lips, H. M. (1991). *Women, men, and power.* Mountain View, CA: Mayfield Publishing.

Lisak, D. (1995). Integrating a critique of gender in the treatment of male survivors of childhood abuse. *Psychotherapy, 32*(2), 258–269.

MacIntosh, H. B., & Johnson, S. (2008). Emotionally focused therapy for couples and childhood sexual abuse survivors. *Journal of Marital and Family Therapy, 34*(3), 298–315.

McGregor, K., Glover, M., Gautam, J., & Julich, S. (2010). Working sensitively with child abuse survivors: What female child sexual abuse survivors want from health professionals. *Women and Health, 50*(8), 737–755.

Mejia, X. E. (2005). Gender matters: Working with adult male survivors of trauma. *Journal of Counseling and Development, 83,* 29–40.

Millwood, M. (2011). Empathic understanding in couples with a female survivor of childhood sexual abuse. *Journal of Couple and Relationship Therapy, 10,* 327–344.

Nelson, B. S., & Wampler, K. S. (2002). Further understanding the systemic effects of childhood sexual abuse: A comparison of two groups of clinical couples. *Journal of Child Sexual Abuse, 11*(3), 85–106.

Orenduff, S. R. (2000). Childhood maltreatment and malevolence: Quantitative findings. *Clinical Psychology Review, 20*(8), 997–1018.

Pandit, M., ChenFeng, J. & Kang, Y. J. (in press). Becoming socio-culturally attuned: A study of therapist experience. *Contemporary Family Therapy.*

Pandit, M., ChenFeng, J. L. & Kang, Y. J. (2015). SERT therapists' experience of practicing sociocultural attunement. In C. Knudson-Martin, M. A. Wells & S. K. Samman (Eds.), *Socio-emotional relationship therapy: Bridging emotion, societal context, and couple interaction* (pp. 67–78). New York, NY: Springer.

Savla, J. T., Roberto, K. A., Jaramillo-Sierra, A. L., Gambrel, L. E., Karimi, H., & Butner, L. M. (2013). Childhood abuse affects emotional closeness with family in mid- and later life. *Child Abuse and Neglect, 37,* 388–399.

Silverstein, R., Bass, L. B., Tuttle, A. R., Knudson-Martin, C., & Huenergardt, D. (2009). Relational orientations: A contextual framework of assessment and practice. In C. Knudson-Martin & A. R. Mahoney (Eds.), *Couples, gender, and power: Creating change in intimate relationships* (pp. 297–316). New York, NY: Springer Publishing Company.

Ward, A., & Knudson-Martin, C. (2012). The impact of therapist actions on the balance of power within the couple system: A qualitative analysis of therapy sessions. *Journal of Couple and Relationship Therapy, 11*(3), 221–237.

Weiselquist, J. (2009). Interpersonal forgiveness, trust, and the investment model of commitment. *Journal of Social and Personal Relationships, 26*(4), 531–548.

Wells, M. A. (in press). Gender, power, and trust in couple therapy with survivors of childhood abuse. *Journal of Couple and Relationship Therapy.*

Relational Justice: Addressing Gender and Power in Clinical Practices for Infidelity

Kirstee Williams and Lana Kim

At its worst infidelity can paralyze couples and clinicians alike. At its best it can transform relationships. Yet, infidelity's power for transformation or dissolution rests on important factors of which gender, power, and culture are an integral part (Williams 2011). Though research has long shown that who has the affair, why an individual has an affair, and how couples respond once the secret is out are related to these important socio-contextual variables (Atkins et al. 2001; Glass 2003; Treas and Giesen 2000), they are seldom explicitly addressed in therapy sessions (Williams 2011; Williams and Knudson-Martin 2013). In this chapter, we present the research-based Relational Justice Approach to couple therapy for infidelity that we developed in response to these concerns.

Our approach to research and practice has been heavily influenced by our training and experience as members of the Socio-Emotional Relationship Therapy (SERT) research team during our doctoral studies in California. This clinical approach centralizes sociocultural attunement to gender and power (Knudson-Martin and Huenergardt 2010, "Bridging Emotion, Societal Discourse, and Couple Interaction in Clinical Practice," 2015). Kirstee is a heterosexual European American woman raised in a conservative southern town in the USA who has returned to the same community and is currently serving as Director of an MFT program with an otherwise all-male graduate faculty. Her clinical work and research focus on heterosexual and same-sex couples experiencing varying types of affairs. Lana's interest in the intersection between gender, power, and infidelity is framed by her experience as a Canadian-born Korean ethnic who has

K. Williams (✉)
Behavioral and Social Sciences Department, Lee University, Cleveland, TN, USA

L. Kim
Marriage and Family Therapy Department, Valdosta State University, Valdosta, GA, USA

© American Family Therapy Academy 2015
C. Knudson-Martin et al. (eds.), *Socio-Emotional Relationship Therapy*,
AFTA SpringerBriefs in Family Therapy, DOI 10.1007/978-3-319-13398-0_10

done extensive work with heterosexual couples wherein the wives have engaged in affairs. She currently teaches in an MFT program in the southern USA that espouses the values of diversity, inclusion, and social justice.

The purpose of this chapter is to discuss how practitioners can centralize socio-contextual issues in treating affairs. We posit that foregrounding gender and power in clinical practice for infidelity is an ethical issue that demands critical attention. We will further explore how gender and power organize infidelity, how clinicians tend to unintentionally miss these factors, and which clinical steps are necessary for incorporating gender and power into couple therapy for affairs.

Importance of Gender, Power, and Context

"I know it's me...I just know it! You can't tell me that if you were happy you would have done this to us." The heterosexual European American couple[1] sitting in front of Kirstee replays a scene we have seen over and over again. A wife who has learned about an affair is earnestly searching for something, anything that will adequately explain why her husband would prefer another woman's arms to her own. In the larger social context, it is inferred that if a man in a heterosexual relationship has an affair, something must be wrong with his partner.

The societal context also affects same-sex couples, as illustrated in the following male client's remark: "I don't know how to explain to him that I want a monogamous relationship ... he feels that I am a prude ... in the gay community we don't have much support for this kind of thing." Some have affairs when they are not able to engage more powerful partners to attend to their concerns (see Knudson-Martin, "When Therapy Challenges Patriarchy: Undoing Gendered Power in Heterosexual Couple Relationships," 2015). For example,

> I don't know what to tell you other than I was unhappy. I tried to tell my partner but she was always too busy with work. We don't have many other lesbian friends in our area and I felt really alone. Then I met Heather, and she was great! She was everything my partner didn't have time to be.

These conversations are telling; while vastly different between couples, they voice a similar tale. It is a tale about gender, a tale about power, a tale about affairs. Infidelity is gendered (Glass 2003; Williams 2011). Research has shown that women tend to link their own unfaithful behavior as stemming from relationship dissatisfaction, whereas men report their extramarital involvement as more of a desire for sexual excitement (Blow and Hartnett 2005; Glass 2003). Statistics also continue to suggest that more men than women are unfaithful (Allen and Baucom 2004; Atkins et al. 2001; Blow and Hartnett 2005).

---

[1] Case details in all clinical examples have been modified to protect client confidentiality.

Infidelity is also about power. As Scheinkman (2005) clearly articulates, until very recently patriarchy has allowed infidelity to solely be a man's privilege. In a recent study conducted in the Netherlands, data from 1,561 professionals revealed an extraordinary relationship between power and infidelity (Lammers et al. 2011). Results suggested that elevated power (i.e., measured via the individual's hierarchical position in the workplace) is positively associated with infidelity because power "increases one's sense of confidence in the ability to attract partners" (Lammers et al. 2011, p. 1191). The researchers found that as power increased, both men's and women's propensity toward infidelity also increased (Lammers et al. 2011). Power in relationships is also reflected in who notices and attends to the other (Knudson-Martin and Mahoney 2009). Historically, male partners have affairs from a position of privilege that discourages attention to other, while women may seek another partner from an invalidating, one-down position in the primary relationship.

When gender and power processes are not addressed, both partners are inadvertently blamed for equally contributing to a relational context that sets the stage for an affair (e.g., Brown 2005; Moultrup 2005; Olmstead et al. 2009). As a result, clinical work may unintentionally promote power imbalances that make it difficult to establish a foundation for mutually supportive intimate relationships (Knudson-Martin and Huenergardt 2010; Scheinkman 2005; Weingarten 1991), as well as limit a couple's ability to build emotional connection (Greenberg and Goldman 2008), which is key in couple affair recovery. Thus, we first set out to study how current therapy models address gender and power contexts in infidelity work (Williams and Knudson-Martin 2013). Our grounded theory analysis found that mostly they do not.

How Therapists Miss the Gender Context

Traditional infidelity practice tends to follow three phases: (1) crisis management and assessment, (2) working through how the affair occurred, and (3) forgiveness and moving forward (Williams 2011). While these phases are necessary steps in infidelity recovery, they tend not to incorporate gender and power processes. In fact, our research has found five conditions that limit attention to gender and power, and these occur throughout most infidelity approaches to varying degrees across clinical phases (Williams and Knudson-Martin 2013).

Speaking as Though (or Assuming) Partners are Equal

Language of presumed partner equality frequently invades couple sessions. When therapists are informed solely by traditional systemic thinking, they can inadvertently define relationship problems through a micro-lens. They may make statements that highlight what they perceive as the interrelated process that motivated the affair. For example, "It sounds like both of you may not have noticed one another's cues that something was missing from the relationship." By speaking as though partners are equal, the ways in which power processes factor into an affair are unintentionally missed (Williams and Knudson-Martin 2013). Yet, from a socio-contextual lens, a partner engaging in an affair from a one-down position may be attempting to equalize the imbalance of power, whereas a partner in the dominant power position may engage in infidelity based on feelings of entitlement (Williams and Knudson-Martin 2013). However, most approaches to infidelity tend to apply a "victim/perpetrator" lens similarly to all couples without taking into consideration how gender constructions or patterns of inequality may have influenced the decision to engage in an affair (Williams and Knudson-Martin 2013). This can unwittingly reify power differentials.

For example, in working with a heterosexual couple in which the husband has had the affair and the wife is in the one-down position, a clinician may typically suggest the following to facilitate a relational repair: "In order for your husband to connect with where you are, you have to speak up. You need to clearly let him know what it is you need, because he can't read your mind." Rather than the husband needing to learn what it means to attune and learn how to share the relationship work, this strategy implies that it is the female partner's responsibility to move the relationship forward. It allows the male partner's experience to organize the couple's healing and reinforces traditional gendered disparities.

Reframing Infidelity as a Relationship Problem

Framing infidelity as a relationship problem is one of the most common interventions utilized to address infidelity. This implies that both partners contribute equally to an affair without considering how societal gender or power processes embedded in couple dynamics may be precursors to the development of an affair (Williams and Knudson-Martin 2013). It can be problematic because it is another way in which clinicians can inadvertently invite the more relationally oriented partner, often a woman in a one-down position, to take an even greater sense of responsibility for the relationship, while the more individually focused partner defers his or her sense of accountability or relational responsibility. "It sounds like you and your partner are coming to an understanding of what was missing. It's important that you [betrayed partner] continue to remember that it takes two to tango," implying that his affair is somehow also her fault.

Limiting Discussion of Societal Context to Background

Clinical models for infidelity may incorporate diversity, culture, and religion in their initial assessment of the factors influencing infidelity. However, a discussion of these issues commonly remains in the background and is not integrated into the overall treatment plan on a session-by-session or phase-by-phase basis (Williams and Knudson-Martin 2013). For example, from a position of cultural sensitivity, clinicians may explore the cultural norms that surround the infidelity. That is, they may make the initial connection between cultural norms and affairs but fail to centralize a way of working with these contextual issues and, therefore, fail to see the ongoing ways in which gender and power are shaped by culture and are playing out in the development of the affair and therapeutic change process.

Not Considering Impact of Gender on Relationship Dynamics

Discussion of how to work with relationship dynamics in therapy for infidelity tends to favor a microsystemic lens that explores couple dynamics within the context of communication, commitment, intimacy, and connection rather than the impact of gender and power on these relationship-building processes (Williams and Knudson-Martin 2013). Failure to include the societal context in therapy can bolster the problematic effects that unexamined gender and power issues can have on couple dynamics, as illustrated throughout this volume.

Limiting Discussion of Ethics to How to Position Around Infidelity

Therapy models for infidelity tend to focus on ethical issues related to safe sex, secrecy, respecting cultural differences, boundaries, and conflicts of interest, as well as the need for therapists to examine their own personal values. However, in general, they do not raise ethical concerns regarding power and equality in the context of couples healing from affairs (Williams and Knudson-Martin 2013).

Integrating the Societal Context into Therapy

Identifying conditions that limit attention to gender and power allowed us to better integrate these socio-contexts into the development of the Relational Justice Approach (Williams 2011; Williams et al. 2013). Then, as a follow up, we conducted a task analysis to operationalize the ways in which clinicians can incorporate gender and power processes into sessions (Williams et al. 2013). We used task analysis to analyze therapist interventions and client couple interactions in order to discover how various therapeutic processes facilitate the development of mutual support for couples recovering from affairs.

The task analysis began by first identifying a sample of successful change events in which couples demonstrated mutual support in session (Williams et al. 2013). The change events were drawn from videotaped couple therapy sessions of MFT doctoral students who had received training in the socio-emotional approach (SERT; Knudson-Martin and Huenergardt 2010, "Bridging Emotion, Societal Discourse, and Couple Interaction in Clinical Practice," 2015) and were working with heterosexual couple cases dealing with "traditional" infidelity; instances in which one partner had engaged in sexual activity with someone outside the relationship. Watching the videotapes allowed us to look for moments in which we (i.e., the research team) thought the four components of mutual support called the Circle of Care in SERT (i.e., attunement, mutual influence, shared vulnerability, and shared relational responsibility) were occurring between the partners in session.

Overall, our sample consisted of 13 successful change events and seven unsuccessful change events identified from 15 tapes of couple therapy sessions involving infidelity (Williams et al. 2013). These change events were transcribed and broken into multiple sequences. Therapists contributing tapes ($N = 6$) ranged in age from 25 to 57, with a diverse range of ethnicities, including European American, East Indian, Korean, and Swedish. Five of the therapists were female and one was male; however, all of the identified change events were from sessions conducted by women. Client couples ($N = 5$) were also diverse, ranging in age from 30 to 60; married 8 to 35 years; and included European American, Latina, and Korean ethnicities. All were heterosexual and included men ($N = 4$) and one woman who had engaged in infidelity.

Our analysis of the 20 change events led us to our empirical model, which is composed of five core components (Williams et al. 2013). Two of the components—(a) attention to power dynamics and (b) attunement to gender context—provide the foundation for the three remaining components: (c) creating space for alternate gender discourses, (d) pursuing relational responsibility of the more powerful partner, and (e) deepening experience of mutual support.

Attention to Power Dynamics

Not surprisingly, a couple's ability to move toward a mutually supportive relationship appears to rest in a therapist's ability to attend to power dynamics. We see this exemplified through two important strategies: (a) strong leadership and (b) not relating to the couple from a position of assumed equality (Williams et al. 2013). In our analysis, we found that power was not determined solely by who had engaged in the affair, but also on the gendered power patterns that underlie heterosexual relationships. Using a gendered lens for understanding power processes appears central to fostering mutual support. It was also clear in our analysis that successful resolution required persistent efforts by the therapist to engage the powerful partner and support the less powerful partner. Techniques fluctuated from helping the couple stay on task to structuring the session to initially engage the powerful partner in therapy and therapist willingness to challenge power positions (Williams et al. 2013).

Therapists who attend to power dynamics avoid using language that imply equality such as "both of you," and are attentive to how gender discourses organize each person's contribution to relationship maintenance. In unsuccessful change events, therapists appeared to talk to the couple from a framework of assumed equality (Williams et al. 2013). This is most visible when the affair is discussed as resulting from relationship problems as opposed to connected to contextual issues of gender and power.

Attunement to Gender Context

A second necessary component underlying successful change is the therapist's attunement to societal and cultural expectations regarding gender (Williams et al. 2013). Key elements are: (a) voicing gendered experiences and (b) making the link between gender and power explicit. Our research found that when therapists were first able to voice an understanding of clients' unspoken gendered experiences, the couples in our sample appeared receptive to alternate gender discourses that would foster mutuality. For example, Kirstee worked with a gay couple with whom she used masculine discourses regarding the expectation that "men should be competent and know how to handle things" to contextualize their struggle and open space for alternate possibilities: "When your partner is angry about what happened around the affair, you don't know how to fix it... and this seems to stir feelings of inadequacy in you?"

Creating Space for Alternate Gender Discourses

We found that change events that successfully fostered mutuality did not simply identify the presence of stereotypic gender patterns, but instead created space for alternate gender discourses by highlighting and privileging new ways of being in a relationship beyond scripted gender training (Williams et al. 2013). Therapists do this by attuning to the female partner's sense of reality and facilitating the male partner's attunement toward her experience as well. Supporting the powerful partner to move toward vulnerability is also a necessary step in this process.

We have found a growing trend in our work with heterosexual women who have been unfaithful. Though research suggests that women report relationship dissatisfaction as a primary motivator for an affair, sometimes it is more complex. For example, Lana worked with a case in which the couple had presented for therapy due to the wife's affair with her work supervisor. Unsurprisingly, she expressed an overwhelming sense of shame and remorse for her behavior. She concluded that she must have a character flaw and reasoned that only someone with serious problems could step outside of a relationship when they had a "good" man. Her partner agreed as he offered numerous examples of the ways in which he had continuously sought to meet her needs, which included sharing in the household labor, taking active part with childcare, arranging leisure activities, etc. It was clear that this meant to the couple that they shared contemporary gender role ideals and believed their relationship to be one of equals.

At first glance, it was easy to join with the couple's conceptualization of what was taking place and assume that they shared the relationship work. However, upon further exploration, it became apparent that while he made sincere efforts to fulfill his spousal role and provide tangible support, unbeknownst to him he remained fairly disconnected from her emotional experience. Conversely, she monitored his day-to-day moods, especially noticing times that he seemed stressed, tense, or irritable. On these occasions, she would take extra care to gingerly step around him. Yet, this was not overtly stated. It became more evident that the egalitarian ideals the couple seemingly espoused were actually imbalanced when the couple started to equate having a "good marriage" to one in which there was no interpersonal conflict and the wife took extra care not to distress him.

In this relationship, masculine and feminine gendered discourses existed in binary fashion and intersected in ways that limited the full spectrum of gender role enactments. From a feminine discourse perspective, the female partner tried not to burden her husband with her day-to-day emotional stress, and masculine discourses also reinforced this self-reliant orientation. Through the lens of patriarchy, we see that society tends to privilege masculine definitions of individual strength by placing autonomy and independence at the helm. This inherently suggests that across genders, rationality, self-support, and invulnerability are the markers of self-agency and individual success (Loscocco and Walzer 2013). Consequently, both women and men aspire for self-reliance and regard this as the elusive gold standard. However, latent societal pressure to demonstrate that one is unaffected or able to endure struggles without overtly needing emotional support hinders a couple's chances for deepening emotional intimacy and engaging mutually in the Circle of Care (Huenergardt and Knudson-Martin 2009; Knudson-Martin and Huenergardt, "Bridging Emotion, Societal Discourse, and Couple Interaction in Clinical Practice," 2015).

Women like the one in the case above may report that they are coupled with "good" men who "try" hard in the relationship. The fact that they are unfaithful is unsettling for both partners because they assume that the relationship itself is fine. From a feminine discourse perspective, women perceive that a "good" man is one who is willing to break traditional gender stereotypes and play a more active role in household and childcare-related tasks. They automatically assume that this bending of traditional gender roles is an indication that their relationship is equal. Consequently, women in these relationships interpret tangible support from their partners as emotional connection and do not express additional expectations for deeper levels of emotional intimacy. Thus, it is important for the therapist to look beyond the couple's generalized statements about egalitarian ideals and explore their gendered expectations that organize beliefs about men's ability for emotional caretaking as well as the idea that individual success is defined as appearing invulnerable and a "rational" rather than relational orientation.

When therapists try to help offset the constraints imposed by sociocultural gendered discourses and open space for alternative experiences of mutual vulnerability in session, it is important to avoid thinking in terms of the gender binary, but rather to think of gender as a fluid continuum. Also, therapists need to actively focus on emotional experience and legitimize the idea that both partners have a desire for emotional connection and human capacity for emotional caregiving. Therapists can then begin to deconstruct and name the ways in which societal gendered discourses limit mutual vulnerability.

Because there is a strong societal pressure for men to be invulnerable and for women to want "tough" men, demonstrations of male vulnerability in the therapeutic process can prompt a female partner to protect or interrupt him. Therapists will need to hold the space for this by overtly framing the male partner's vulnerability as a valuable relational action and, if need be, help the female partner be more patient with his taking on more emotional work and seeking to build relational connection. We have found that when men begin to see how meaningful these new ways of being in relationship are for their partner, it is tremendously affirming for them.

Techniques in the task analysis found to help facilitate male partner attunement and vulnerability include: asking him to inquire about his partner's experience, directly asking about his strategies for limiting vulnerability, naming the discourses that limit vulnerability for both partners, asking about strategies for maintaining vulnerable engagement, and asking him to give voice to vulnerable emotions (Williams et al. 2013).

Pursuing Relational Responsibility of Powerful Partner

In our study, balancing relational responsibility seemed to be accomplished through direct experiential work that motivated the powerful partner to assume more of the emotional caretaking (Williams et al. 2013). Therapist actions, such as structured enactments focusing on relational responsibility, appeared to create space for the powerful partner to develop a relational vision, as well as not reinforce the less powerful partner carrying responsibility for the relationship alone.

One example of working with invisible power and creating shifts in relational responsibility is illustrated in Kirstee's work with a heterosexual couple in which the husband had the affair. This was a conservative Christian couple, married 30 years, both in their fifties. They subscribed to traditional gender roles that were organized by their religious belief system. The husband, although humiliated, distraught, and sincerely repentant, struggled to engage in meaningful conversations with his wife around the affair. This was problematic because, even though the husband had the affair, the wife would plead with him to engage with her, a clear function of his power position. Kirstee quickly realized that the only way to impact his willingness to be more vulnerable and engage with her was to draw out his sense of responsibility for his wife's healing. Only then was he willing to engage. Enactments became critical for structured conversations in which he was supported in the moment-by-moment relational repair. His emotional presence was fueled by Kirstee's strong affirmation of his ability and intention to help his wife. Over time he began to do the relational work on his own to the surprise and delight of his wife.

Power dynamics are more easily spotted in traditional couples but more difficult to discern when invisible power, power that is latent in societal norms and expectations, is at play (see Knudson-Martin, "When Therapy Challenges Patriarchy: Undoing Gendered Power in Heterosexual Couple Relationships," 2015). For instance in the couple that Lana worked with above, in which both partners challenged many aspects of traditional gender roles, invisible power kept the female partner focused on emotionally attending to her husband's moods and making self-sacrificing accommodations based upon it. When this was enacted in session, Lana overtly focused the couple's attention to what was happening in the moment to help them begin to notice and attend to a relational dynamic that felt so natural, but was constraining their movement toward mutuality.

When the male partner realized how his moods would shut his partner down and motivate her to keep her experience hidden from him, he expressed sadness. He wondered how he could not have known he was having this effect on her and wished that he had. Lana then named the context around his sadness, the sense that he was so peripheral to her experience. He agreed and said that he wanted to be closer to her. Lana also commented on the loneliness that that must have created for both of them, then asked the partners to envision what they hoped could be different. She wondered aloud, so both could hear, that as he learned to notice how he shaped his partner's experience, if it would also be important for her to not minimize her feelings, but to let him know directly when he was not meeting her needs. Lana noticed that in subsequent sessions he was becoming more self-reflective and relationally aware by recognizing how he was shaping the emotional safety in sessions. For example, when he noticed his wife becoming silent in session he would stop and check in with her by asking, "You look bothered by what I said; I must not have gotten something right."

New Experience of Mutual Support

Focusing on the process of mutual support and validating each partner's contribution were keys in the task analysis. These tasks were accomplished through interventions such as naming the processes that facilitate mutual support, facilitating mutual engagement through enactment, and asking about new emotional experiences of mutual support (Williams et al. 2013). Our analysis revealed that these strategies seemed to help the couple build awareness of the behavioral and experiential elements of mutual support. It was also clear that validation of the couple's progress toward mutual support was important, along with continued awareness of how power differences had previously limited their mutuality.

For couples in our study who were able to achieve a state of mutual support, we observed an increased ability to engage in sharing previously unvoiced experiences of one another (Williams et al. 2013). This ranged from expressing emotional pain connected to the affair to expressing a sense of feeling heard and understood by the other. Body language also indicated engagement and connection as they were turned toward one another, participating actively in conversation, maintaining eye contact, and touching each other. We noticed that across successful change events client couples appeared to adopt relational processes that included vulnerability, attunement, and relational responsibility, particularly and notably with the powerful partner first, which then resulted in the less powerful partner reciprocating.

Putting It All Together

It is critical to remember that engaging in an affair is not indicative of residing in the power position prior to the affair. This challenges the common misconception and frequently debated issue of whether and if the partner who engaged in the affair is always in a position of power, particularly when the woman has had the affair. We have found that an affair can be a way to gain power as well as an enactment of it. In order for therapy to be successful, it is critical for therapists to be able to recognize the ways in which power is distributed in the relationship regardless of who has been unfaithful, and connect how gender discourses relate to these power dynamics.

The following steps can be a useful guide for approaching this work. First, rather than simply assuming that shared relational distress is the problem, attention to working with power imbalances of the relationship throughout the clinical processes is critical. Secondly, understanding the link between power and infidelity can be complex and will be overlooked altogether if therapists assume couples are equal. Third, linking the societal context (i.e., gender and cultural discourses) to power patterns is an essential step in working with couples in session. These conceptual linkages create scaffolding for a therapeutic process that helps couples reorganize imbalances that limit mutuality and relational options. For additional information on how to apply the Relational Justice Approach, see Williams (2011) and Williams et al. (2013).

References

Allen, E. S., & Baucom, D. H. (2004). Adult attachment patterns of extradyadic involvement. *Family Process, 43*(4), 467–488. doi:10.1111/j.1545-5300.2004.00035.x.

Atkins, D. C., Baucom, D. H., & Jacobson, N. S. (2001). Understanding infidelity: Correlates in a national random sample. *Journal of Family Psychology, 15*, 735–749. doi:10.1037/0893-3200.15.4.735.

Blow, A., & Hartnett, K. (2005). Infidelity in committed relationships II: A substantive review. *Journal of Marital and Family Therapy, 31*, 217–233. doi:10.1111/j.1752-0606.2005.tb01556.x.

Brown, E. M. (2005). Split self affairs and their treatment. *Journal of Couple & Relationship Therapy: Innovations in Clinical and Educational Interventions, 4*, 55–69. doi:10.1300/J398v04n02_06.

Glass, S. P. (2003). *Not just friends: Rebuilding trust and recovering your sanity after infidelity.* New York, NY: Free Press.

Greenberg, L. S., & Goldman, R. N. (2008). *Emotion-focused couples therapy: The dynamics of emotion, love, and power.* Washington, DC: American Psychological Association.

Huenergardt, D., & Knudson-Martin, C. (2009). Gender and power as a fulcrum for clinical change. In C. Knudson-Martin & A. Mahoney (Eds.), *Couples, gender, and power: Creating change in intimate relationships* (pp. 337–361). New York, NY: Springer Publishing Company.

Knudson-Martin, C. (2015). When therapy challenges patriarchy: Undoing gendered power in heterosexual couple relationships. In C. Knudson-Martin, M. A. Wells, & S. K. Samman (Eds.), *Socio-emotional relationship therapy: Bridging emotion, societal context, and couple interaction.* (pp. 15–26). New York, NY: Springer.

Knudson-Martin, C., & Huenergardt, D. (2010). A socio-emotional approach to couples therapy: Linking social context and couple interactions. *Family Process, 49*(3), 369–384. doi:10.1111/j.1545-5300.2010.01328.x.

Knudson-Martin, C., & Huenergardt, D. (2015). Bridging emotion, societal discourse, and couple interaction in clinical practice. In C. Knudson-Martin, M. A. Wells, & S. K. Samman (Eds.), *Socio-emotional relationship therapy: Bridging emotion, societal context, and couple interaction.* (pp. 1–13). New York, NY: Springer.

Knudson-Martin, C., & Mahoney, A. R. (Eds.). (2009). *Couples, gender, and power: Creating change in intimate relationships.* New York, NY: Springer Publishing Company.

Lammers, J., Stoker, J. I., Jordan, J., Pollmann, M., & Stapel, D. A. (2011). Power increases infidelity among men and women. *Psychological Science, 22*(9), 1191–1197. doi:10.1177/0956797611416252.

Loscocco, K., & Walzer, S. (2013). Gender and the culture of heterosexual marriage in the United States. *Journal of Family Theory & Review, 5,* 1–14. doi:10.1111/jftr.12003.

Moultrup, D. (2005). Undercurrents. *Journal of Couple & Relationship Therapy: Innovations in Clinical and Educational Interventions, 4,* 31–40. doi:10.1300/J398v04n02_04.

Olmstead, S. B., Blickup, R. W., & Mills, L. I. (2009). Helping couples work toward the forgiveness of marital infidelity: Therapists' perspectives. *The American Journal of Family Therapy, 37*(1), 48–66. doi:10.1080/01926180801960575.

Scheinkman, M. (2005). Beyond the trauma of betrayal: Reconsidering affairs in couples therapy. *Family Process, 44*(2), 227–244. doi:10.1111/j.1545-5300.2005.00056.x.

Treas, J., & Giesen, D. (2000). Sexual infidelity among married and cohabiting Americans. *Journal of Marriage and Family, 62*(1), 48–60. doi:10.2307/1566686.

Weingarten, K. (1991). The discourse of intimacy: Adding a social constructionist and feminist view. *Family Process, 30,* 285–306. doi:10.1111/j.1545-5300.1991.00285.x.

Williams, K. (2011). A socio-emotional relational framework for infidelity: The relational justice approach. *Family Process, 50*(4), 516–528. doi:10.1111/j.1545-5300.2011.01374.x.

Williams, K., Galick, A., Knudson-Martin, C., & Huenergardt, D. (2013). Toward mutual support: A task analysis of the relational justice approach to infidelity. *Journal of Marital and Family Therapy, 39*(3), 285–298. doi:10.1111/j.1752-0606.2012.00324.x.

Williams, K., & Knudson-Martin, C. (2013). Do therapists address gender and power in infidelity? A feminist analysis of the treatment literature. *Journal of Marital and Family Therapy, 39*(3), 271–284. doi:10.1111/j.1752-0606.2012.00303.x.

Relational Spirituality, Gender, and Power: Applications to Couple Therapy

Elisabeth Esmiol Wilson

A growing body of research links relational spirituality to health and well-being (Peterman et al. 2002). Additionally, recent studies cite relational spirituality as an important aspect of healthy couple relationships (Esmiol et al. 2014; Mahoney 2010; Mahoney et al. 2009; Sandage and Williamson 2010). Interestingly, a relational spirituality seems to draw on some of the same relational competencies promoted by relational feminism (Esmiol Wilson et al. 2014; Knudson-Martin et al. 2014). My interest in spirituality and feminism began early: I was raised in Hawaii by a single European American mother in a predominantly Asian community with a rich native Hawaiian heritage. Spirituality has long been an important part of my life, evolving over time with experience in different spiritual contexts. Training in Socio-Emotional Relationship Therapy (SERT) helped me see that gendered power between couples can surface in spiritual styles. Drawing on recent research as well as examples from my own clinical practice and supervision of clinicians in training, this chapter explores the connection between gendered power and relational spirituality and the clinical implications of a relationship-friendly spirituality on couple relationships.

Intersection of Gendered Power and Relational Spirituality

A relational feminist perspective is grounded in the practice of *mutuality* between partners (Fishbane 2011; Jordan 2009). Mutuality involves power sharing and egalitarian ideas demonstrated through reciprocal interactions. According to SERT, four key practices referred to as the Circle of Care are necessary for mutuality: (1) shared

E.E. Wilson (✉)
Department of Marriage and Family Therapy, Pacific Lutheran University,
Tacoma, WA, USA

© American Family Therapy Academy 2015
C. Knudson-Martin et al. (eds.), *Socio-Emotional Relationship Therapy*,
AFTA SpringerBriefs in Family Therapy, DOI 10.1007/978-3-319-13398-0_11

vulnerability, (2) mutual attunement, (3) shared relational responsibility, and (4) mutual influence (Esmiol Wilson et al. 2014; Knudson-Martin and Huenergardt 2010, "Bridging Emotion, Societal Discourse, and Couple Interaction in Clinical Practice," 2015). The practice of relational spirituality also involves mutuality—between the Divine and human (Idel 1990; Ladinsky 2006). While different religious beliefs and traditions uniquely contextualize how people connect with God, relational spirituality transcends religious lines even while being more in alignment with some religious contexts than others. From Christian and New Age spirituality to the mysticism of Jewish Kabbalah and Islamic Sufism, relational spiritual practices share a focus on intimate union with a relational God (Bagasra 2004; Idel 1990; Lahood 2010; Sandage Hill and Vaubel 2011). What is of interest here is how relational spirituality impacts gendered power in couple relationships.

A Relationship-Friendly Spirituality

Gender and power dynamics influence all aspects of our lives from our spirituality to our human relationships (Fishbane 2011; Mahoney 2010). In the context of two genders, some couples share relational power and connect in non-gendered, mutually reciprocal interactions, while others seem unable to reach these ideals (Jonathan and Knudson-Martin 2012; Knudson-Martin and Mahoney 2009b). This gap between belief and action occurs when some couples talk about ideals of relationship equality yet deny the influence of gender and power on their actions and decision-making (Knudson-Martin and Mahoney 2009a).

Relational patterns with the Divine can mirror relational patterns with one's partner (Esmiol Wilson et al. 2014; McDonald et al. 2005). Couples practicing mutuality versus those struggling to practice mutuality seem to engage with both God and each other in (1) more intimate versus obligation-based relational patterns and (2) more mutually reciprocal versus non-reciprocal directions of dialogue (Esmiol Wilson et al. 2014). Thus, some forms of spirituality are more relationship-friendly than others. In the examples that follow, I illustrate how the obligation-based, non-reciprocal dialogue relationship patterns demonstrated by Rachel and Tom limit their mutuality and contrast this with Lisa and David, whose intimate and reciprocal patterns promote each aspect of the Circle of Care (Fig. 1).[1]

Obligation-Based and Non-reciprocal Dialogue

Rachel and Tom came to counseling seeking premarital therapy. Their obligation-based interactions focused on duty to God and each other, demonstrating a lack of mutuality, while their non-reciprocal dialogue privileged the male perspective and revealed a gendered power disparity. A European American couple in their early

---

[1] All names and identifying information have been changed to protect confidentiality.

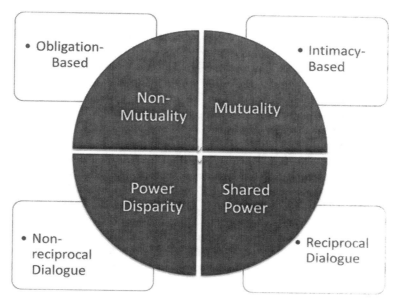

Fig. 1 Spiritual and couple relational patterns

thirties with no children and no prior marriages, both expressed a deep faith in God and were active members of their local Seventh-day Adventist (SDA) church. While not SDA myself, the couple was referred to me due to my background studying Christian spirituality, which they stated was a significant reason in their seeing me as a clinician.

Spiritual patterns. For Tom "going to church every Sabbath shows God that I'm doing what God expects of me." Such statements seemed more focused on a dutiful obligation to the Divine. Rachel described a spiritual relationship based more on intimacy and connection, yet she seemed vulnerable to Tom's influence and prone to silencing her voice in favor of his obligatory way of practicing spirituality.

> I know I should, but I don't read my Bible every day like Tom. I feel close to God in my everyday life, like at random times driving my car and a song comes on that speaks to me, but I should read scripture more.

Rachel's dialogue with God tended to be marked by moments of intimacy followed by minimizing and silencing the significance of her own experiences. Tom's dialogue with God included "listening to God's voice in scripture," feeling guilty, and then "confessing my sin and asking for forgiveness." The dialogue seemed one-sided with Tom's view directing how "best" to converse with God.

Similar couple patterns. The couple demonstrated similar patterns in their relationship with each other. Tom shared: "I end dates early if I feel we're being sexually tempted" and "I tell Rachel her clothes and posture lead to more temptation and frustration." Notice the one-sided, non-power-sharing direction of communication from Tom to Rachel in these statements. Tom seemed to direct their dialogue about sexual purity, making decisions about when and how to spend time together, instead of engaging in mutual dialogue about their shared relational and spiritual struggles to stay sexually "pure." This one-sided pattern of communication, with Tom holding more power than Rachel, was similar to the non-reciprocal communication Tom experienced in his spiritual life with God. Rachel felt Tom silencing her and struggled to tell him, "I just want sometimes to be able to sit together and hold hands and tell each other 'I love you' without feeling guilty about it becoming a sexual purity thing."

Non-mutuality in the Circle of Care. Couple relational patterns impact every aspect of the Circle of Care, in this case limiting Rachel and Tom's practice of mutuality. Both Rachel and Tom struggled with *shared vulnerability*, though in different ways. Rachel invalidated her expressions of vulnerability with God and with Tom, while Tom avoided his vulnerable feelings through rigid patterns of spiritual practice. For example, he prayed, "God, I'm sorry, I need to pray and confess more," instead of more openly admitting "God, I love Rachel and sometimes my body responds so strongly I don't know what to do." Preoccupied with his guilt and shame, he struggled to feel *mutually attuned* to God or to Rachel's love and forgiveness. Rachel seemed more able to feel God's love for her and similarly seemed able to attune to Tom's feelings of shame, although she was unsure how to help him. Tom's difficulty attuning to Rachel was a source of pain, highlighting their gendered-power imbalance (see Knudson-Martin, "When Therapy Challenges Patriarchy: Undoing Gendered Power in Heterosexual Couple Relationships," 2015). They lacked *shared relational responsibility*, as Rachel carried the burden of noticing their lack of connection and the negative impact on their relationship. Yet she had little room to voice her concerns and even less ability to influence Tom. He held much more power in their relationship, influencing Rachel's view of herself and their relationship, as well as her relationship with God. Similarly neither experienced *mutual influence* with God, as both felt somewhat powerless and more prone to accepting spiritual blame than proactively asking God for help.

Intimacy-Based and Reciprocal Dialogue

In contrast, Lisa and David demonstrated more relationally mutual patterns of interaction. Their intimacy-based interactions focused on connection with God and each other, demonstrating relational mutuality, while their reciprocal dialogue made space for mutual understanding and revealed a sharing of power. They were a recently married Hispanic couple in their early forties, with one child between them and two children each from former marriages. The couple came to counseling to find better ways of coping with increasing stress due to conflicts with David's teenage son and Lisa's ex-husband. Having a clinician who respected and could integrate their Catholicism into therapy was important to both of them and especially to Lisa.

Spiritual patterns. While expressed differently, both Lisa and David described an intimate spiritual connection with God marked by different degrees of reciprocal dialogue. When asked how she experienced God, Lisa shared, "I talk to God all the time, out loud, in my head, when cleaning the house, it doesn't matter. He's always listening and sometimes talking back, reminding me he's got my back." Lisa experienced deeply intimate, reciprocal dialogues with God, while David's relational spirituality was harder to assess. I was careful to distinguish between David's more private expressions of faith (e.g., "I don't talk about it much, not like Lisa") and his less verbally developed relational connection with God (e.g., "God's always there; I don't need to say much"). Lisa's experiences of reciprocal communication with God and David's experiences of implicit, mutual understanding seemed similar to their couple relational patterns.

Similar couple patterns. Lisa constantly talked in therapy, openly sharing her feelings with David, yet added, "Sometimes I just don't know what he's thinking or feeling." David seemed open to hearing Lisa and enjoyed her sharing, yet often felt he did not have much to add. When I invited David to process, he could express feeling a secure connection with Lisa as partners, lovers, and parents. My concern was supporting David in formulating his words, even if in a simple statement of "I hear you and agree." This meant Lisa might also need to leave more space for David to find his words. Despite these needed changes in their communication, their couple relational pattern, like their spirituality, seemed based on an intimate connection.

Mutuality in the Circle of Care. Lisa easily and openly expressed *shared vulnerability* with God and with David. With encouragement, David expressed more vulnerable feelings of concern for his teenage son and sadness around Lisa's stress. I wondered how a spiritual practice of sharing his vulnerable feelings with God might impact David's ability to share with Lisa. The couple also experienced *mutual attunement,* though David seemed more able to feel what Lisa was feeling. She needed to remind herself to "slow down and listen, because that's when I start realizing what he's thinking and feeling." Her experience with God was similar as Lisa predominantly talked in prayer, yet spent less time attuning to God. Together they *shared relational responsibility* for their couple needs. David said, "I want to be able to say 'we need to talk,' even if it's hard sometimes for me." And as Lisa reciprocated by giving David "space and time" to share, his ability to share facilitated their mutual attunement. Lisa and David also shared, "We've seen God answer prayer and seen Him act in our life," demonstrating *mutual influence* on a spiritual level. They also took turns influencing each other, such as David responding to her requests for more emotional conversations despite the challenge of verbalizing his feelings.

Relational Spirituality and the Implications for Clinical Practice

As we begin to see how specific spiritual practices and ways of interacting with God directly intersect couples' attempts at mutuality (Mahoney 2010; Sandage and Williamson 2010), the importance of attending to relational spirituality in clinical practice becomes apparent. Clinicians are increasingly open to and even recommend incorporating spirituality in couple therapy (Carlson et al. 2002; Richards and Bergin 2005). Attending to relational spirituality has particular relevance for supporting couples struggling to live out relationally mutual patterns of interaction. The following clinical recommendations outline how to address these dynamics at both the divine and human levels. Additionally, each is illustrated with a brief clinical example and linked to the SERT competencies outlined in the chapter "Bridging Emotion, Societal Discourse, and Couple Interaction in Clinical Practice" (Knudson-Martin and Huenergardt 2015; Knudson-Martin et al. 2014).

Identify Enactments of Cultural Discourses: SERT Competency 1

In my own clinical practice and supervision of clinicians in training, *identifying enactments of cultural discourses* includes assessing religious and spiritual messages and listening specifically for relational spirituality dynamics. While lack of familiarity or comfort with various spiritual practices may lead some clinicians to shy away from addressing spiritual issues (Walsh 2008), spirituality is an important cultural and relational issue. Specifically, I encourage clinicians in training to reflect on similarities between addressing couple relational interactions and the divine–human interactions in relational spirituality. It is helpful to specifically listen for (1) more intimate versus duty-bound, obligation-based relational patterns and (2) more mutually reciprocal versus hierarchical, non-reciprocal directions of dialogue (Esmiol Wilson et al. 2014).

When working with Michelle and Jill, a Latina and European American lesbian couple in their mid-30s, assessing spiritual relational patterns involved acknowledging their spiritual hurts. Specifically, I helped the couple differentiate painful experiences in leaving their Evangelical community from their fledging attempts at connecting with God in new spiritual contexts. Larger cultural discourses around spirituality and sexuality were incorporated into therapy as both women explored how these messages impacted their faith practices and their couple relationship. Expanding conversations to include how couples think about God, what they talk to God about, and how they experience themselves with God are all important in understanding the larger sociocultural context.

Attune to Underlying Sociocultural Emotion: SERT Competency 2

As clinicians assess spiritual contexts, they need to understand that changing couple relational patterns can actually alter how couples interact with God (Cattich and Knudson-Martin 2009). Clinicians can also guide couples to see how these larger spiritual discourses can influence their couple relationship. Seeing the intersection between their spiritual experience and their couple relationship occurs as clients begin to *attune to underlying sociocultural emotion*. For example, only when Tom began to hear the pain behind Rachel's desire for more intimacy was he able to connect the effect of his shame-based, spiritual obligations with Rachel's distress. A possible question to help explore this intersection is, "How does your sense of 'how God views you' impact your couple relationship?" Tom's answer became, "I can see that my guilt and struggle to accept God's love, and even the fact that He made my sexuality, makes Rachel feel like I push her away from me and hurts our relationship." Attuning to the emotional aspect of spiritual experiences helps make the influence of the larger context visible in their everyday couple interactions.

Identify Relational Power Dynamics: SERT Competency 3

Research supports the need for clinicians to *identify relational power dynamics* and help couples become aware of discrepancies in their struggle to practice mutuality (e.g., Fishbane 2011; Knudson-Martin and Huenergardt 2010; Williams et al. 2012). While this intervention often feels more confrontational, helping couples see their power imbalances and the lack of reciprocity in both spiritual and couple interactions is key to changing patterns. With Genelia and James, an East Indian Catholic couple grieving multiple miscarriages, I began by exploring the complex power dynamics around gender and spirituality.

James came into therapy saying, "We believe miscarried babies are in Heaven, so there's no need to keep grieving, and besides we have one healthy child. But my wife is having trouble moving on with the life God's given us." Genelia seemed silenced and even reprimanded by her "more holy" husband, withdrawing further from him and increasing his frustration that she was not able to "trust God." I made their power structure visible by highlighting their pattern.

> James, it seems like your faith in God helps you with the loss of your babies. Yet when you try to use God to comfort Genelia, she feels like you're saying she's not a "good Catholic" and shouldn't share her hurt with you. It seems like you're using your faith to put her down, even if this isn't at all what you want. Then you feel her pulling away instead of you being able to comfort her and feel close to her like you want to.

In identifying the couple's relational power dynamics, I highlighted that James's use of spiritual power over Genelia may not be intentional but nevertheless hurts her and silences her. I was also careful to frame their power dynamics in terms of their relational goals: James wants to "comfort her" and "feel close to her" and she wants to "share her hurt" with him. By recognizing James' relational desires to comfort his wife, I set the stage to help James, the more powerful partner, move toward vulnerability and the next SERT competency.

Facilitate Relational Safety: SERT Competency 4

Once couples see their power discrepancies, I *facilitate relational safety* by supporting the less powerful partner's voice and encouraging vulnerability from the more powerful partner. Intervening according to discrepancies in gendered power is essential, regardless of which partner the couple views as more spiritual. In certain spiritual contexts, faithfully pursuing the Divine and being perceived as "close to God" may lead to a privileged role (Ladinsky 2006; Lahood 2010). However, for couples struggling to practice relational mutuality, being male seems to carry an even stronger level of privilege and power than being spiritual.

Adam and Sarah, a European American Mormon couple in their early thirties with five children, both considered Adam more spiritual. In contrast, Youssef and Shereen, a Sunni Muslim couple in their mid-thirties with one child, both considered Shereen more spiritual. Yet for both couples, male privilege seems to disempower the wives. While addressing parenting issues in couple therapy, Adam used phrases such as "God revealed to me" and "as the spiritual leader of the home" to dismiss Sarah's views. Youssef similarly dismissed Shereen's belief that "Allah has a plan for us," calling her "naive" during therapy sessions addressing their financial crisis. Regardless of which partner has more spiritual status, I facilitate relational safety by first encouraging vulnerability in the partner with more gendered power.

As Adam described his experience of parenting with Sarah, I helped him move from criticism to vulnerability saying, "I imagine it's almost a powerless feeling not being able to work together no matter how hard you try." Adam's ability to show Sarah his feelings of powerlessness and even loss around wanting a closer parenting relationship helped him shift from the spiritual expert discrediting her views to a partner open to new ways of parenting together. To similarly access Youssef's vulnerable emotions, I asked him, "What is it like seeing how close Shereen is to Allah?" I searched for the vulnerability behind his dismissive comments, stating, "I wonder if you ever feel on the outside, separate from her special bond with Allah?" Gradually, Youssef identified feeling isolated from an important part of Shereen's life that he did not understand and feeling fear of her trying to assert power over him. I then supported Shereen in voicing her desire to "face this financial mess together," stressing her desire for power with him, rather than power over him (Fishbane 2011).

Foster Mutual Attunement: SERT Competency 5

The benefits of egalitarian power dynamics (e.g., Day and Acock 2013; Fishbane 2011; Knudson-Martin 2013) strongly support the need for clinicians to facilitate mutually supportive relationships. The task in helping couples aspiring to a relationship-friendly spirituality involves fostering the Circle of Care in both their spiritual and couple relationships. This proves challenging, however, when stark power differences exist, for example, as occurred between Genelia and James, the second-generation East Indian Catholic couple. They described holding egalitarian ideals, yet at the start of therapy, James appeared to hold more spiritual power as the "holy one" and he had difficulty being vulnerable and attuning to Genelia's grief. Yet helping them *foster mutual attunement* allowed this couple to experience exceptions to their traditional gendered stereotypes and see how mutuality actually benefited them.

James had difficulty both sharing his own feelings and being able to feel Genelia's deep loss around their multiple miscarriages. He was also unable to see the impact of his spirituality on Genelia, who seemed more shamed into silence, believing "I'm not being faithful enough, I suppose." James's inability to experience mutuality with God, and to sense God's sadness with them in their loss, only compounded Genelia's grief. To help James attune to his wife, I helped him identify with her pain (SERT Competency 3) and then fostered his attunement to her (SERT Competency 4) through encouraging him to initiate dialogue and understanding. He learned to ask her, "Can you tell me more?" and emotionally identify with her many-layered losses associated with unmet hopes and longings, changes in gendered and cultural identity, and the hardship of physically bearing and losing each baby.

Create a Relationship Model Based on Equality: SERT Competency 6

As therapists modeling mutuality to our clients, our clinical work needs to include both their couple and spiritual experiences. I do not shy away from helping clients engage in more relational spiritual practices, yet I maintain a respectful and collaborative approach, following clients' lead as spiritual "experts" in their own lives. For Lisa and David, the Latin American couple in their early forties, one therapeutic goal was helping David verbalize his private and vulnerable emotions with Lisa. Through in-session enactments, I asked Lisa to sit quietly, validating David's desire to share and encouraging him to focus on his emotions and tell Lisa what he was experiencing. However, I also invited David to notice similar patterns in his relationship with God. I suggested that David experiment with spiritual practices of mutuality, such as focusing on his emotions and sharing these with God to foster a more vulnerable connection with God.

Research indicates that increased mutuality with God positively impacts relational spirituality as much as a lack of mutuality negatively impacts relationship with God (Gardner et al. 2008). Using relational spiritual practices identified by clients and consistent with their faith traditions is critical. David shared his assumption that "God already knows what I'm feeling," while acknowledging "I guess I feel kind of closer to God when I share my feelings with God in these new ways." With Lisa, I asked her to identify spiritual exercises which helped her slow down and listen to God, similar to her goal of listening to David. These parallel couple and spiritual experiences helped both Lisa and David embrace the positive aspects of increased mutuality, not only with each other but also with God. As they engaged more consistently in spiritual relational practices, they were able to *create a relationship model based on equality* that included both their couple and spiritual relationships.

Facilitate Shared Relational Responsibility: SERT Competency 7

Solidifying a relationship model based on equality requires that couples share responsibility for the well-being of their relationship with God and each other. I intentionally highlight the moments of mutuality. For example, with the East Indian Catholic couple I stated, "James, I see when you talk about all the different parts of Genelia's loss, you begin to share what's been hard for you too." As he began to express shared vulnerability, I also asked questions to deepen his relational responsibility, such as "How do you think it impacts her when you share some of the reasons why her loss is so big and hurts so much?" In these moments, James began to recognize the impact of his actions on Genelia stating, "When I share my hurts she doesn't feel so alone, and realizes I hurt too" and "I think talking about her hurt feels like I understand her and she's not crazy for still being so sad." I purposely focused on working with James first, identifying him as the partner holding more power and therefore the one to take the first steps toward *facilitating shared relational responsibility*. As James realized he was equally responsible for dealing with the relational impact of their miscarriages on their marriage, he was able to better attend to Genelia's well-being and I began to see more evidence of the Circle of Care between them. I similarly invited both Genelia and James to examine how taking responsibility for mutually engaging with God, such as being vulnerable about their loss in prayer, positively impacted their connection with God. James shared, "Its hard feeling the hurt but when I take the initiative and pray about it, I feel God's closeness in a new way."

Final Thoughts: Modeling Mutuality

Attending to the nuances of gender, power, and spirituality in couple dynamics poses many challenges. Gender and power issues are deeply embedded in the larger societal context and easy for clinicians to overlook, while spirituality sometimes has therapists feeling out of our depths of clinical training (Walsh 2008). Simply navigating the complex and multilayered issues inherent in the intersection of all these dynamics can be daunting. I often remind myself and my supervisees that even when we are not sure of where these intersections will lead us or what mistakes we may make along the way, ignoring these issues would be a greater disservice to our clients. Part of helping couples achieve a relationship-friendly spirituality involves modeling mutuality, embracing our own vulnerability, and being influenced by the specific needs unique to each of our clients.

References

Bagasra, A. (2004). Psychology of the sufi mystics of Islam. *Journal of Theta Alpha Kappa, 28*(1), 16–31.

Carlson, T. D., Kirkpatrick, D., Hecker, L., & Killmer, M. (2002). Religion, spirituality, and marriage and family therapy: A study of family therapists' beliefs about the appropriateness of addressing religious and spiritual issues in therapy. *The American Journal of Family Therapy, 30*(2), 157–171.

Cattich, J., & Knudson-Martin, C. (2009). Spirituality and relationship: A holistic analysis of how couples cope with diabetes. *Journal of Marital and Family Therapy, 35*(1), 111–124.

Day, R. D., & Acock, A. (2013). Marital well-being and religiousness as mediated by relational virtue and equality. *Journal of Marriage and Family, 75*(1), 164–177. doi:10.1111/j.1741-3737.2012.01033.x.

Esmiol Wilson, E., Knudson-Martin, C., & Wilson, C. (2014). Gendered power, spirituality, and relational processes: Experiences of Christian physician couples. *Journal of Couple and Relationship Therapy, 13*(4), 312–338.

Fishbane, M. D. (2011). Facilitating relational empowerment in couple therapy. *Family Process, 50*, 337–352.

Gardner, B. C., Butler, M. H., & Seedall, R. B. (2008). En-gendering the couple-deity relationship: Clinical implications of power and process. *Contemporary Family Therapy: An International Journal, 30*(3), 152–166.

Idel, M. (1990). *Kabbalah: New perspectives.* New York, NY: Yale University Press.

Jonathan, N., & Knudson-Martin, C. (2012). Building connection: Attunement and gender equality in heterosexual relationships. *Journal of Couple and Relationship Therapy, 11*, 95–111.

Jordan, J. (2009). *Relational-cultural therapy.* Washington, DC: American Psychological Association.

Knudson-Martin, C. (2013). Why power matters: Creating a foundation of mutual support in couple relationships. *Family Process, 52*, 5–18.

Knudson-Martin, C. (2015). When therapy challenges patriarchy: Undoing gendered power in heterosexual couple relationships. In C. Knudson-Martin, M. A. Wells, & S. K. Samman (Eds.), *Socio-emotional relationship therapy: Bridging emotion, societal context, and couple interaction.* (pp. 15–26). New York, NY: Springer.

Knudson-Martin, C., & Huenergardt, D. (2010). A socio-emotional approach to couple therapy: Linking societal context and couple interaction. *Family Process, 49*(3), 369–384.

Knudson-Martin, C., & Huenergardt, D. (2015). Bridging emotion, societal discourse, and couple interaction in clinical practice. In C. Knudson-Martin, M. A. Wells, & S. K. Samman (Eds.), *Socio-emotional relationship therapy: Bridging emotion, societal context, and couple interaction.* (pp. 1–13). New York, NY: Springer.

Knudson-Martin, C., Huenergardt, D., Lafontant, K., Bishop, L., Schaepper, J. & Wells, M. (2014). Competencies for addressing gender and power in couple therapy: A socio-emotional approach. *Journal of Marital and Family Therapy.*. doi:10.1111/jmft.12068 (Advance online publication).

Knudson-Martin, C., & Mahoney, A. R. (Eds.). (2009a). *Couples, gender, and power: Creating change in intimate relationships.* New York, NY: Springer Publishing Company.

Knudson-Martin, C., & Mahoney, A. R. (2009b). Gendered power in cultural contexts: Capturing the lived experiences of couples. *Family Process, 48*, 5–8.

Ladinsky, D. (2006). *I heard God laughing: Renderings of Hafiz.* London: Penguin Books.

Lahood, G. (2010). Relational spirituality, part 2: The belief in others as a hindrance to enlightenment: Narcissism and the denigration of relationship within transpersonal psychology and the new age. *International Journal of Transpersonal Studies, 29*(1), 58–78.

Mahoney, A. (2010). Religion in families, 1999–2009: A relational spirituality framework. *Journal of Marriage and Family, 72*(4), 805–827.

Mahoney, A., Pargament, K., & DeMaris, A. (2009). Couples viewing marriage and pregnancy through the lens of the sacred: A descriptive study. *Research in the Social Scientific Study of Religion, 20*, 1–45.

McDonald, A., Beck, R., Allison, S., & Norsworthy, L. (2005). Attachment to God and parents: Testing the correspondence versus compensation hypotheses. *Journal of Psychology and Christianity, 24*(1), 21–28.

Peterman, A. H., Fitchett, G., Brady, M. J., Hernandez, L., & Cella, D. (2002). Measuring spiritual well-being in people with cancer: The functional assessment of chronic illness therapy–spiritual well-being scale (FACIT-Sp). *Annals of Behavioral Medicine, 24*(1), 49–58.

Richards, P. S., & Bergin, A. E. (2005). *A spiritual strategy for counseling and psychotherapy* (2nd ed.). Washington, DC: American Psychological Association.

Sandage, S. J., Hill, P. C., & Vaubel, D. C. (2011). Generativity, relational spirituality, gratitude, and mental health: Relationships and pathways. *The International Journal for the Psychology of Religion, 21*, 1–16.

Sandage, S. J., & Williamson, I. (2010). Relational spirituality and dispositional forgiveness: A structural equations model. *Journal of Psychology and Theology, 38*(4), 255–266.

Walsh, F. (2008). Religion, spirituality and the family: Multifaith perspectives. In F. Walsh (Ed.), *Spiritual resources in family therapy* (pp. 3–30). New York, NY: Guilford Press.

Williams, K., Galick, A., Knudson-Martin, C., & Huenergardt, D. (2012). Toward mutual support: A task analysis of the relational justice approach to infidelity. *Journal of Marital and Family Therapy, 39*(3), 285–298. doi:10.1111/j.1752-0606.2012.00324.x.

Engaging Power, Emotion, and Context in Couple Therapy: Lessons Learned

Carmen Knudson-Martin, Melissa A. Wells and Sarah K. Samman

Power, emotion, and societal context come together with force in couple interactions. The chapters in this book describe what members of the Socio-Emotional Relationship Therapy (SERT) team have learned about engaging these issues. As part of the SERT study group (see Knudson-Martin and Huenergardt, "Bridging Emotion, Societal Discourse, and Couple Interaction in Clinical Practice," 2015; Knudson-Martin et al. 2014) and editors of this book, we have learned that doing so requires courage, vision, and persistence (e.g., Samman and Knudson-Martin, "Relational Engagement in Heterosexual Couple Therapy: Helping Men Move from "I" to "We"," 2015; Waters and Lawrence 1994), especially when entering into the dynamics of gendered power with heterosexual couples. We have had to recognize what we were socialized not to see and confront ideas about what it means to be "neutral" when the playing field is not equal (Knudson-Martin 1997). The work is inevitably personal as well as professional.

The Three I's: Guiding Strategies

As women, we see male colleagues sometimes more able to challenge gendered power processes directly or have their interventions more readily received by clients. Each of us sometimes experiences internal trepidation as we enter the potent

C. Knudson-Martin (✉)
Counseling Psychology Department, Lewis & Clark College, Portland, OR, USA

M.A. Wells · S.K. Samman
Department of Counseling and Family Sciences,
Loma Linda University, Loma Linda, CA, USA

© American Family Therapy Academy 2015
C. Knudson-Martin et al. (eds.), *Socio-Emotional Relationship Therapy*,
AFTA SpringerBriefs in Family Therapy, DOI 10.1007/978-3-319-13398-0_12

confluence of gender, power, and context at play in couple therapy. Three I's—Identify, Interrupt, and Invite—help us focus and engage. In this chapter, we discuss our lessons learned as we challenge the legacies of patriarchy.

Identify

Gendered power persists because it is embedded in gender norms and its processes often seem normal as part of taken-for-granted realities. Equality is an ideal difficult to translate into day-to-day reality (Coontz 2005; Deutsch 2007). Therapists need a critical contextual framework to recognize power processes and track them with couples (Estrella et al. "Expanding the Lens: How SERT Therapists Develop Interventions that Address the Larger Context," 2015; Pandit et al. "SERT Therapists' Experience of Practicing Sociocultural Attunement," 2015). The questions in Table 1 (Knudson-Martin, "When Therapy Challenges Patriarchy: Undoing Gendered Power in Heterosexual Couple Relationships," 2015) and the Circle of Care (Knudson-Martin and Huenergardt, "Bridging Emotion, Societal Discourse, and Couple Interaction in Clinical Practice," 2015) help bring unexamined ideas about equality and mutual support from the shadows to the forefront.

Melissa: Identifying invisible power is a process that usually begins for me with sociocultural attunement to the couple. As I go "larger" into context, I have discovered that this promotes a sense of safety between me and each partner that is foundational to the more powerful partner's subsequent expression of emotional vulnerability, accountability, and experimenting with new relational approaches beyond gendered ways. I am explicit with my clients about the importance of examining the impact of the larger social context on their identities and relationships. As we engage in these socio-contextual conversations, I sense that they experience freedom from fear of being judged and instead feel understood and validated.

For instance, in the process of socioculturally attuning with a man[1] who identifies as Latin American and readily acknowledged a need to fit the "macho man" image, we were able to recognize a major societal influence. He shared a story of the pressure of this cultural demand in order to meet the expectations of his traditional Latina mother. Later in the session, when it was time to interrupt the flow of power in his interactions with his wife, he seemed to "feel safe, and as a result we could start getting somewhere" (D. Huenergardt, SERT group notes, 9/23/2009). Indeed, in our SERT clinical group, we realized early on that "you have to do the socio-emotional attunement before you challenge the power structure directly ... you can't really (interrupt power) too much until (clients) feel felt" (C. Knudson-Martin, SERT group notes, 10/07/2009).

---

[1] Identifiable details in case examples have been removed or modified.

Carmen: As a woman in a "senior" position, I'm still getting used to the power that I hold in relation to students and clients. Opening myself to take in my client's experience and identify power processes can feel vulnerable to me, too. It's easier for me to see women's vulnerability. I sometimes have a harder time with men's, especially if they seem to resist my empathy or seem particularly invested in "being right" or knowledgeable. These male responses can inspire gendered feelings of both helplessness and challenge for me. And, as Melissa pointed out, creating a context of safety for both partners means I also need to facilitate relational accountability. When I think about helping new therapists identify how sociocultural and power processes are part of a particular case, being able to understand and engage with the more powerful partner while also making visible the effects of his actions on his partner and the relationship can seem like juggling a lot of relationship balls at once.

Sarah: Like Melissa and Carmen, I believe it is imperative to identify the nuanced ways sociocultural contexts and experiences impact the couple relationship in order to make sense of the couple's desired outcomes (Knudson-Martin et al. 2014). I cannot understand power dynamics without empathy and understanding of both partners' contexts. Compassion for the client's sociocultural experience (as well my own) goes a long way when working with powerful partners who may, and often do, trigger feelings of uncertainty, confusion, and doubt in my ability to successfully work with difficult and pervasive patriarchal legacies.

Recognizing the many ways patriarchal legacies challenge me personally and professionally is an ongoing learning process. My research on how therapists can increase and sustain male relational engagement in heterosexual couple therapy (Samman and Knudson-Martin, "Relational Engagement in Heterosexual Couple Therapy: Helping Men Move from "I" to "We"," 2015) has made me keenly aware of how difficult it can be to identify power inequities. In those moments of uncertainty, I've found it helpful to explore the couple's experience of mutual relational responsibility, or lack thereof. Focusing on the degree to which partners share a sense of responsibility for the well-being of the other and the relationship and mutually engage emotionally brings hidden power differences to light and helps me recognize opportunities to interrupt the flow of power by intentionally working with the more powerful person first (Knudson-Martin et al. 2014).

Carmen: I've watched Sarah and Melissa beautifully join with the experience of powerful male partners while still making the power disparities visible and highlighting the consequences for their female partners. Often, it is only when processing our experiences after the session that it becomes obvious how much internal apprehension we may also have experienced when allowing ourselves to engage as vulnerable women on one hand and influential therapists on the other. Working from a relationship model based on shared relational responsibility and mutual support helps us maintain focus and makes it easier to identify and interrupt clinically relevant power processes.

Interrupt

Once we developed an "eye" for power and other sociocultural processes, our SERT group started to recognize them regularly; in fact, it became almost impossible not to see them. Learning how to use our power as therapists to interrupt the usual flow of gendered power was more challenging. We had to take the balance of power into account when crafting a clinical response (Estrella et al., "Expanding the Lens: How SERT Therapists Develop Interventions that Address the Larger Context," 2015). A useful rule of thumb is to begin by encouraging the vulnerability and relational responsibility of the male or more powerful partner (Knudson-Martin and Huenergardt 2010; Knudson-Martin et al. 2014).

Melissa: Interrupting power can be daunting for me. Overcoming my trepidation typically is embedded in mustering my courage to "stretch" in order to connect with the more powerful partner in a way that is validating while also challenging power processes. For instance, with one Jewish-identified male client who avoided expressing his own vulnerable emotions by shrugging his shoulders and saying, "it doesn't matter," I persisted. Had I not been willing to follow my own understanding of how male gender socialization often limits the expression of emotion to anger for most men, I would have missed an opportunity to help my client claim more of his emotional world. Instead, I wondered out loud what else he might possibly have felt in the situation that we were exploring. He listened intently as I softly elaborated my sense of how fear and sadness may have had a strong hold on him in that situation. Tears rolled down his cheeks, and he nodded his assent. Accessing these vulnerable emotions then facilitated our work on gendered power interactions of the couple.

Importantly, not all of my attempts to interrupt power meet with success. I can often find myself wondering what just happened when I miss an opportunity to recognize and interrupt invisible power. It is at times such as these that my SERT supervision is so helpful. "This is how we learn from our clients. We don't just learn from our successes, but the (times) that don't go the way we thought it would" (D. Huenergardt, SERT group notes, 10/21/2009).

Carmen: Interrupting power processes is never just a one-time strategy. Perhaps the most important thing I've learned from our years of research is that, like Melissa, therapists have to be willing to play this role over and over again. We need to find creative ways to engage so that habitual societal discourses cannot take over (ChenFeng and Galick, "How Gender Discourses Hijack Couple Therapy—and How to Avoid It," 2015). Sarah and I were especially interested to find that validating men's relational intentions and then *immediately* highlighting the impact of their behavior on the female partner is particularly effective in catalyzing heterosexual men to break power patterns that discourage attunement to their female partners (Samman and Knudson-Martin, "Relational Engagement in Heterosexual Couple Therapy: Helping Men Move from "I" to "We"," 2015). In supervising new therapists, I find that once they experience how interrupting the usual flow of power facilitates positive relational change, they are more willing to take the risk (see Esmiol Wilson, "Relational

Spirituality, Gender, and Power: Applications to Couple Therapy," 2015; Wells and Kuhn, "Couple Therapy with Adult Survivors of Child Abuse: Gender, Power, and Trust," 2015; Williams and Kim, "Relational Justice: Addressing Gender and Power in Clinical Practices for Infidelity," 2015).

Sarah: Though I have been working on gender and power issues with the SERT clinical research group over the last two years, I still often find it difficult to feel competent or comfortable interrupting power inequities. It is one thing to identify power inequities and the sociocultural contexts influencing their expression in therapy and quite another to strategically and successfully interrupt the process!

For example, I worked with a couple identifying as Italian American who had been living together for five years. The male partner had only recently been diagnosed with a chronic illness, and his female partner, who was very religious and relationally oriented, willingly took on the caregiving role. It took a few sessions to work through the many sociocultural expectations that influenced their interactions and reinforced power disparities through his sense of "entitlement" and her feelings of "responsibility." I found it much more difficult to interrupt these processes and bring them into their immediate awareness, particularly when the male partner would insist it was her *choice* to provide care at all hours. It was only through my own courage and persistence that I felt confident enough to highlight the ways his underlying sense of need and fear of abandonment distanced him from the woman he loved through its presentation as a sense of entitlement and silencing of her needs. Once we created the space for her to speak up about her desires and needs of *him*, the conversations began to shift and slowly rebalance the inequities in the relationship.

Invite

We have also learned that it is not enough to track power processes and make them visible. Therapists must find ways to invite partners to enact alternative gender discourses. This requires therapist leadership (Williams et al. 2013), either by identifying and expanding upon what partners are already doing that resists unequal power or by inviting them to experiment with another way of relating, such as asking the male partner to listen to and take in his partner's anger or supporting a less powerful partner to stick with a thought that she is doubtful about expressing and helping the couple experience a positive outcome from enacting something new.

Melissa: I have noticed that discovering an opening from the more powerful partner on alternative ways of relating is a key aspect of changing gendered power interactions. With male clients, it can often be that we need to expand beyond a common male gender-stereotypical "fix the problem" discourse to helping him listen to his female partner and validate what he has heard. This attunement exercise sounds simple enough, but is a quick way to encounter the taken-for-granted sociocultural messages that men draw upon in their approaches to their couple relationship. With one male partner who practiced listening to his wife's story that inferred her wish for them to buy a horse, I needed to help him set aside the discourse of "what's the point of this conversation if we can't afford to do this?" to consider how to simply take in her perspective and reflect back what he heard. He struggled to move away from engaging in a defensive mode of who's right and who's wrong, yet discovered in this enactment (replete with therapist coaching on reflecting) that it opened the possibility for the couple to connect in a new way. "The work then is about how to attune him to her so that he can actually hear her, respond to her not out of his guilt (or defensiveness), but from his own connection with her" (D. Huenergardt, SERT group notes, 8/05/2009).

Carmen: One of the things I was surprised to learn is how much men like invitations that help them successfully engage with their partners. I should not have been surprised. When partners are able to share relational responsibility, men no longer feel incompetent in the relational arena. This is true for same-sex partners as well (Richards et al., "Building a Circle of Care in Same-Sex Couple Relationships: A Socio-Emotional Relational Approach," 2015). It's not just about learning the right skill. New skills can be helpful, but if the power balance has not changed, they are met with skepticism by less powerful partners. Repeatedly demonstrating an ongoing attitude that you matter and your needs or opinions matter to me is what creates success. Part of supervising new therapists is helping them develop a vision of possibility so that they can persist in making space for couples to experiment with and positively experience alternatives that create new neural pathways that help men and women resist societal gender and power processes (Fishbane and Wells, "Toward Relational Empowerment: Interpersonal Neurobiology, Couples, and the Societal Context," 2015).

Sarah: I've had similar experiences. Though I value the benefits of developing specific skills that may be useful for both partners, the reality is these skills can also be used to continue to reinforce inequity in the relationship. For example, in the Italian couple in which the male partner was diagnosed with a chronic illness, he often interrupted his partner with, "*I* feel that you talk too much and it drives me nuts." It comes as no surprise that his partner often shut down in session. Clearly, this is not how a skill such as I-statements is used in an equal relationship and why it is fundamentally important for the powerful partner to engage differently with the less powerful partner for the skills to work successfully toward a mutually supportive relationship.

I invited the male partner to resist his tendency to impose his perspective and try a listening position. This worked best when I also highlighted his relational desires and successes, "I know how much you care about her. Did you notice how she sat up straighter and her eyes lit up when you asked her to tell you more?" Over time, he learned to genuinely acknowledge his automatic self-focused behaviors as well as take relational responsibility and extend relational repair: "I'm sorry, I didn't mean to interrupt you. I really do value what you're saying." The female partner eventually felt confident enough to block his tendency to interrupt her by saying, "I would like to hear you out as soon as I finish what I was saying." Upon reflection, the male partner shared how differently it felt for him to acknowledge his automatic silencing of her voice and to recognize the positive impact their changes were having on their relationship as a result.

Carmen: In the example above, Sarah provided leadership that helped the couple create a new, more mutual relationship experience. Several of our research projects have found that this is critical to transforming unequal power (Samman and Knudson-Martin, "Relational Engagement in Heterosexual Couple Therapy: Helping Men Move from "I" to "We"," 2015; Williams et al. 2013). Many in our group learned to interrupt unequal power dynamics by pointing them out. "Sean, I notice that you vigorously express your point. Have you noticed how Shana seems to shut down when all your energy comes at her like that? What do you think makes that happen?" But the next step of inviting something new can challenge our ideas about therapist roles.

Therapists may not have a vision of what would help couples step out of limiting gender and power patterns, or we may fear being too directive or imposing our values. We also come up against anxiety or discomfort when trying to undo societally reinforced gender and power patterns. I have found that my supervisees often need help actually thinking about other possible options. This is an example of how latent power associated with gender norms limits the choices people consider (see Knudson-Martin, "When Therapy Challenges Patriarchy: Undoing Gendered Power in Heterosexual Couple Relationships," 2015). My supervisees also often seem to need a "green light" and support from me to cross over an invisible line that keeps them from actively engaging with their clients to provide leadership that catalyzes something new.

The Three C's: Keys to Engagement

The inevitably personal nature of our professional work demands attuning to our own vulnerability as we resonate with our clients to provide a safe space for them to identify and practice new relational approaches in their couple relationships. Staying true to our social justice, social constructionist view of our couples' problems when challenged by a powerful partner in session is not easy. The reasons for being derailed in our work with gender and power can be many. All too often we have found ourselves tempted to put on a pathologizing lens when confronted with gendered power dynamics. Yet, we continue to discover how to hold onto our relational values that inform us of the need to resist patriarchy, both professionally and personally.

The three C's—Compassion, Curiosity, and Courage—are a good reminder for what we hold dear as we enter into the active process of undoing gender inequality. Bringing compassion to our therapeutic conversations is the heart-connecting aspect of our work. It helps us want to experience each partner's humanity and their desires to be known and valued and to build relationship. Curiosity helps us better grasp and resonate with each person's sense of identity and ways of relating. We want to know the details of what happens for them, how it feels, and how each partner responds to the other. Approaching with curiosity minimizes the therapist–client hierarchy and communicates respect and interest in the unique aspects of each couple's sociocultural story. It invites multiple realities and begins to liberate both therapist and client from the taken-for-granted to activate what might be.

Most importantly, summoning courage to empathetically draw attention to power disparities evident in session provides the key to opening new possibilities for our couples. We find that when we persistently resist patriarchy *with* couples, our courage is contagious. As interpersonal neurobiology indicates (see Fishbane and Wells, "Toward Relational Empowerment: Interpersonal Neurobiology, Couples, and the Societal Context," 2015), emotional attunement and compassion can be bidirectional. Couples may invigorate their own three C's. The neuroplasticity involved in the brain's capacity to change and the corresponding relational plasticity can help the couple explore and process where they are now, what they would like to do about the influence of larger social contexts, and where they would like to be in the future.

Taking the steps to identify and perform the relational processes involved in experiencing a mutually supportive relationship is an act of both social resistance and creativity. It is always challenging and even more so when gendered power imbalances intersect with the effects of poverty, race, and other inequities, and when the consequences include or are related to complex issues such as depression, addictions, or violence. The research and practice models offered in this volume provide an important foundation from which to confront and transform destructive power disparities and are fertile for continued exploration, integration, and development. We invite researchers and clinicians working across the many factors that contribute to relationship distress to further expand our growing understanding of how to undo, rather than reinforce, societal power processes and engage with clients to catalyze the relational possibilities inherent in the connections among emotion, societal context, and couple interaction.

References

ChenFeng, J. L., & Galick, A. (2015). How gender discourses hijack couple therapy—and how to avoid it. In C. Knudson-Martin, M. A. Wells, & S. K. Samman (Eds.), *Socio-emotional relationship therapy: Bridging emotion, societal context, and couple interaction.* (pp. 41–52). New York, NY: Springer.

Coontz, S. (2005). *Marriage, a history: From obedience to intimacy or how love conquered marriage.* New York, NY: Viking.

Deutsch, F. M. (2007). Undoing gender. *Gender and Society, 21,* 106–127. doi:10.1177/0891243206293577.

Esmiol Wilson, E. (2015). Relational spirituality, gender, and power: Applications to couple therapy. In C. Knudson-Martin, M. A. Wells, & S. K. Samman (Eds.), *Socio-emotional relationship therapy: Bridging emotion, societal context, and couple interaction.* (pp. 133–144). New York, NY: Springer.

Estrella, J., Kuhn, V. P., Freitas, C. J., & Wells, M. A. (2015). Expanding the lens: How SERT therapists develop interventions that address larger context. In C. Knudson-Martin, M. A. Wells, & S. K. Samman (Eds.), *Socio-emotional relationship therapy: Bridging emotion, societal context, and couple interaction.* (pp. 53–65). New York, NY: Springer.

Fishbane, M. D., & Wells, M. A. (2015). Toward relational empowerment: Interpersonal neurobiology, couples, and the societal context. In C. Knudson-Martin, M. A. Wells, & S. K. Samman (Eds.), *Socio-emotional relationship therapy: Bridging emotion, societal context, and couple interaction.* (pp. 27–40). New York, NY: Springer.

Knudson-Martin, C. (1997). The politics of gender in family therapy. *Journal of Marital and Family Therapy, 23,* 431–447.

Knudson-Martin, C. (2015). When therapy challenges patriarchy: Undoing gendered power in heterosexual couple relationships. In C. Knudson-Martin, M. A. Wells, & S. K. Samman (Eds.), *Socio-emotional relationship therapy: Bridging emotion, societal context, and couple interaction.* (pp. 15–26). New York, NY: Springer.

Knusdon-Martin, C., & Huenergardt, D. (2010). A socio-emotional approach to couples therapy: Linking social context and couple interactions. *Family Process, 49*(3), 369–384. doi:10.1111/j.1545-5300.2010.01328.x.

Knudson-Martin, C., Huenergardt, D., Lafontant, K., Bishop, L., Schaepper, J., & Wells, M. (2014). Competencies for addressing gender and power in couple therapy: A socio-emotional approach. *Journal of Marital and Family Therapy.* Advance online publication. doi: 10.1111/jmft.12068.

Knudson-Martin, C., & Huenergardt, D. (2015). Bridging emotion, societal discourse, and couple interaction in clinical practice. In C. Knudson-Martin, M. A. Wells, & S. K. Samman (Eds.), *Socio-emotional relationship therapy: Bridging emotion, societal context, and couple interaction.* (pp. 1–13). New York, NY: Springer.

Pandit, M., ChenFeng, J. L., & Kang, Y. J. (2015). SERT therapists' experience of practicing sociocultural attunement. In C. Knudson-Martin, M. A. Wells, & S. K. Samman (Eds.), *Socio-emotional relationship therapy: Bridging emotion, societal context, and couple interaction.* (pp. 67–78). New York, NY: Springer.

Richards, J. C., Jonathan, N., & Kim, L. (2015). Building a Circle of Care in same-sex couple relationships: A socio-emotional relational approach. In C. Knudson-Martin, M. A. Wells, & S. K. Samman (Eds.), *Socio-emotional relationship therapy: Bridging emotion, societal context, and couple interaction.* (pp. 93–105). New York, NY: Springer.

Samman, S. K., & Knudson-Martin, C. (2015). Relational engagement in heterosexual couple therapy: Helping men move from "I" to "We." In C. Knudson-Martin, M. A. Wells, & S. K. Samman (Eds.), *Socio-emotional relationship therapy: Bridging emotion, societal context, and couple interaction.* (pp. 79–91). New York, NY: Springer.

Waters, D. B., & Lawrence, E. C. (1994). *Competence, courage, and change: An approach to family therapy.* New York: Norton.

Wells, M. A., & Kuhn, V. P. (2015). Couple therapy with adult survivors of child abuse: Gender, power, and trust. In C. Knudson-Martin, M. A. Wells, & S. K. Samman (Eds.), *Socio-emotional relationship therapy: Bridging emotion, societal context, and couple interaction.* (pp. 107–119). New York, NY: Springer.

Williams, K., Galick, A., Knudson-Martin, C., & Huenergardt, D. (2013). Toward mutual support: A task analysis of the relational justice approach to infidelity. *Journal of Marital and Family Therapy, 39*(3), 285–298. doi:10.1111/j.1752-0606.2012.00324.x.

Williams, K., & Kim, L. (2015). Relational justice: Addressing gender and power in clinical practices for infidelity. In C. Knudson-Martin, M. A. Wells, & S. K. Samman (Eds.), *Socio-emotional relationship therapy: Bridging emotion, societal context, and couple interaction.* (pp. 121–132). New York, NY: Springer.